FANNY KEMBLE
The American Journals

FANNY KEMBLE

The American Journals

—

COMPILED AND EDITED BY

ELIZABETH MAVOR

WEIDENFELD AND NICOLSON
LONDON

First published in Great Britain in 1990 by
George Weidenfeld and Nicolson Limited
91 Clapham High Street London SW4 7TA

British Library Cataloguing in Publication Data
Kemble, Fanny 1809–1893
  Fanny Kemble: the American journals
  1. Acting. Kemble, Fanny
  I. Title II. Mavor, Elizabeth 1927–
  792.028092

ISBN 0 297 81128 2

Photoset by Deltatype Ltd, Ellesmere Port, Cheshire
Printed in Great Britain by
Butler & Tanner Ltd, Frome and London

For Ann Strenger

Contents

Acknowledgements

I should like to thank the Bodleian Library for permission to photograph the printed journals of Fanny Kemble in their possession, and also the Butler Library Columbia University for kindly lending the microfilm of Fanny's annotated copy of the journal.

I am also grateful for Rosemary Legge's help in preparing the manuscript for publication.

Introduction

'I keep a voluminous journal,' wrote Fanny Kemble to a friend, adding that she also scrawled doggerel, 'to ease my heart of its pressing emotions, much as a bird sings, with as little method, purpose or trouble.'[1]

She was in fact a natural writer – 'wrote exactly as she talked,' comments Henry James, 'observing, asserting, complaining, confiding, contradicting, crying out and bounding off, always effectually communicating.'[2]

She had much to communicate, for, as she wrote up those days of the early 1830s, England was painfully converting from an agricultural to an industrial society. She personally was to make some thirty trips across the Atlantic, first under sail, then steam; would do the London to Brighton journey in both old and new style, six hours by coach, she tells us, two by train. She would even sit beside Stephenson on the *Rocket*'s experimental trip between Liverpool and Manchester, falling *en route* 'most horribly in love' with the grave ex-platelayer.

A post-Regency pop-star, she went everywhere, met everyone. 'I have seen Manchester powerlooms, spinning jennies, cotton factories,' she lightly boasted, 'Birmingham, its button-making, pin-making, plating, stamping . . .'[3] She milled among the ecstatic London crowds during the 1831 Reform Bill fever and heard someone shout out 'The People's triumph!' and a voice reply 'No – they don't yet, but they will!'[4] Much later she would even witness the beginnings of Women's Emancipation. Most importantly, for the purposes of this book, she was one of the first writers to chronicle the New America, and the only woman to record life first-hand on a Southern plantation.

It could be said that in describing contemporary America she was jumping on a bandwagon. Americans had already been affronted by Mrs Frances Trollope's account of their society in

Domestic Manners of the Americans, a publication causing Mr Sam Weller to propose shipping Mr Pickwick off to the States in order that he should come back and 'write a book about the 'Merrikins as'll pay all his expenses and more if he blows 'em up enough.'[5] Fanny's intention in publishing her America book was not so much to blow it up, as to provide a modest sum with which to repay her kind and impecunious Aunt Dall, who had accompanied Fanny and her father on their theatrical tour of the States. The *Journal of a Residence on a Georgian Plantation* was to be published for rather different reasons.

As it was, the publication of the *American Journal* disastrously undermined her marriage, even though it won her not altogether desired publicity. 'The city is in an uproar,' wrote a close friend of its reception in New York. 'Nothing else is talked of . . . in the country houses . . . and Wall Street . . . people seem to think there never was such ingratitude!'[6] Meanwhile, Edgar Allen Poe, reviewing it for the *Southern Literary Messenger*, complained of its free style, and also of the use of certain vulgar words, in particular 'dawdled', 'gulped', 'pottering', and 'grumpily'.

Back in England the *Edinburgh Review* was favourable, its critic enjoying 'all the freshness, confidence and indiscretion'[7] of Fanny's pages, but *The Times* complained of 'Extravagance without fancy, coarseness without humour . . .'[8] and the *Atheneum* stuffily identified it as 'one of the most deplorable exhibitions of vulgar thinking and vulgar expression that it was ever our misfortune to encounter.'[9] In fact from first page to last the *Journal* is a wonderfully vivacious charivari of American life, and this was recognized by the young Princess Victoria who, having dutifully castigated it as 'pertly and oddly written', 'not well bred', ended up by freely admitting, 'It amuses me . . .'[10]

The *Journal of a Residence on a Georgian Plantation* was another matter. It was kept for Fanny's friend, Elizabeth Dwight Sedgwick, and of the experience that lay before her Fanny had reservations. 'I am going prejudiced against slavery,' she wrote. 'Nevertheless I go prepared to find many mitigations . . . much kindness on the part of the masters, much content on that of the slaves . . . you may rely on the carefulness of my observation.'[11]

She was of course to find the experience worse, far far worse than she had ever imagined, and the winter sojourn at her husband's Georgia plantation finally sealed the fate of their tempestuous marriage.

In the interests of family loyalty the *Plantation Journal* was not published until thirty years after her visit, and then at a critical moment of the Civil War, shortly after Gettysburg. In England, for the most part sympathetic to the South, few journals even recorded its publication. Though portions of the book were read out in the House of Commons, and it was influential in causing the Manchester cotton operatives to boycott American cotton, the London daily press barely noticed it. In the States, however, it was another story. *Harper's Monthly* considered it 'the most powerful anti-slavery book yet written' and the *Atlantic Monthly* told its readers 'A sadder book the human hand never wrote . . .' further commenting, 'a noble service nobly done!'[12]

This seems fair judgement. No one has seriously challenged the candid descriptions of life as it was then lived in that country where 'horses were more costly to keep than coloured folk'. Few would disagree with Henry James's opinion that it contains 'easily the best of her prose,' or that it evokes in a masterly way the very great beauty of the tragic and tainted South.

> The sun went down . . . a sort of dreamy stillness seemed creeping over the world and into my spirit as the canoe just tilted against the steps that led to the wharf, raised by the scarce perceptible heaving of the water. A melancholy, monotonous boat-horn sounded from a distance up the stream, and presently, floating slowly down with the current, huge shapeless, black, relieved against the sky, came one of those rough barges piled with cotton, called hereabouts Ocane boxes . . . upon this great tray are piled the swollen apoplectic looking cotton bags, to the height of ten, twelve and fourteen feet. This huge water-wagon floats lazily down the river, from the upper country to Darien . . .[13]

It is a description that achieves what she is particularly good at, the literal and symbolic perception of the Southern essence.

To compare Fanny Kemble with other women diarists is difficult. The range of her experience was both deeper and broader than that of most men, let alone women, of the time. For this reason she makes writers such as Fanny Burney or Harriet Wilson seem almost provincial. And although both Fannys wrote lambent English prose, there is a candour, an unselfregarding humour in the Kemble writing which is absent from that of the other Fanny.

As someone remarked, 'She persists in calling a male fowl a cock and her ambulatory pedestals legs . . .'[14] There is also a spontaneity in the writing, one knows there was no painful re-working in the studio. Hers are out-of-doors impressions, taken on the spot, and all the more sparkling for that. Her love for the world of nature sometimes approaches Dorothy Wordsworth's. But while Dorothy allowed that world with its subtle mysteries to speak for itself, Fanny was a more active celebrant, and her *Benedicite* is written with the passion of an artist. 'As I held the first violets in my hand it seemed to me I liked them better than husband or child, and I have felt a positive thrill in watching shadow and sunshine in hill country which nothing but some moral beauty should cause . . .'[15] thus occupying a position somewhere between that of Dorothy's famous brother and Emily Brontë.

Fanny was very much better educated than the considerably well-educated women of her own time – and since. She was exceedingly musical and knew a great deal about the natural world. Being fluent in French, German and Italian, she had read many of the European classics in the original, and was of course familiar with the great English writers, Shakespeare in particular. Yet there was little of the blue-stocking about her, because her cultivation was only a part of her great passion for life in all its aspects. For she was a woman wonderfully alive, appearing to live more intensely than other people, to enjoy as well as to suffer more, so that reading her is to understand exactly what Sidney Smith meant when, seeing her for the last time, he said, 'If I'm alive at all when you return I shall most likely be paralytic in body and mind, but come and give one look at me, and I shall flash up for a moment and feel some bright vision of other times is come back.'[16]

It is her own bright vision of other times that is Fanny Kemble's unique achievement as a writer, and by the same token it is painful to cut anything at all that she wrote. But, as she said herself, she wrote voluminously, and to cut has been a sad necessity for the purposes of this book.

Fanny's *American Journal* was first published in 1835, both in this country and the United States, and was reissued in facsimile in New York in 1970. Personal names left blank in previous editions have now been completed and corrected following reference to Fanny's own annotated copy kindly lent in microfilm by the Butler Library, Columbia University.

The *Plantation Journal*, first published in 1863, was reissued here in 1961, and in America in 1984. The two journals now appear for the first time in one volume.

1

Before America

The Kembles, suitably enough for a great acting family, seem to have materialized out of the Herefordshire mists. Roger Kemble, Fanny's grandfather, had no record of his parents' origins. He was born in 1731, became a strolling player, and at twenty-two married Sarah, the seventeen-year-old ward of a strolling manager. For a number of years the pair performed in public squares, taverns and barns, in the course of which Sarah produced eight sons and four daughters. The family often went hungry, and Fanny's father, Charles, remembered as a boy stealing and eating raw turnips from the fields.

Understandably, neither parent wanted their children to follow them as actors, but of the eight who survived, all were at one time or another on the stage.

In spite of their humble beginnings the family rise was rapid. They made their London début under Sheridan's exacting dominion at Drury Lane, and by 1802 were established in their own theatre at Covent Garden. The success was marked by the founder grandparents having their portraits painted by Sir Thomas Lawrence – hers 'the portrait of an old lioness', someone remarked, though all contemporaries spoke of Roger Kemble's polished manners and his wife's vivacious conversational powers.

Their son, Charles, Fanny's father, was in turn to marry an actress. Thérèse De Camp was the daughter of a French Revolutionary captain who had married a Swiss farmer's daughter. The family moved to London where the captain gave flute lessons, his small daughter, Thérèse, joining Texier's troupe as a child actress, often performing in benefit performances for the French *émigrés*. The child became exceedingly popular with members of the aristocracy, including the Prince Regent, 'one of whose favourite jokes', according to Fanny, 'was to place my mother under a huge glass bell, made to cover some group of precious Dresden china, where her tiny figure and flashing face produced even a more beautiful effect than the costly work of art . . .'[1]

Fanny, the third child of Charles and Thérèse, was born at Newman Street, Oxford Road, London, on 27 November 1809. From the start her temperament seems to have been a worrying combination of charm and waywardness. Fanny herself admitted to a childish excitability of temperament, probably inherited from her mother, also 'the sort of ecstasy which anything beautiful gives me'. Many years later, a family friend spoke of her as having been 'a source of perpetual worry to her parents . . .'[2] Certainly, all the evidence points to her being very difficult to handle. Before she was five the family moved to to Westbourne Green next to Fanny's aunt, the renowned Mrs Siddons. Hoping perhaps that their mutinous child might be awed into obedience by her formidable aunt, Fanny was taken to be interviewed by the great actress. The little girl climbed on to her aunt's lap, gazed earnestly into her face and cried out 'What beautiful eyes you have!'[3] At which, all stern resolutions cast aside, Mrs Siddons collapsed in laughter.

At five Fanny was in desperation despatched to another aunt, a Mrs Twiss, who ran a small dame school in Bath – the first of a number of educational establishments Fanny was to patronize. Here, apart from plunging head first over the Twiss banisters, though without apparent injury, little was accomplished, and Fanny soon returned home to be taught by Aunt Dall, her mother's sister. At seven she was once more hopefuly packed off, this time to the 'Rue tant perd tant paie' at Boulogne where Madame Faudier, 'sallow and grim but still vivacious', ran a school with her daughter 'unforgettable', according to Fanny, 'in salmon coloured merino'.[4]

At Madame Faudier's music, dancing and Italian were taught, and the foundations laid for Fanny's later skill in languages, though for Madame Faudier coping with her difficult, vivacious pupil was to prove an uphill task. Seeing a child climbing out on the leads of the Faudier establishment, a passer-by reported the incident. 'Ah,' was Madame Faudier's tired riposte, 'ah, ce ne peut être que cette *diable* de Kemble!'[5]

The *diable* left two years later, bearing off most of the school prizes, and returning home to two more years of Aunt Dall and regular readings from Milton with her father. At about this time she and her sister and two brothers were given a toy theatre, 'with a *real* blue silk curtain, a *real* set of footlights . . .'[6] They put on *The Miller and his Men*, *Blue Beard* and *The Gypsies' Curse*. This was after being taken to Astley's to see their first plays: *Meg Murdoch or the Mountain Hag* and *Hippolita Queen of the Amazons*, which appealed particularly to Fanny since the Queen was mounted on a 'snow-white *live* charger!'

Meanwhile, eleven now, and plotting to poison her sister, Adelaide, with privet berries, the *diable* was most timely whisked off to Paris to her final and most successful educational establishment, smartly situated in the Champs Elysées.

Mrs Rowden, the principal of the school, and authoress of *The Pleasures of Friendship*, boasted Mary Russell Mitford and Lady Caroline Lamb as former pupils, and in later years Fanny much enjoyed repeating an anecdote of the latter's fatuity: 'Gueth how many pairth of thtockings I have on!' she (Lady Caroline) demanded of an astonished dancing partner, and on his expressing amazed inability to guess, told him 'Thixth!'[7]

Mrs Rowden clearly ran an excellent school. The girls were allowed to wander at will in the romantic Parc Manceaux, a deliciously neglected *jardin anglais*. They were taken to the Luxembourg Palace to see the modern painters David and Gerard, and, under Mrs Rowden's direction, regularly took part in performances of the plays of Racine and Corneille.

Fanny spent three years at Mrs Rowden's, significantly, perhaps, remaining at school during the holidays. Her father crossed the channel to see her, however, and took her out to '*déjeuner à la fourchette* at the Café Riche' as she later recalled, or 'dinner in the small *cabinet* at the Trois Frères', followed afterwards by the theatre. When almost sixteen she emerged, not only more biddable it seems, but able to read Latin, speak French, Italian and German fluently, play the piano and sing. On the way home in the channel packet her bonnet ritually blew off into the sea and was lost. She was – for all practical purposes – of age.

By now the Kembles had moved to Weybridge, then a remote and picturesque village three hours' coach drive from London. Their rented cottage was bounded on one side by Portmore Park, then falling into a pleasingly romantic ruin, and on the other by the empty mansion of Oatlands. Here Charles Kemble came down each Saturday from London, leaving on Monday morning for the theatre and their town house in Soho Square.

The three years the family spent at Weybridge were among the happiest of Fanny's life, for it was a period of luxurious consolidation of all she had learned in Paris. Here, like some heroine of Sensibility, she lay beneath the Park oaks, a cabbage leaf of fresh strawberries at her elbow, a scatter of moss roses beside her, composing poetry or omnivorously reading German romances, Wieland's *Oberon*, Goethe's *Wilhelm Meister*. Sometimes she took long dreaming walks, attended by her terrier, a large Newfoundland and a cat, through the deserted Park; at other times she joined her mother on that exacting lady's fishing expeditions, or her brothers at cricket and shooting practice. On the eve of her sixteenth birthday this idyllic period of her life was interrupted by a severe attack of smallpox, an illness which left her considerably disfigured.

Fortunately, neither her temperament nor her immediate circumstances allowed of repining. Covent Garden, the family theatre, was at that time undergoing a managerial and financial crisis; its proprietors, of whom her father was one, enmeshed in the processes of an expensive lawsuit. Fanny's response was to embark on an historical novel and a play, no doubt with the idealistic intention of shoring up the family fortunes.

She had by now begun to take an interest in Covent Garden, had met there and been charmed by Mendelssohn, then a youth of nineteen. She had also encountered Weber: 'a little thin man', she recorded in her journal, 'lame of an foot . . .'

Meanwhile, affairs at the theatre were fast moving from bad to worse. For a time it looked as though Charles Kemble might be called on for the enormous sum of £27,000 to prop up the Garden's dwindling finances. It was a sum he did not have. His income was currently £1,800 a year, out of which he had to support a wife and three children, besides keeping his eldest son at Cambridge, which was costing £300 a year.

It was now that the idea of going on the stage first began to take shape in Fanny's mind. It was not a profession that appealed to her, however: 'utterly distasteful' she'd write of it time and again, 'a vocation which I never liked or honoured.'[8] Left to her own devices she would undoubtedly have preferred to be a writer.

In her memoirs Fanny describes taking her mother aside and asking her to try her out with a recitation from the *Merchant of Venice*. The chosen speech was one spoken by Portia – 'my ideal of a perfect woman' Fanny writes, adding 'the wise, witty woman loving with all her soul, and submitting with all her heart to a man whom everybody but herself (who was the best judge) would have judged her inferior . . .'[9] It was to prove an uncannily accurate forecast of her own case.

Her mother listened attentively to the recitation, remarked that there was hardly passion enough in the part to test any tragic power Fanny might possess, and advised her daughter to go away and study the part of Juliet.

Not long after, Charles Kemble took his daughter to Covent Garden to ascertain whether her voice was strong enough for her to be an actress. The stage 'with its racks of pasteboard and canvas streets, forests, banqueting-halls and dungeons'[10] both appalled and fascinated Fanny. Three weeks later she was acting.

It is intriguing the extent to which the producers of the time sought for authenticity in their costumes. Fanny tells how for *Romeo and Juliet* the paintings and engravings of Raphael, Titian, Giorgione and Bronzino were closely studied in order to produce accurate effects. It was finally decided, however, that Fanny would look best in plain white satin, her hair dressed as she usually wore it. The next question was who should play Romeo. Her younger brother, Henry, was suggested, but the audition broke down in 'cockadoodles from Henry and an explosion of giggles – and Mr Abbot was decided upon instead'.[11] Mr Abbot, old enough to be Fanny's father, was given in moments of emotion to serious instability about the legs. Fanny later maintained that her best Romeo of all had been Miss Ellen Tree. Miss Tree apparently fenced exceedingly well, and the only disagreement had been that in keeping with the part Miss Tree had proposed lifting Fanny – 'a solid little lady', according to another actor – and this Fanny had sternly refused.

'We drove to the theatre very early,' Fanny wrote of this first night, 'while the late autumn sunlight yet lingered in the sky; it shone into the carriage upon me, and as I screened my eyes from it, my mother said "Heaven smiles on you my child." '[12]

Heaven smiled indeed, but Fanny was also well supported by her family. Her father was playing Mercutio, her mother, who had left the stage twenty years before, taking a minor rôle in order to guide her daughter through her part. Behind the scenes was dear Aunt Dall, acting as Fanny's maid and dresser.

5

Later she remembered every detail of that first tremendous performance. How she waited, crying with nerves, in her dressing room till the dreaded signal 'Miss Kemble called for the stage ma'am!' rang out – at which she heard someone growl, 'Never mind 'em Miss Kemble, don't think of 'em any more than if they were so many rows of cabbages!'[13]

When she reached the stage, half the cast were waiting like worker bees to cluster protectively round her. The audience meanwhile, was in a state of uproar welcoming her mother on stage once again.

'Nurse!' called my mother, and out waddled Mrs Davenport, and, turning back, called in her turn, 'Juliet!' My aunt gave me an impulse forward, and I ran straight across the stage, stunned with the tremendous shout that greeted me, my eyes covered with mist, and the green baize flooring of the stage feeling as if it rose up against my feet; but I got hold of my mother, and stood like a terrified creature at bay confronting the huge theatre full of gazing human beings . . .[14]

It was at this moment that the Kemble genes asserted themselves. She began to forget herself – 'for aught I knew, I was Juliet; the passion I was uttering sending hot waves of blushes all over my neck and shoulders, while the poetry sounded like music to me as I spoke it, with no consciousness of anything before me, utterly transported into the imaginary existence of the play.'[15]

There was tumultuous applause. Congratulations. Tears. Embraces. 'A general joyous explosion of unutterable relief!' With this one performance she had become a star, and for the time being Covent Garden was saved.

Adulation of the kind so familiar to us now followed instantly: daily newspaper raves, shop windows hung with engravings taken from a Lawrence sketch of her, which was further reproduced on plates, cups and saucers and gentlemen's neckerchiefs. With the adulation came a touch of quite possessive affection: 'Mrs Siddons through the diminishing end of an opera glass', commented one critic, while another likened her fondly to a Shetland pony, and yet another enumerated her 'diminutive stature, defective features'[16] which conspired to make everyone adore her all the more.

Fanny's life changed totally. She was now acting three times a week, though not yet allowed into the green room for fear of meeting undesirable associates. Her salary was thirty guineas a week, an impressive sum, which meant her 'faded, threadbare, turned and died [sic] frocks' could be exchanged for fashionable gowns. Far more important to Fanny was that she could now afford to buy her father a horse and herself take riding lessons at Captain Fossard's. The Captain's instruction was taken 'without stirrup, without holding the reins, with our arms behind us, and as often as not sitting left-sided on the saddle . . .'[17] One day, in the course of this strenuous tuition a middle-aged lady and a young girl came to watch. The lady was the Duchess of Kent and the young girl Princess Victoria.

Fanny and her father now went on tour with *Venice Preserved*, *The Grecian Daughter* and the wildly sentimental *Gamester*, playing at Bath, Edinburgh, Dublin, Liverpool, Manchester and Birmingham. At Glasgow, with its 'dull, dark handsome square,' the audience alarmed her by its stillness, its strained attention. Riding in Princes Street in Edinburgh, she was stopped one day by none other than Sir Walter Scott. 'You appear to be a very good horsewoman,' said he in his delightful rich burr, 'which is a great merit in the eyes of an old Border-man!'[18]

At Liverpool, fêted wherever she went, Fanny was conducted like some sprig of the aristocracy over the splendid docks, the cemetery, spirited away on a steam engine 'at the rate of five and thirty miles per hour,' sitting beside the great Stephenson himself, 'a stern-featured man' she noted, 'with a dark and deeply marked countenance . . .'[19]

By New Year 1831 she was off again, this time to play at Brighton, enlivening the tedious six-hour coach journey by discussing Hamlet's madness with another passenger who turned out to be one of Dr Burney's sons. When they were not talking, she read *Sir Launcelot du Lac*, though with impatience, 'their deadly blows and desperate thrusts, their slashing, gashing, mashing, mangling, and hewing bore me to death . . .'[20]

Fanny's intellect as well as her aesthetic sense was ever on the alert. She would notice, for instance, how the chalk at Brighton had been washed from the cliffs to form 'a deep embossed silver embroidery along the coast as far as the eye could see,' at the same time as she was entertaining grave thoughts on the afterlife. She found fault with the notion 'that all spirit is after death to form but one whole spiritual existence, a sort of *lumping* which I object to,' adding mutinously, 'I should like always to be able to know myself from somebody else!'[21]

A celebrity now, she was meeting celebrities: Lord Gray, the Duke of Bedford, Lord Russell, Sidney Smith, the poet Campbell, and Lord Melbourne. Lord and Lady Dacre became particular friends, and their house (The Hoo, in Hertfordshire) a second home. Lady Dacre was not only a blue-stocking, Fanny tells us, but a sculptor, and 'the finest female rider and driver in England: that is saying in the world!'[22]

In May 1831 she accepted, though with some misgivings, Lord Francis Egerton's invitation to act in an amateur production of *Hernani* down at Oatlands. Here, among a sparkling assembly, she was presented to the Queen, who greatly admired her acting. Fanny herself gives us an unmistakably Walpole-like glimpse of the green room after this performance: 'rouge, swords, wine, moustaches, soda water . . .'[23]

She also accompanied Elizabeth Fry, the prison reformer, to Newgate. By now such a visit had become heartlessly fashionable among the well-to-do. 'I felt broken-hearted for *them*,' commented Fanny, who would have much preferred to sit with the convicts, 'and ashamed for *us*'.[24]

She participated in the more conventional social round with an equally critical eye, noting one miserable upper-class ménage with dismay: 'What could, would, or *should* a woman do in such a case,' the twenty-year-old girl asked herself, 'Endure and endure till her heart broke, I suppose!' She then added, with what would prove a terrible irony, 'Somehow I don't think a man would have the heart to *break* one's heart; but to be sure I don't know. . . '[25]

She and her father continued touring, but by now they were beginning to discuss the possibility of taking themselves to America to improve their fortunes. Fanny was not enthusiastic. America had no grey abbeys, she ruminated after the style of Jane Austen's Catherine Morland, no ruined cloisters, no 'great, old time-stained weather-beaten, ivy-mantled churches or tombs. . . .'[26]

Common sense asserted itself nonetheless – the Covent Garden lawsuit still dragging on and due anytime to go before the Lords finally persuaded her: '. . . the best thing I can do will be to take ship from Liverpool and sail to the United States!' she wrote, adding mournfully, 'But I do hate the very thought of America!'[27]

By the autumn of 1831, their first English tour was over, and Fanny and her father back at their London home in Great Russell Street. Worry over the fortunes of Covent Garden had undermined Charles Kemble's health; he had inflammation of the lungs and was spitting blood. By the beginning of 1832 Fanny had definitely made up her mind to go to America, work till she had made £10,000, and then come home to England. Her own play *Francis I* was already in rehearsal, but the proceeds from it were already mortgaged to pay for a commission in the army for her younger brother, Henry. 'Good God,' she wrote, 'what will become of us!'

Francis I was a success. 'A historical play,' she commented, 'written by a girl of seven and acted by the authoress at one and twenty.' She went on to acknowledge 'its entire lack of merit'.[28]

Plans had by this time been drawn up for the American adventure. By June Fanny had played for the last time at Covent Garden. By 1st July they were in Edinburgh, and booked to work their way down to Liverpool, Fanny playing Juliet once more, as well as taking parts in *The Gamester* and her own play, *Francis I.*

Still in Edinburgh on 7th July she parted sorrowfully from her mother who was returning home. They were not to meet again for two years. While her father sobbed his heart out, Fanny looked out of the lodging house window and watched the white column of smoke rising from her mother's ship as it lay under Newhaven. Then 'I saw the steamer had left the shore, and was moving fast towards Inchkeith, the dark smoky wake that lingered behind it showing how far it had already gone from us. . . .'[29]

In spite of her full repertoire she found time before leaving her favourite city to visit the Edinburgh Phrenological Museum with her friend, George Combe. Here she describes sitting on the ground, her lap full of skulls, and thinking of Hamlet. 'One of the best specimens of the human skull, it seems, is Raphael's,' she wrote in her journal, 'a cast of whose head I held lovingly in my hands wishing it had been the very house where once abode that spirit of immortal beauty . . .'[30]

The following day was their last in Edinburgh. She spent it riding out towards the Pentland Hills and lamenting privately '. . . it is the terrible distance, the slowness and uncertainty of communication; it is that dreadful America.'[31]

On 19th July they reached Liverpool, where cholera had broken out. There was still a fortnight of their tour to run. They moved on to Manchester where they played *Francis* and *School for Scandal* to packed houses, then, returning in melancholy triumph, Fanny, her father and Aunt Dall boarded the *Pacific* for America on Wednesday, 1 August 1832.

'The foreboding with which I left my own country was justified,' she commented years later, 'neither of us ever had a home again in England.'[32]

2

Journal

1 August – 13 October 1832

Wednesday, August 1st, 1832
Another break in my journal, and here I am on board the *Pacific*,
bound for America, having left home, and all the world behind. –
Well! . . .

I had a bunch of carnations in my hand, which I had snatched
from our drawing-room chimney; – English flowers! – dear English
flowers! they will be withered long before I again see land, but I will
keep them until I once more stand upon the soil on which they
grew.

The sky had become clouded, and the wind blew cold.

Came down and put our narrow room to rights.

Worked at my Bible cover till dinner time. We dined at half-past
three. – The table was excellent – cold dinner, because it was the
first day – but every thing was good; and champagne, and dessert,
and every luxury imaginable, rendered it as little like a ship-dinner
as might be. The man who sat by me was an American; very good-
natured, and talkative. Our passengers are all men, with the
exception of three; a nice, pretty-looking girl, who is going out with
her brother; a fat old woman, and a fat young one. I cried almost
the whole of dinner-time. . . .

I am weary and sad, and will try to go and sleep. – It rains: I
cannot see the moon.

Thursday, 2d [August 1832]
It rained all night, and in the morning the wind had died away, and
we lay rocking, becalmed on the waveless waters. At eight o'clock
they brought me some breakfast, after which I got up; while
dressing, I could not help being amused at hearing the cocks

11

crowing, and the cow lowing, and geese and ducks gabbling, as though we were in the midst of a farm-yard. . . .

Friday, 3d [August 1832]
Breakfasted at eight; got up, and dressed, and came upon deck. The day was lovely, the sea one deep dark sapphire, the sky bright and cloudless, the wind mild and soft, too mild to fill our sails, which hung lazily against the masts, – but enough to refresh the warm summer's sky, and temper the bright sun of August that shone above us.

Walked upon deck with Miss Hodgkinson* and Captain Whaite: the latter is a very intelligent, good-natured person; rough and bluff, and only seven and twenty; which makes his having the command of a ship rather an awful consideration.

At half-past eleven got my German, and worked at it till half-past one, then got my work; and presently we were summoned on deck by sound of bell, and oyes! oyes! oyes! – and a society was established for the good demeanour and sociability of the passengers. My father was in the chair. . . . A badge was established, rules and regulations laid down, a code framed, and much laughing and merriment thence ensued.

Worked till dinner-time. After dinner, went on deck, took a brisk walk for half an hour with Captain Whaite. . . .

Wednesday, 15th [August 1832]
Here's a lapse! thanks to head winds, a rolling sea, and their result, sickness, sadness, sorrow. I've been better for the last two days, thank God! and take to my book again.

Rose at eight, dawdled about, and then came up stairs. Breakfasted, sat working at my Bible cover till lunchtime.

Somebody asked me if I had any of Mrs Siddons's hair; I sent for my dressing-box, and forthwith it was over-hauled, to use the appropriate phrase, by half the company, whom a rainy day had reduced to a state of worse than usual want of occupation.

The rain continued all day; we ladies dined in the round-house, the room down stairs being too close. . . . As evening came on, the whole of the passengers collected in the round-house. . . .

* The Hodgkinsons, both brother and sister, were to become lifelong friends of Fanny's. Charles Hodgkinson was the son of a tenant of the Duke of Norfolk.

Afterwards they fell to singing; while they did so, the sky darkened tremendously, the rain came pelting down, the black sea swelled, and rose, and broke upon the ship's sides into boiling furrows of foam, that fled like ghosts along the inky face of the ocean. The ship scudded before the blast, and we managed to keep ourselves warm by singing.

After tea, for the first time since I have been on board, got hold of a pack of cards (oh me, that it ever should come to this!) and initiated Miss Hodgkinson in the mysteries of the intellectual game. Mercy! how my home rose before me as I did so. Played till I was tired; dozed, and finally came to bed. . . .

Friday, 17th [August 1832]
On my back all day: mercy, how it ached too! the ship reeled about like a drunken thing. I lay down and began reading Byron's life. As far as I have gone (which is to his leaving England) there is nothing in it but what I expected to find, – the fairly sown seeds of the after-harvest he bore. Had he been less of an egotist, would he have been so great a poet? – I question it. . . .

Ate nothing but figs and raisins; in the evening some of our gentlemen came into our cabin, and sat with us; I, in very desperation and seasickness, began embroidering one of my old nightcaps, wherein I persevered till sleep overtook me.

Saturday, 18th [August 1832]
Rose at about half-past eight, dawdled about as usual, breakfasted in the round-house – by the by, before I got out of bed, read a few more pages of Byron's life. . . .

Our company consists chiefly of traders in cloth and hardware, clerks, and counting-house men – a species with but few peculiarities of interest to me, who cannot talk pounds, shillings, and pence, as glibly as less substantial trash. Most of them have crossed this trifling ditch half a dozen times in their various avocations. But though they belong to the same sort generally, they differ enough individually for the amusement of observation. . . .

Sunday, 19th [August 1832]
Did not rise till late – dressed and came on deck. The morning was brilliant; the sea, bold, bright, dashing its snowy crests against our

ship's sides, and flinging up a cloud of glittering spray round the prow.

I breakfasted – and then amused myself with finding the lessons, collects, and psalms for the whole ship's company. After lunch, they spread our tent, a chair was placed for my father, and the little bell being rung, we collected in our rude church.

It affected me much, this praying on the lonely sea, in the words that at the same hour were being uttered by millions of kindred tongues in our dear home. There was something, too, impressive and touching in this momentary union of strangers, met but for a passing day, to part perhaps never to behold each other's faces again, in the holiest of all unions, that of Christian worship. . . .

After prayers, wrote journal. Some sea weed floated by the ship to-day, borne from the gulf stream; I longed to have it, for it told of land: gulls too came wheeling about, and the little petterels [sic] like sea-swallows skimmed round and round, now resting on the still bosom of the sunny sea, now flickering away in rapid circles like black butterflies. They got a gun, to my horror, and wasted a deal of time in trying to shoot these feathered mariners; but they did not even succeed in scaring them.

We went and sat on the forecastle to see the sun set: he did not go down cloudless, but dusky ridges of vapour stretched into ruddy streaks along the horizon, as his disc dipped into the burnished sea. The foam round the prow, as the ship made way with all sail set before a fair wind, was the most lovely thing I ever saw. Purity, strength, glee, and wondrous beauty were in those showers of snowy spray that sprang up above the black ship's sides, and fell like a cataract of rubies under the red sunlight.

We sat there till evening came down; the sea, from brilliant azure grew black as unknown things, the wind freshened, and we left our cold stand to walk, or rather run, up and down the deck to warm ourselves. . . .

Came back to our gipsy encampment, where, by the light of a lantern, we supped and sang sundry scraps of old songs. At ten came to bed. . . .

Monday, 20th [August 1832]
Wrote journal, walked about, worked at my cap, in the evening danced merrily enough, quadrilles, country dances, La Boulangère, and the monaco; fairly danced myself tired.

Came to bed. But oh! not to sleep – mercy, what a night! The wind blowing like mad, the sea rolling, the ship pitching, bouncing, shuddering, and reeling, like a thing possessed.

I lay awake, listening to her creaking and groaning, till two o'clock, when, sick of my sleepless berth, I got up and was going up stairs, to see, at least, how near drowning we were, when Dall, who was lying awake too, implored me to lie down again. I did so for the hundred and eleventh time, complaining bitterly that I should be stuffed down in a loathsome berth, cabined, cribbed, confined, while the sea was boiling below, and the wind bellowing above us.

Lay till daylight, the gale increasing furiously; boxes, chairs, beds, and their contents, wooden valuables, and human invaluables, rolling about and clinging to one another in glorious confusion. At about eight o'clock, a tremendous sea took the ship in the waist, and rushing over the deck, banged against our skylight, and bounced into our cabin.

Three women were immediately apparent from their respective cribs, and poor Henrietta[†] appeared in all her lengthy full-length, and came and took refuge with me. As I held her in my arms, and put my cloak round her, she shook from head to foot poor child! – I was not the least frightened, but rather excited by this invasion of Dan Neptune's; but I wish to goodness I had been on deck. Oh, how I wish I had seen that spoonful of salt water flung from the sea's boiling bowl! . . .

Thursday, 23d [August 1832]
A curious thought, or rather a fantastical shadow of a thought, occurred to me to-day in reading a chapter in the Corinthians about the resurrection. I mean to be buried with Harriet's[*] ring on my finger; will it be there when I rise again? – What a question for the discussers of the needle's point controversy. . . .

Friday, 24th [August 1832]
Rose late after a fair night's sleep – came up to the round-house. After breakfast, worked and walked for an immense time.

Read a canto in Dante: just as I had finished it, 'A sail! a sail!' was cried from all quarters.

---

* Harriet St Leger, Fanny's 'dearest friend'.
† Miss Hodgkinson.

Remembering my promise to dear Harriet, I got together my writing materials, and scrawled her a few incoherent lines full of my very heart.

The vessel bore rapidly down upon us, but as there was no prospect of either her or our lying-to, Mr Hodgkinson tied my missive, together with one Mr Staley* had just scribbled, to a lump of lead, and presently we all rushed on deck to see the ship pass us.

She was an English packet, from Valparaiso, bound to London; her foremast had been carried away, but she was going gallantly before the wind. As she passed us, Mr Hodgkinson got up into the boat to have a better chance of throwing. I saw him fling powerfully, – the little packet whizzed through the air, but the distance was impossible, and the dark waters received it within twenty feet of the ship, which sailed rapidly on, and had soon left us far behind. I believe I screamed, as the black sea closed over my poor letter. . . .

The letter was to Harriet St Leger, twelve years older than Fanny, who lived at Ardgillan Castle in Ireland.

'The device of her family is "Haut et Bon!"' wrote Fanny of her friend, 'it was her description. She was about thirty years old when I met her . . . tall and thin, her figure wanted roundness and grace, but it was straight as a dart, and the vigorous elastic active movements of her limbs, and firm, fleet springing step of her beautifully made feet and ankles, gave to her whole person and deportment a character like that of Atalanta.'[1]

Fanny jokingly called Harriet, who was of a studious turn, 'Plato in Petticoats,' but for Fanny Harriet was always to be 'the dearest friend I have ever known' and she was to write to her every week and occasionally twice a day for forty years.

They hardly ever met, Harriet leading a secluded life in Ireland. 'I cut down trees, I play with my dog,' she wrote. 'I dig, I carry potatoes to the donkeys, I listen to the music of the mind . . .'[2] Occasionally she and her friend Alice Wilson visited the European watering places. People noted her oddly clumsy boots, made by a man's shoemaker, and her garments, appallingly badly cut, though made of the finest wool. Her character seems to have been austere, and at least outwardly serene, providing a good balance for Fanny's passionate and ebullient nature.

* Mr Staley was a Yorkshire businessman. He was one of Fanny's many admirers, and remained a lifelong friend.

Saturday and Sunday [25 and 26 August 1832]
Towards evening got up and came on deck: – The sky was a mass of stormy black, here and there edged with a copper-looking cloud, and breaking in one or two directions into pale silvery strata, that had an unhealthy lightning look: a heavy black squall lay ahead of us, like a dusky curtain, whence we saw the rain, fringe-like, pouring down against the horizon. The wind blew furiously. I got cradled among the ropes, so as not to be pitched off when the ship lurched, and enjoyed it all amazingly.

It was sad and solemn, and, but for the excitement of the savage-looking waves, that every now and then lifted their overwhelming sides against us, it would have made me melancholy: but it stirred my spirits to ride over these huge sea-horses, that came bounding and bellowing round us.

Remained till I was chilled with the bitter wind, and wet through with spray; – walked up and down the deck for some time – had scarce set foot within the round house, when a sea took her in midships, and soused the loiterers. Sat up, or rather slept up, till ten o'clock, and then went down to bed. . . .

Wednesday, 28th [29 August 1832]
Skipped writing on Tuesday – so much the better – a miserable day spent between heart-ache and side-ache.

Rose late, breakfasted with Henrietta, afterwards went and sat on the forecastle, where I worked the whole morning, woman's work, stitching. . . .

Finished my work, and then, tying on sundry veils and handkerchiefs, danced on deck for some time; – I then walked by the light of the prettiest young moon imaginable.

Afterwards sat working and stifling in the round-house till near ten, and then, being no longer able to endure the heat, came down, undressed, and sat luxuriously on the ground in my dressing-gown drinking lemonade.

At twelve went to bed; the men kept up a horrible row on deck half the night; singing, dancing, whooping, and running over our heads. . . .

Thursday, 29th [30 August 1832]

I sat down stairs in my cabin all day; the very spirit of doggerel possessed me, and I poured forth rhymes as rapidly as possible. – Wrote journal; in looking over my papers, fell in with the *Star of Seville** – some of it is very good. I'll write an English tragedy next.

Dined at table – our heroes have drunk wine, and are amicable. After dinner, went on deck, and took short walk; saw the sun set, which he did like a god, as he is, leaving the sky like a geranium curtain, which overshadowed the sea with rosy light – beautiful!

Came down and sat on the floor like a Turkish woman, stitching, singing, and talking, till midnight; supped – and to bed. My appetite seems like the Danaïde's tub, of credible memory. . . .

Saturday Night Song

Come fill the can again, boys,
One parting glass, one parting glass;
Ere we shall meet again, boys,
Long years may pass, long years may pass. . . .

Sunday, September 2d [1832]

Rose at half-past six: the sun was shining brilliantly; woke Henrietta and went on deck with her. The morning was glorious, the sun had risen two hours in the sky, the sea was cut by a strong breeze, and curled into ridges that came like emerald banks crowned with golden spray round our ship; she was going through the water at nine knots an hour.

I sat and watched the line of light that lay like a fairy road to the east – towards my country, my dear, dear home.

Breakfasted at table for the first time since I've been on board the ship – I did hope, the last. After breakfast, put my things to rights, tidied our cabin for prayers, and began looking out the lessons; while doing so, the joyful sound, 'Land, land!' was heard aloft. I rushed on deck, and between the blue waveless sea, and the bright unclouded sky, lay the wished-for line of darker element. 'Twas Long Island: through a glass I described the undulations of the coast, and even the trees that stood relieved against the sky.

Hail, strange land! my heart greets you coldly and sadly! Oh, how I thought of Columbus, as with eyes strained and on tiptoe

---

* One of Fanny's plays.

our water-weary passengers stood, after a summer's sail of thirty days, welcoming their mother earth!

The day was heavenly, though intensely hot, the sky utterly cloudless, and by that same token, I do not love a cloudless sky. . . .

After dinner, sat in my cabin some time – walked on deck; when the gentlemen joined us we danced the sun down, and the moon up. The sky was like the jewel-shop of angels; I never saw such brilliant stars nor so deep an azure to hang them in. The moon was grown powerful, and flooded the deck, where we sat playing at blind man's buff, magic music, and singing, and talking of shore till midnight, when we came to bed. . . .

Tuesday, September 4th [1832] New York, America
It is true, by my faith! it is true; there it is written, here I sit, I am myself and no other, this is New York and nowhere else – Oh! 'singular, strange!'

Our passengers were all stirring and about at peep of day, and I get up myself at half-past six. Trunks lay scattered in every direction around, and all were busily preparing to leave the good ship *Pacific*. Mercy on us! it made me sad to leave her and my shipmates. . . .

We breakfasted, and packed ourselves into our shawls and bonnets, and at half-past nine the steam-boat came alongside to take us to shore: it was different from any English steam-boat I ever saw, having three decks, and being consequently a vessel of very considerable size. We got on board her all in the rain and misery, and as we drifted on, our passengers collected to the side of the boat and gave 'The dear old Lady' three cheers. Poor ship! there she lay – all sails reefed, rocking in melancholy inaction, deserted by her merry inmates, lonely and idle – poor *Pacific!* . . .

Mr Staley and Mr Hodgkinson went to secure apartments for us at the American Hotel; and after bidding good-by [*sic*] to the sea, we packed ourselves into a hackney coach, and progressed.

The houses are almost all painted glaring white or red; the other favourite colours appear to be pale straw colour and grey. They have all green venetian shutters, which give an idea of coolness, and almost every house has a tree or trees in its vicinity, which looks pretty and garden-like.

We reached our inn, – the gentlemen were waiting for us, and led us to our drawing-room. I had been choking for the last three hours, and could endure no more, but sobbed like a wretch aloud.

There was a piano in the room, to which I flew with the appetite of one who has lived on the music of the speaking-trumpet for a month; that, and some iced lemonade and cake, presently restored my spirits. I went on playing and singing till I was exhausted, and then sat down and wrote journal. . . .

Our dinner was a favourable specimen of eating as practised in this new world; every thing good, only in too great a profusion, the wine drinkable, and the fruit beautiful to look at: in point of flavour it was infinitely inferior to English hothouse fruit, or even fine espalier fruit raised in a good aspect. Every thing was wrapped in ice, which is a most luxurious necessary in this hot climate; but the things were put on the table in a slovenly, outlandish fashion; fish, soup, and meat, at once, and puddings, and tarts, and cheese, at another once; no finger glasses, and a patched tablecloth – in short, a want of that style and neatness which is found in every hotel in England. . . .

Wednesday, 5th [September 1832]
I have been in a sulky fit half the day, because people will keep walking in and out of our room, without leave or licence, which is coming a great deal too soon to Hope's idea of Heaven.* I am delighted to see my friends, but I like to tell them so, and not that they should take it for granted.

When I made my appearance in my dressing gown (my clothes not being come, and the day too hot for a silk pelisse) great was my amazement to find our whole ship's company assembled at the table. After breakfast they dispersed, and I sat writing journal, and playing, and singing. . . .

At half-past three we walked down to the quay to convoy them to their steamboat, which looked indeed like a 'castle on the main'. We saw them on board, went down and looked at the state cabin, which was a magnificent room, and would have done charmingly for a galopade. We bade our new friends, whom I like better than some old ones, good-by, and walked briskly on to the battery, to see them as they passed it. . . .

* Thomas Hope (1770?–1831), traveller and virtuoso, author of *Anastasius*, where his idea of Heaven is presumably to be found.

Came home up Broadway, which is a long street of tolerable width, full of shops, in short the American Oxford Road, where all people go to exhibit themselves and examine others.

The women that I have seen hitherto have all been very gaily dressed, with a pretension to French style, and a more than English exaggeration of it. They all appear to me to walk with a French shuffle, which, as their pavements are flat, I can only account for by their wearing shoes made in the French fashion, which are enough in themselves to make a waddler of the best walker that ever set foot to earth. Two or three were pretty girls; but the town being quite empty, these are probably bad specimens of the graces and charms that adorn Broadway in its season of shining.

Came home and had tea; After which crossed the Park (a small bit of grass enclosed in white palings, in plain English, a green) to the theatre. Wallack was to act in *The Rent Day*. Mercy, how strange I felt as I once more set foot in a theatre; the sound of the applause set my teeth on edge. The house is pretty though rather gloomy, well formed, about the size of the Haymarket, with plenty of gold carving, and red silk about it, looking rich and warm.

The audience was considerable, but all men; scarce, I should think, twenty women in the dress circle, where, by the by, as well as in the private boxes, I saw men sitting with their hats on. . . .

Came to bedroom at eleven, remained up till one, unpacking goods and chattels. Mercy on me, what a cargo it is! They have treated us like ambassadors, and not one of our one and twenty huge boxes have been touched.

Thursday, 6th [September 1832]
Rose at eight. After breakfast, began writing to my brother; while doing so they brought up Captain Whaite's and Mr Staley's cards. I was delighted to see our dear Captain again, who, in spite of his glorious slip-slop, is a glorious fellow. They sat some time. . . . When they were all gone, finished letter and wrote journal.

Unpacked and sorted things. Opened with a trembling heart my bonnet box, and found my precious *Dévy* squeezed to a crush – I pulled it out, rebowed, and reblonded, and reflowered it, and now it looks good enough 'pour les thauvages mamthelle Fannie.' Worked at my muslin gown; in short, did a deal. . . .

This hotel reminds me most extremely of our 'iligant' and untidy apartments in dear, nasty Dublin, at the Shelbourne. The paper in our bedroom is half peeling from the walls, our beds are without curtains, then to be sure there are pier looking-glasses, and one or two pieces of showy French furniture in it. 'Tis customary, too, here, I find, for men to sleep three or four in a room; conceive an Englishman shown into a dormitory for half-a-dozen; I can't think how they endure it; but, however, I have a fever at all those things.

My father asked me, this evening, to write a sonnet about the wild pigeons welcoming us to America; I had thought of it with scribbling intent before, but he wants me to get it up here, and that sickened me. . . .

Friday, 7th [September 1832]

. . . My father proposed to us a walk, and we accordingly sallied forth. We walked to the end of Broadway, a distance of two miles, I should think, and then back again. The evening was most lovely. The moon was lighting the whole upper sky, but every now and then, as we crossed the streets that led to the river, we caught glimpses of the water, and woody banks, and the sky that hung over them; which all were of that deep orange tint, that I never saw, but in Claude's pictures.

After walking nearly a mile up Broadway, we came to Canal Street: it is broader and finer than any I have yet seen in New York; and at one end of it, a Christian church, copied from some Pagan temple or other, looked exceedingly well, in the full flood of silver light that streamed from heaven. . . .

The street was very much thronged, and I thought the crowd a more civil and orderly one, than an English crowd. The men did not jostle or push one another, or tread upon one's feet, or kick down one's shoe heels, or crush one's bonnet into one's face, or turn it round upon one's head, all which I have seen done in London streets. . . .

I observed that the young men to-night invariably made room for women to pass, and many of them, as they drew near us, took the segar [sic] from their mouth, which I thought especially courteous. They were all smoking, to a man, except those who were spitting, which helped to remind me of Paris, to which the whole place bore a slight resemblance. . . .

Sunday, 9th [September 1832]

Rose at eight. While I was dressing, Dall went out of the room, and presently I heard sundry exclamations: 'Good God, is it you! How are you? How have you been?' I opened the door, and saw my uncle.*

After breakfast, went to church with my father. . . . The church we went to is situated half way between the Battery and our hotel. It is like a chapel in the exterior, being quite plain, and standing close in among the houses; the interior was large and perfectly simple. The town is filling, and the church was well attended. 'T is long since I have heard the church service so well read; with so few vices of pronunciation, or vulgarisms of emphasis. Our own clergy are shamefully negligent in this point. . . . The organ and chanting were very good; infinitely superior to the performances of those blessed little parish cherubim, who monopolize the praises of God in our churches, so much to the suffering of all good Christians not favoured with deafness.

The service is a little altered – all prayers for our King, Queen, House of Lords, Parliament, etc., of course omitted: in lieu of which they pray for the President and all existing authorities. Sundry repetitions of the Lord's Prayer, and other passages, were left out; they correct our English, too, substituting the more modern phraseology of those, for the dear old-fashioned them, which our prayer-book uses: as 'spare thou those, O God,' instead of 'spare thou them, O God, which confess their faults.' . . .

I do nothing but look out of window all the blessed day long: I did not think in my old age to acquire so Jezebel† a trick; but the park (as they entitle the green opposite our windows) is so very pretty, and the streets so gay, with their throngs of smartly dressed women, and so amusing with their abundant proportion of black and white caricatures, that I find my window the most entertaining station in the world. . . .

Several of the black women I saw pass had very fine figures; (the women here appear to me to be remarkably small, my own being, I should think, the average height;) but the contrast of a bright blue, or pink crape bonnet, with the black face, white teeth, and glaring blue whites of the eyes, is beyond description grotesque. . . .

* Vincent De Camp, her mother's brother – also an actor.

† The proud and infamous wife of Ahab, King of Israel.

The evening was very beautiful, and we walked as far as Canal Street and back. During our promenade, two fire engines passed us, attended by the usual retinue of shouting children; this is about the sixth fire since yesterday evening. They are so frequent here, that the cry 'Fire, fire!' seems to excite neither alarm nor curiosity, and except the above mentioned painstaking juveniles, none of the inhabitants seem in the least disturbed by it.

We prosecuted our walk down to the Battery, but just as we reached it, we had to return, as 't was tea-time. I was sorry: the whole scene was most lovely. The moon shone full upon the trees and intersecting walks of the promenade, and threw a bright belt of silver along the water's edge. The fresh night wind came over the broad estuary, rippling it, and stirring the boughs with its delicious breath. A building, which was once a fort, from whence the Americans fired upon our ships, is now turned into a sort of *café*, and was brilliantly lighted with coloured lamps, shining among the trees, and reflected in the water. The whole effect was pretty, and very Parisian. . . .

Tuesday, 11th [September 1832]
This day week we landed in New York; and this day was its prototype, rainy, dull, and dreary; with occasional fits of sunshine, and light delicious air, as capricious as a fine lady. . . .

I wish I could make myself draw. I want to do every thing in the world that can be done, and, by the by, that reminds me of my German, which I must *persecute*.

At four o'clock sent for a hair-dresser, that I might in good time see that I am not made an object on my first night. He was a Frenchman, and after listening profoundly to my description of the head-dress I wanted, replied, as none but a Frenchman could, 'Madame, la difficulté n'est pas d'executer votre coiffure mais de la bien concevoir.' However, he conceived and executed sundry very smooth-looking bows, and, upon the whole, dressed my hair very nicely, but charged a dollar for so doing; O nefarious.

Dall and I dined tête-à-tête; the evening was sulky – I was in miserable spirits. . . .

Had tea at eight, and embroidered till midnight. The wind is rioting over the earth. I should like to see the Hudson now. The black clouds, like masses of dark hair, are driven over the moon's pale face, the red lights and fire engines are dancing up and down the streets, the church bells are all tolling – 't is sad and strange.

Wednesday, 12th [September 1832]

Rose at eight. After breakfast, heard my father say Hamlet. How beautiful his whole conception of that part is, and yet it is but an actor's conception too. . . .

To-night, as I stood watching that surpassing sunset, I would have given it all – gold, and purple, and all – for a wreath of English fog stealing over the water. . . .

Friday, 14th [September 1832]

. . . Drove all about New York, which more than ever reminded me of the towns in France: passed the Bowery theatre, which is a handsome, finely-proportioned building, with a large brazen eagle: this is nefarious! We passed a pretty house, which Colonel Sibell* called an old mansion; mercy on me, him, and it! Old! I thought of Warwick Castle, of Hatfield, of Checquers [*sic*], of Hopwood – old, and there it stood, with its white pillars and Italian-looking portico, for all the world like one of our own cit's[†] yesterday-grown boxes. . . .

Saturday, 15th [September 1832]

Sat stitching all the blessed day. So we are to go to Philadelphia before Boston. I'm sorry. The Hones[‡] will be disappointed, and I shall get no riding, *che seccatura* ['What a bore!']

At five dressed, and went to the Hones', where we were to dine. This is one of the first houses here, so I conclude that I am to consider what I see as a tolerable sample of the ways and manners of being, doing, and suffering of the best society in New York.

There were about twenty people; the women were in a sort of French demi-toilette, with bare necks, and long sleeves, heads frizzed out after the very last petit courier, and thread net handkerchiefs and capes; the whole of which, to my English eye, appeared a strange marrying of incongruities.

The younger daughter of our host is beautiful; a young and brilliant likeness of Ellen Tree,[§] with more refinement, and a smile that was, not to say a ray, but a whole focus of sun rays, a perfect

* Another of their friends from the *Pacific*.
† Current slang for the 'residences' of the *nouveaux riches*.
‡ Philip Hone, former Mayor of New York City.
§ Ellen Tree (Mrs Charles Kean) 1805–80, actress.

blaze of light; she was much taken up with a youth, to whom, my neighbour at dinner informed me, she was engaged.

The women here, like those of most warm climates, ripen very early, and decay proportionably [sic] soon. They are, generally speaking, pretty, with good complexions, and an air of freshness and brilliancy, but this, I am told, is very evanescent; and whereas, in England, a woman is in the full bloom of health and beauty from twenty to five-and-thirty, here they scarcely reach the first period without being faded and looking old. They marry very young, and this is another reason why age comes prematurely upon them. . . .

The dinner was plenteous, and tolerably well dressed, but ill served: there were not half servants enough, and we had neither water-glasses nor finger-glasses. Now, though I don't eat with my fingers (except peaches, whereat I think the aborigines, who were paring theirs like so many potatoes, seemed rather amazed) yet do I hold a finger-glass at the conclusion of my dinner a requisite to comfort. After dinner we had coffee, but no tea, whereat my English taste was in high dudgeon. . . .

Sunday, 16th [September 1832]
. . . Dined at five; after dinner, went on with my letter to John,* and wrote an immense one to dear Harriet, which kept me pen in hand till past twelve.

A tremendous thunderstorm came on, which lasted from nine o'clock till past two in the morning: I never saw but one such in my life; and that was our memorable Weybridge storm, which only exceeded this in the circumstance of my having seen a thunderbolt fall during that paroxysm of the elements. But this was very glorious, awful, beautiful, and tremendous.

The lightning played without the intermission of a second, in wide sheets of purple glaring flame that trembled over the earth for nearly two or three seconds at a time; making the whole world, river, sky, trees, and buildings, look like a ghostly universe cut out in chalk. The light over the water, which absolutely illumined the shore on the other side with the broad glare of full day, was of a magnificent purple colour. The night was pitchy dark, too; so that between each of these ghastly smiles of the devil, the various pale

---

* Fanny's elder brother.

steeples and buildings, which seemed at every moment to leap from nothing into existence, after standing out in fearful relief against a background of fire, were hidden like so many dreams in deep and total darkness.

God's music rolled along the heavens; the forked lightnings now dived from the clouds into the very bosom of the city, now ran like tangled threads of fire all round the blazing sky. 'The big bright rain came dancing to the earth,' the wind clapped its huge wings, and swept through the dazzling glare; and as I stood, with eyes half veiled (for the light was too intense even upon the ground to be looked at with unshaded eyes), gazing at this fierce holyday of the elements – at the mad lightning – at the brilliant shower, through which the flashes shone like daylight – listening to the huge thunder, as its voice resounded, and its heavy feet rebounded along the clouds – and the swift spirit-like wind rushing triumphantly along, uttering its wild paean over the amazed earth; – I felt more intensely than I ever did before the wondrous might of these, God's powerful and beautiful creatures. . . .

Monday, 17th [September 1832]
Rose at eight. At twelve, went to rehearsal.

The weather is intolerable; I am in a state of perpetual fusion. The theatre is the coolest place I have yet been in, I mean at rehearsal; when the front is empty, and the doors open, and the stage is so dark that we are obliged to rehearse by candle-light. That washed-out man who failed in London when he acted Romeo with me is to be my Fazio; let us hope he will know some of his words to-morrow night, for he is at present most innocent of any such knowledge.

After rehearsal, walked into a shop to buy some gauze. . . . We dined at three. . . .

At seven, went to the theatre. It was my dear father's first appearance in this new world, and my heart ached with anxiety. The weather was intensely hot, yet the theatre was crowded: when he came on, they gave him what everybody here calls an immense reception; but they should see our London audience get up, and wave hats and handkerchiefs, and shout welcome as they do to us. The tears were in my eyes, and all I could say was, 'They might as well get up, I think.'

My father looked well, and acted beyond all praise; but oh, what a fine and delicate piece of work this is! There is not one sentence, line, or word of this part which my father has not sifted grain by grain; there is not one scene or passage to which he does not give its fullest and most entire substance, together with a variety that relieves the intense study of the whole with wonderful effect. I think that it is impossible to conceive Hamlet more truly, or execute it more exquisitely than he does. The refinement, the tenderness, the grace, dignity, and princely courtesy with which he invests it from beginning to end, are most lovely; and some of the slighter passages, which, like fine tints to the incapable eyes of blindness, must always pass unnoticed, and, of course, utterly uncomprehended, by the discriminating public, enchanted me.

Although the New York Evening Post *was to describe Charles Kemble's performance as that of '. . . the gallant and the finished gentleman'; 'a picture of unaffected courtliness', the Americans found his acting dull. They could make nothing of his deliberate and pregnant pauses, and they found him slow – he was, after all, fifty-eight. But next night was* Fazio, *a torrid melodrama, in which, appearing before her American audience for the first time, Fanny was to play Bianca. She was cast opposite Mr Keppel: 'That washed out man who failed in London when he acted Romeo with me . . .'*

Tuesday, 18th [September 1832]
Rose at eight. At eleven, went to rehearsal. Mr Keppel is just as nervous and as imperfect as ever: what on earth will he, or shall I, do to-night!

Came home, got things out for the theatre, and sat like any stroller stitching for dear life at my head-dress. . . .

At half-past six, went to the theatre. They acted the farce of *Popping the Question* first, in order, I suppose, to get the people to their places before the play began. Poor Mr Keppel was gasping for breath; he moved my compassion infinitely; I consoled and comforted him all I could, gave him some of my lemonade to swallow, for he was choking with fright; sat myself down with my back to the audience, and up went the curtain.

Owing to the position in which I was sitting, and my plain dress, most unheroine-like in its make and colour, the people did not know me, and would not have known me for some time, if that stupid man had done as I kept bidding him, gone on; but instead of doing so, he stood stock still, looked at me, and then at the audience, whereupon the latter caught an inkling of the truth, and gave me such a reception as I get in Covent Garden theatre every time I act a new part.

The house was very full; all the Hones were there, and Colonel Sibell. Mr Keppel was frightened to death, and in the very second speech was quite out: it was in vain that I prompted him; he was too nervous to take the word, and made a complete mess of it. This happened more than once in the first scene; and at the end of the first act, as I left the stage, I said to Dall, 'It's all up with me, I can't do anything now;' for having to prompt my Fazio, frightened by his fright, annoyed by his forgetting his crossings and positions, utterly unable to work myself into any thing like excitement, I thought the whole thing must necessarily go to pieces.

However, once rid of my encumbrance, which I am at the end of the second act, I began to move a little more freely, gathered up my strength, and set to work comfortably by myself; whereupon, the people applauded, I warmed (warmed, quotha? the air was steam) and got through very satisfactorily, at least so it seems.

My dresses were very beautiful; but oh, but oh, the musquitoes [sic] had made dreadful havoc with my arms, which were covered with hills as large and red as Vesuvius in an eruption. . . .

Came to bed at half past twelve; weary, and half melted away. The ants swarm on the floors, on the tables, in the beds, about one's clothes; the plagues of Egypt were a joke to them: horrible! it makes one's life absolutely burdensome, to have creatures creeping about one, and all over one, night and day, this fashion; to say nothing of those cantankerous stinging things, the musquitoes.

Whatever the shortcomings of poor Mr Keppel, Fanny's very appearance was to guarantee the performance instant success.

'The curtain rose', reported the New York Mirror, *'and discovered two characters, the one a man, the other a young female, slight but gracefully formed seated at a table, drawing, with her back partly towards the audience, so as to preclude any immediate recognition. Her companion had proceeded sometime in his opening speech before she turned and discovered a sweet new face, glowing with soul and feeling, and the large, dark eyes of Miss Fanny Kemble half lifted to the audience who returned their glances with long, hearty, and reiterated thunders of applause. The deafening peals*

29

at length died away into a hushed and pervading silence, and the low tones of a silvery voice rose in the silence, tremulously sweet, and at once seducing every heart!'[3]

This particular notice pleased Fanny, who found it *'written with great taste and feeling . . . evidently not the produce of a common hack,'* though she modestly acknowledged that the praise was *'excessive, and far beyond my deserts.'* In other critiques she thought she discerned *'the provincial dread of praising too much.'[4]*

New York society was now standing back to take stock of Fanny. Philip Hone, former Mayor of New York City, confessed he had never seen an audience so moved and delighted. At the same time he noticed about her an air *'of indifference and nonchalance'* and remarked with considerable insight, *'I am of the opinion that she does not like her profession; necessity rather than choice has led her to adopt it.'[5]* This perceptive onlooker further noticed that Fanny preferred the company of married men and that she treated the attentions of any single man with marked ungraciousness.

Thursday, 20th [September 1832]

Rose at eight. After breakfast, went to rehearse *Romeo and Juliet*.

Poor Mr Keppel is fairly laid on the shelf; I'm sorry for him! What a funny passion he had, by the by, for going down upon his knees. In *Fazio*, at the end of the judgement scene, when I was upon mine, down he went upon his, making the most absurd, devout looking *vis-à-vis* I ever beheld: in the last scene, too, when he ought to have been going off to execution, down he went again upon his knees, and no power on earth could get him up again, for Lord knows how long. Poor fellow, he bothered me a good deal, yet I'm sincerely sorry for him.

At the end of our rehearsal, came home. The weather is sunny, sultry, scorching, suffocating. . . .

By the by, Essex* called his morning to fetch away the Captain's claret jug: he asked my father for an order; adding, with some hesitation, 'It must be for the gallery, if you please, sir, for people of colour are not allowed to go to the pit, or any other part of the house.' I believe I turned black myself, I was so indignant. . . .

Friday, 21st [September 1832]

Rose at eight. After breakfast went to rehearsal. *The School for*

---

* The black servant of the captain of the *Pacific*.

Scandal; Sir Peter, I see, keeps his effects to himself; what a bore this is, to be sure! . . .

They were talking of Mr Keppel. By the by, of that gentleman; Mr Simpson sent me this morning, for my decision, a letter from Mr Keppel, soliciting another trial, and urging the hardness of his case, in being condemned upon a part which he had had no time to study. My own opinion of poor Mr Keppel is, that no power on earth or in heaven can make him act decently; however, of course, I did not object to his trying again; he did not swamp me the first night, so I don't suppose he will the fifth.

We dined at five. Just before dinner, received a most delicious bouquet, which gladdened my very heart with its sweet smell and lovely colours: some of the flowers were strangers to me.

After dinner, Colonel Sibell called, and began pulling out heaps of newspapers, and telling us a long story about Mr Keppel, who, it seems, has been writing to the papers, to convince them and the public that he is a good actor, at the same time throwing out sundry hints, which seem aimed our way, of injustice, oppression, hard usage, and the rest on 't. . . .

When they were gone, went to the theatre; the house was very good, the play, *The School for Scandal*. I played pretty fairly, and looked very nice.

The people were stupid to a degree, to be sure; poor things! it was very hot. Indeed, I scarce understand how they should be amused with *The School for Scandal*; for though the dramatic situations are so exquisite, yet the wit is far above the generality of even our own audiences, and the tone and manners altogether are so thoroughly English, that I should think it must be for the most part incomprehensible to the good people here. . . .

Saturday 22d [September 1832]
Rose at eight. After breakfast, dawdled about till near one o'clock: got into a hackney coach with Dall, and returned all manner of cards.

Went into a shop to order a pair of shoes. The shopkeepers in this place, with whom I have hitherto had to deal, are either condescendingly familiar, or insolently indifferent in their manner. Your washerwoman sits down before you, while you are standing speaking to her; and a shop-boy bringing things for your inspection, not only sits down, but keeps his hat on in your drawing-room. The worthy man to whom I went for my shoes was so amazingly ungracious, that at first I thought I would go out of the shop; but recollecting that I should probably only go farther and fare worse, I gulped, sat down, and was measured.

All this is bad: it has its origin in a vulgar misapprehension, which confounds ill breeding with independence, and leads people to fancy that they elevate themselves above their condition by discharging its duties and obligations discourteously. . . .

Sunday, 23d [September 1832]

Rose at eight. After breakfast, went to church with Dall. There is no such thing, I perceive, as a pew-opener; so, after standing sufficiently long in the middle of the church, we established ourselves very comfortably in a pew, where we remained un-molested.

The day was most lovely, and my eyes were constantly attracted to the church windows, through which the magnificent willows of the burial-ground looked like golden-green fountains rising into the sky. . . .

Monday, 24th [September 1832]

Rose at eight: went and took a bath. After breakfast, went to rehearsal: *Venice Preserved*, with Mr Keppel, who did not appear to me to know the words even, and seemed perfectly bewildered at being asked to do the common business of the piece. 'Mercy on me! what will he do tonight?' thought I. . . .

Dined at three: after dinner, played and sang through *Cinderella*; wrote journal: at six, went to the theatre.

My gown was horribly ill-plaited, and I looked like a blue-bag. The house was very full, and they received Mr Keppel with acclamations and shouts of applause.

When I went on, I was all but tumbling down at the sight of my Jaffier* who looked like the apothecary in *Romeo and Juliet*, with the addition of some devilish red slashes along his thighs and arms.

The first scene passed well and so: but, oh, the next, and the next, and the next to that. Whenever he was not glued to my side (and that was seldom), he stood three yards behind me; he did nothing but seize my hand, and grapple to it so hard, that unless I

---

* Mr Keppel as the hero.

had knocked him down (which I felt much inclined to try), I could not disengage myself.

In the senate scene, when I was entreating for mercy, and struggling, as Otway has it, for my life, he was prancing round the stage in every direction, flourishing his dagger in the air: I wish to Heaven I had got up and run away; it would but have been natural, and have served him extremely right.

In the parting scene – oh what a scene it was! – instead of going away from me when he said 'farewell for ever,' he stuck to my skirts, though in the same breath that I adjured him, in the words of my part, not to leave me, I added, aside, 'Get away from me, oh do!' When I exclaimed, 'Not one kiss at parting,' he kept embracing and kissing me like mad; and when I ought to have been pursuing him, and calling after him, 'Leave thy dagger with me,' he hung himself up against the wing, and remained dangling there for five minutes.

I was half crazy! and the good people sat and swallowed it all: they deserved it, by my troth, they did. I prompted him constantly, and once, after struggling in vain to free myself from him, was obliged, in the middle of my part, to exclaim, 'You hurt me dreadfully, Mr Keppel!' He clung to me, cramped me, crumpled me – dreadful! . . .

We came home tired, and thoroughly disgusted, and found no supper. The cooks, who do not live in the house, but come and do their work, and depart home whenever it suits their convenience, had not thought proper to stay to prepare any supper for us: so we had to wait for the readiest things that could be procured out of doors for us – this was pleasant – very!

At last appeared a cold boiled fowl, and some monstrous oysters, that looked for all the world like an antediluvian race of oysters, 'for in those days there were giants'.* Six mouthfuls each: they were well-flavoured; but their size displeased my eye, and I swallowed but one, and came to bed. . . .

Sunday, 30th [September 1832]
. . . Select specimens of American pronunciation:

vaggaries	vagaries
ad infinnitum	*ad infinitem*
vitupperate	vituperate

* Genesis, 6, 4.

Monday, 8th [October 1832]

Rose (oh, horror!) at a quarter to five. Night was still brooding over the earth. Long before I was dressed the first voice I heard was that of Colonel Sibell, come to look after our luggage, and see us off.

To lend my friend a thousand pounds (if I had it) I could; to lend him my horse, perhaps I might; but to get up in the middle of the night, and come dawdling in the grey cold hour of the morning upon damp quays, and among dusty packages, except for my own flesh and blood, I could not. Yet this worthy man did it for us; whence I pronounce that he must be half a Quaker himself, for no common episcopal benevolence could stretch this pitch.

Dressed, and gathered together my things, and at six o'clock, just as the night was folding its soft black wings, and rising slowly from the earth, we took our departure from that mansion of little ease, the American,* and our fellow-lodgers the ants, and proceeded to the Philadelphia steam-boat, which started from the bottom of Barclay Street.

We were recommended to this American hotel as the best and most comfortable in New York; and truly the charges were as high as one could have paid at the Clarendon, in the land of comfort and taxation. The wine was exorbitantly dear; champagne and claret about eleven shillings sterling a bottle; sherry, port, and madeira, from nine to thirteen. The rooms were a mixture of French finery, and Irish disorder and dirt; the living was by no means good; the whole house being conducted on a close scraping system of inferior accommodations and extravagant charges. . . . In short, nothing can exceed the want of order, propriety, and comfort in this establishment, except the enormity of the tribute it levies upon pilgrims and wayfarers through the land. And so, as I said, we departed therefrom nothing loath.

The morning was dull, dreary, and damp, which I regretted very much. The steam-boat was very large and commodious, as all these conveyances are. I enquired of one of the passengers what the power of the engine was: he replied that he did not exactly know, but that he thought it was about forty-horse power; and that, when going at speed, the engine struck thirty times in a minute: this appeared to me a great number in so short a time; but the weather shortly became wet and drizzly, and I did not remain

* Their hotel.

on deck to observe. My early rising had made me very sleepy, so I came down to the third deck to sleep.

These steam-boats have three storeys; the upper one is, as it were, a roofing or terrace on the leads of the second, a very desirable station when the weather is neither too foul nor too fair; a burning sun being, I should think, as little desirable there as a shower of rain. The second floor or deck has the advantage of the ceiling above, and yet, the sides being completely open, it is airy, and allows free sight of the shores on either hand. Chairs, stools, and benches, are the furniture of these two decks. The one below, or third floor, downwards, in fact, the ground floor, being the one near the water, is a spacious room completely roofed and walled in, where the passengers take their meals, and resort if the weather is unfavourable. At the end of this room is a smaller cabin for the use of the ladies, with beds and a sofa, and all the conveniences necessary, if they should like to be sick; whither I came and slept till breakfast time. . . .

At about half-past ten we reached the place where we leave the river, to proceed across a part of the State of New Jersey to the Delaware. The landing was beyond measure wretched: the shore shelved down to the water's edge; and its marshy, clayey, sticky soil, rendered doubly soft and squashy by the damp weather, was strewn over with broken potsherds, stones, and bricks, by way of pathway; these, however, presently failed, and some slippery planks half immersed in mud were the only roads to the coaches that stood ready to receive the passengers of the steam-boat. Oh, these coaches! . . . They are shaped something like boats, the sides being merely leathern pieces, removable at pleasure, but which, in bad weather, are buttoned down to protect the inmates from the wet. There are three seats in this machine; the middle one, having a movable leathern strap, by way of a dossier, runs between the carriage doors, and lifts away to permit the egress and ingress of the occupants of the other seats.

Into the one facing the horses Dall and I put ourselves; presently two young ladies occupied the opposite one; a third lady, and a gentleman of the same party, sat in the middle seat, into which my father's huge bulk was also squeezed; finally, another man belonging to the same party ensconced himself between the two young ladies. . . . The third place was amply filled up with baskets and packages of ours, and huge *undoubleableup* coats and cloaks of my father's. For the first few minutes I thought I must have fainted from the intolerable sensation of smothering which I experienced. However, the leathers having been removed, and a little more air obtained, I took heart of grace, and resigned myself to my fate.

Away wallopped [sic] the four horses, trotting with their front, and galloping with their hind legs; and away went we after them, bumping, thumping, jumping, jolting, shaking, tossing, and tumbling, over the wickedest road, I do think the cruellest, hard-heartedest road that ever wheel rumbled upon. Through bog and marsh, and ruts wider and deeper than any Christian ruts I ever saw, with the roots of trees protruding across our path; their boughs every now and then giving us an affectionate scratch through the windows. . . . Bones of me! what a road! . . . Even my father's solid proportions could not keep their level, but were jerked up to the roof and down again every three minutes.

Our companions seemed nothing dismayed by these wondrous performances of a coach and four, but laughed and talked incessantly, the young ladies, at the very top of their voices, and with the national nasal twang. The conversation was much of the genteel shop-keeper kind; the wit of the ladies, and the gallantry of the gentlemen, savouring strongly of tapes and yard measures, and the shrieks of laughter of the whole set enough to drive one into a frenzy.

The ladies were all pretty; two of them particularly so, with delicate fair complexions, and beautiful grey eyes: how I wish they could have held their tongues for two minutes. We had not long been in the coach before one of them complained of being dreadfully sick. This, in such a space, and with seven near neighbours! Fortunately she was near the window; and during our whole fourteen miles of purgatory she alternately leaned from it overcome with sickness, then reclined languishingly in the arms of her next neighbour, and then, starting up with amazing vivacity, joined her voice to the treble duet of her two pretty companions, with a superiority of shrillness, that might have been the pride and envy of Billingsgate. . . .

The few cottages and farm houses which we passed reminded me of similar dwellings in France and Ireland; yet the peasantry here have not the same excuse for disorder and dilapidation as either the Irish or French. The farms had the same desolate, untidy, untended look: the gates broken, the fences carelessly put up, or ill repaired; the farming utensils sluttishly scattered about a littered yard, where the pigs seemed to preside by undisputed right; house-windows broken, and stuffed with paper or clothes; dishevelled women, and barefooted, anomalous looking human young things; – none of the stirring life and activity which such places present in England and Scotland; above all, none of the enchanting mixture of neatness, order, and rustic elegance and comfort, which render so picturesque the surroundings of a farm, and the various belongings of agricultural labour in my own dear country. . . .

At the end of fourteen miles we turned into a swampy field, the whole fourteen coachfuls of us, and, by the help of Heaven, bag and baggage were packed into the coaches which stood on the railway ready to receive us. The carriages were not drawn by steam, like those on the Liverpool rail-way, but by horses, with the mere advantage in speed afforded by the iron ledges, which, to be sure, compared with our previous progress through the ruts, was considerable.

Our coachful got into the first carriage of the train, escaping, by way of especial grace, the dust which one's predecessors occasion. This vehicle had but two seats, in the usual fashion; each of which held four of us. The whole inside was lined with blazing scarlet leather, and the windows shaded with stuff curtains of the same refreshing colour; which, with full complement of passengers, on a fine, sunny, American summer's day, must make as pretty a little miniature hell as may be, I should think. . . .

This rail-road is an infinite blessing; 't is not yet finished, but shortly will be so, and then the whole of that horrible fourteen miles will be performed in comfort and decency in less than half the time.

In about an hour and a half we reached the end of our railroad part of the journey, and found another steam-boat waiting for us, when we all embarked on the Delaware. Again, the enormous width of the river struck me with astonishment and admiration. Such huge bodies of water mark out the country through which they run, as the future abode of the most extensive commerce, and greatest maritime power in the universe. . . .

I sat working, having finished my book, not a little discomfited by the pertinacious staring of some of my fellow-travellers. One woman, in particular, after wandering round me in every direction, at last came and sat down opposite me, and literally gazed me out of countenance.

One improvement they have adopted on board these boats is to forbid smoking, except in the fore part of the vessel. I wish they would suggest that, if the gentlemen would refrain from spitting about too, it would be highly agreeable to the female part of the community. The universal practice here of this disgusting trick makes me absolutely sick: every place is made a perfect piggery of – street, stairs, steam-boat, every where – and behind the scenes; and on the stage at rehearsal I have been shocked and annoyed beyond expression by this horrible custom. To-day, on board the boat, it was a perfect shower of saliva all the time; and I longed to be released from my fellowship with these very obnoxious chewers of tobacco.

At about four o'clock we reached Philadelphia, having performed the journey between that and New York (a distance of a hundred miles) in less than ten hours, in spite of bags, ruts, and all other impediments. The manager came to look after us and our goods, and we were presently stowed into a coach which conveyed us to the Mansion House, the best reputed inn in Philadelphia. . . .

Tuesday, 9th [October 1832]
Rose at half-past eight. Went and took a bath. On my way thither, drove through two melancholy looking squares, which reminded me a little of poor old Queen Square in Bristol.

The ladies' baths were closed, but as I was not particular, they gave me one in the part of the house usually allotted to men's use. I was much surprised to find two baths in one room, but it seems to me that the people of this country have an aversion to solitude, whether eating, sleeping, or under any other circumstances.

I made acquaintance with a bewitching Newfoundland puppy whom I greatly coveted. Came home, dressed, and breakfasted. After breakfast, righted my things, and wrote journal.

Took a walk with my father through some of the principal streets. The town is perfect silence and solitude, compared with New York; there is a greater air of age about it too, which pleases me. The red houses are not so fiercely red, nor the white facings so glaringly white; in short, it has not so new and flaunting a look, which is a great recommendation to me.

The city is regularly built, the streets intersecting each other at right angles. We passed one or two pretty buildings in pure white marble, and the bank in Chestnut Street, which is a beautiful little copy of the Parthenon. The pure, cold, clear-looking marble, suits well with the severe and un-adorned style of architecture; and is in harmony, too, with the extreme brilliancy of the sky, and clearness of the atmosphere of this country. . . .

Wednesday, 10th [October 1832]
Rose at eight. After breakfast, trimmed a cap, and wrote to dear Harriet.

The streets were in an uproar all night, people shouting and bonfires blazing; in short, electioneering fun, which seems to be pretty much the same all the world over. . . .

At twelve o'clock, sallied forth with Dall to rehearsal. The theatre is very pretty; not large, but well sized, and I should think, favourably constructed for the voice. . . .

Dined at three: after dinner read my father some of my journal; went on with letter to Harriet, and then went and dressed myself. Took coffee, and adjourned to the theatre.

The house was very full, but not so full as the Park on the first night of his acting in New York, which accounts for the greater stillness of the audience. I watched my father narrowly through his part to-night with great attention and some consequent fatigue, and the conclusion I have come to is this: that though his workmanship may be, and is, far finer in the hand, than that of any other artist I ever saw, yet its very minute accuracy and refinement renders it unfit for the frame in which it is exhibited. . . .

Now the great beauty of all my father's performances, but particularly of Hamlet, is a wonderful accuracy in the detail of the character which he represents; an accuracy which modulates the emphasis of every word, the nature of every gesture, the expression of every look; and which renders the whole a most laborious and minute study, toilsome in the conception and acquirement, and most toilsome in the execution. But the result, though the natural one, is not such as he expects, as the reward of so much labour. Few persons are able to follow such a performance with the necessary attention, and it is almost as great an exertion to see it understandingly, as to act it. . . .

Kean* and my father are immediately each other's antipodes, and in adopting their different styles of acting, it is evident that each has been guided as much by his own physical and intellectual individuality, as by any fixed principle of art.

The one, Kean, possesses particular physical qualifications; an eye like an orb of light, a voice, exquisitely touching and melodious in its tenderness, and in the harsh dissonance of vehement passion terribly true; to these he adds the intellectual ones of vigour, intensity, amazing power of concentrating effect: these give him an entire mastery over his audience in all striking, sudden, impassioned passages; in fulfilling which, he has contented himself, leaving unheeded what he probably could not compass, the unity of conception, the refinement of detail, and evenness of execution.

My father possesses certain physical defects, a faintness of colouring in the face and eye, a weakness of voice; and the corresponding intellectual deficiencies, a want of intensity, vigour, and concentrating power: these circumstances have led him (probably unconsciously) to give his attention and study to the finer and more fleeting shades of character, the more graceful and delicate manifestations of feeling, the exquisite variety of all minor parts, the classic keeping of a highly wrought whole; to all these, polished and refined tastes, an acute sense of the beauty of harmonious proportions, and a native grace, gentleness, and refinement of mind and manner, have been his prompters; but they cannot inspire those startling and tremendous bursts of passion, which belong to the highest walks of tragedy, and to which he never gave their fullest expression. I fancy my aunt Siddons united the excellences of both these styles. . . .

Friday, 12th [October 1832]
Rose at eight. After breakfast, sat writing journal. . . . At half-past eleven, went to rehearsal.

Afterwards walked down to the riding-school with my father. The horse I was to look at had not arrived; but my father saw the grey. We were there for some time; and during that whole some time a tall, thin, unhappy looking gentleman, who had gotten up upon a great hulking rawboned horse, kept trotting round and

* Edmund Kean (1789–1833), an unrivalled tragic actor.

round, with his legs dangling down, sans stirrups, at the rate of a mile and a quarter an hour; occasionally ejaculating in the mildest of tones, 'keome – keome up;' whereat the lively brute, nothing persuaded, proceeded in the very same pace, at the very same rate; and this went on till I wondered at the man and the beast.

Came home and put out things for the theatre. My cold and cough are dreadful. After dinner, practised: invented and executed a substitute for the *coques de perle* in my Bianca dress; and lay down to rest a little before my work. At six, went to the theatre: the house was very full; and Dall and my father say that I was extremely ungracious in my acknowledgment of their greeting. I cannot tell; I did not mean to be so; I made them three courtesies [*sic*], and what could woman do more? Of course, I can neither feel nor look so glad to see them, as I am to see my own dear London people: neither can I be as profound in my obeisance, as when my audience is civil enough to rise to me: 'there is differences, look you.' . . .

Saturday, 13th [October 1832]
Rose at half-past eight. After breakfast, wrote journal; practised for an hour; got things ready for tomorrow; put on my habit, which I had no sooner done than the perverse clouds began to rain. The horses came at two, but the weather was so bad that I sent them away again. Practised for another hour, read a canto in Dante, and dressed for dinner. After dinner, worked and practised.

Came to my own room, and tried to scribble something for the *Mirror*, at my father's request; the editors having made an especial entreaty to him, that I might write something for them, and also sit to some artist for them. I could not accomplish any thing, and they must just take something that I have by me: as for my physiognomy, that they shall certainly not have with my own good leave. I will never expend so much useless time again as to sit for my picture; nor will I let any unhappy painter again get abused for painting me as I am, which is any thing but what I look like. Lawrence alone could do it: there is no other that could see my spirit through my face; and as for the face without that, the less that is seen of it the better.

Came down to tea, and found a young gentleman sitting with my father; one Mr Pierce Butler. He was a pretty-spoken genteel youth enough: he drank tea with us, and offered to ride with me. He is, it seems, a great fortune; consequently, I suppose (in spite of his inches), a great man. Now I'll go to bed: my cough's enough to kill a horse.

15 October – 30 December 1832

Fanny at this time knew very little if anything of Pierce Butler. He, however, knew something of her, thanks to his English crony, Henry Berkeley. It was Berkeley, Fanny tells us, 'who when we were going to Philadelphia gave my father a letter of introduction to Mr Butler and so was the means of my first acquaintance with that gentleman.'[6]

'In conversation she is very free, but highly educated and accomplished,' Berkeley had written to his friend, 'she puts you out of countenance by cursed apt quotations . . . if you show any French, she kills you with Racine, if Italian, knocks you down with Dante – Rather blue! but mind not obtrusively so . . .' In spite of large hands and large arms, he told Pierce, Fanny was 'right lovely to look upon,' her voice soft and beautiful, her face all expression, 'you will fall in love with her',[7] he promised. And this indeed is what happened.

The man before her was small and well made. 'Marse Pierce, little short one,'[8] as Celia, a Butler slave, affectionately remembered him. S. Weir Mitchell, one of Philadelphia's eminent physicians, referred to 'his singular personal beauty', his 'refined charm of manner.' He rode well, was a talented amateur musician, had studied for the American bar. Descended from a distinguished Irish family, he was heir to one of the largest cotton and rice plantations in the South – a great catch, and rumour had it that he was already engaged to Emily Chapman, the reigning belle of Philadelphia. He had, moreover, S. Weir Mitchell tells us, 'perfect amiability,' though it was that 'of a selfish man',[9] and alas, his credentials – how could the unfortunate Fanny have known – were little better than those of his friend, Henry Berkeley.

'. . . one of the most profligate and unprincipled men I have ever known', wrote Fanny of Berkeley, many years later. 'He was also one of the most agreeable and accomplished. He was the most intimate friend of Pierce Butler who when he first made his acquaintance, was a mere youth, not yet of age. To this Englishman's example and precepts I attribute much of Mr Butler's subsequent profligacy.'[10]

This was in the future, however. Nine days after meeting Pierce, Fanny, apparently unaffected, was writing to a friend of the dearest wish of her heart, 'a cottage near Edinburgh, with an income of two hundred a year, seems to me the most desirable of earthly possessions'.[11]

43

Nevertheless, from now onwards she would regularly receive 'enchanting' and costly nosegays of 'roses, geraniums, rare heaths, and white camellias' from someone who mysteriously signed himself: 'from a Friend'.

Monday, 15th [October 1832]

Rose at eight; took a hot bath. . . . After breakfast, went to rehearsal.

The day was cold, but beautifully bright and clear. The pure, fresh, invigorating air, and gay sunlight, together with the delightfully clean streets, and pretty mixture of trees and buildings in this nice town, caused me to rejoice, as I walked along. . . .

Went and ordered a dress. . . . Came home, put out things for the theatre, practised an hour; dined at three.

After dinner, read a canto in Dante: he is my admiration! – great, great master! – a philosopher profound, as all poets should be; a glorious poet, as I wish all philosophers were. Sketched till dark. Chose a beautiful claret-coloured velvet for Mrs Beverley;* which will cost Miss Kemble eleven guineas, by this living light.

At six, went to the theatre. I never beheld any thing more gorgeous than the sky at sunset. Autumn is an emperor here, clothed in crimson and gold, and canopied with ruddy glowing skies. Yet I like the sad russet cloak of our own autumnal woods. . . .

The play was *Romeo and Juliet*. My father was the 'youngest of that name,' for want of a better, or, rather, of a worse. How beautiful this performance must have been, when the youthful form made that appear natural which now seems the triumph of art over nature. Garrick said, that to act Romeo required a grey head upon green shoulders. Indeed, 't is difficult! Oh, that our sapient judges did but know half how difficult.

It is delightful to act with my father. One's imagination need toil but little, to see in him the very thing he represents; whereas, with all other Romeos, although they were much younger men, I have had to do double work with that useful engine, my fancy: first, to get rid of the material obstacle staring me in the face, and then to substitute some more congenial representative of that sweetest vision of youth and love. Once, only, this was not necessary.†

* The heroine of *The Gamester*.

† Presumably Miss Tree, since Fanny always said she was her best Romeo.

The audience here are, without exception, the most disagreeable I ever played to. Not a single hand did they give the balcony scene, or my father's scene with the friar: they are literally immovable. They applauded vehemently at the end of my draught scene, and a great deal at the end of the play; but they are, nevertheless, intolerably dull; and it is all but impossible to act to them.

Tuesday, 16th [October 1832]
. . . We came in at five o'clock; dressed, and dined. Just as I had finished dinner, a most beautiful, fragrant, and delicious nosegay was brought to me with a very laconic note from a Philadelphia 'friend',* dashed under, as though from a Quaker. Whoever 't is from, Jew or Gentile, Puritan or Pagan, he, she, or it hath my most unbounded gratitude. Spent an ecstatic half hour in arranging my flowers in glasses; gave orders about my Mrs Beverley's gown, and began marking journal; while doing so, a card was brought up. . . .

Thursday, 18th [October 1832]
. . . Returned home at about half-past five, dined at six; found another beautiful nosegay waiting for me, from my unknown furnisher of sweets. This is almost as tantalizing as it is civil; and I would give half my lovely flowers to find out who sends them to me. Distributed them all over the room, and was as happy as a queen. . . .

Tuesday, 23rd [October 1832]
At ten o'clock, went to rehearsal. Rehearsed *The Hunchback*, and then *Fazio*: this is tolerably hard work, with acting every night: we don't steal our money, that's one comfort.

Came home, found a letter for me in a strange hand. Went on with my letter to —;† while doing so, was interrupted by the entrance of a strange woman, who sat herself down, apparently in much confusion. She told me a story of great distress, and claimed my assistance as a fellow-countrywoman. I had not a farthing of money: Dall and my father were out; so I took the reference she gave me, and promised to enquire into her condition.

* Pierce Butler.

† Not filled in by Fanny.

The greatest evil arising from the many claims of this sort which are made upon us, wherever we go, is the feeling of distrust and suspicion which they engender, and the sort of excuse which they teach us to apply plausibly to our unwillingness to answer such demands. 'Oh, ten to one, an impostor,' is soon said, and instances enough may unfortunately be found to prove the probability of such a conclusion. Yet in this sweeping condemnation, one real case of misery may be included, and that possibility should make us pause, for 't is one that, if afterwards detected, may be the source of heavy condemnation, and bitter regret to ourselves. . . .

After dinner, went on writing to —,* till time to go to the theatre. The house was not as full as I had expected, though a good one enough. My father looked wonderfully well and young: there is certainly some difference in acting with him, but this part fatigues me horribly.

Wednesday, 24th [October 1832]
Went to rehearsal at eleven; at half-past one, went with Dall to find out something about my yesterday's poor woman. The worst of it is, that my trouble involves necessarily the trouble of somebody else, as I cannot go trotting and exploring about by myself. The references were sufficiently satisfactory, that is, they proved that she was poor, and in distress, and willing to work. I gave her what I could, and the man by whom she is employed seems anxious to afford her work; so I hope she will get on a little. The 'God bless you,' of gratitude, even if uttered by guileful and unworthy lips, is surely yet a blessing if it alights on those who are seeking to do good. And if I were assured that that woman was the veriest impostor under the sun, I still should hope her prayer might descend with profit on my head; for I was sincere in my desire to do well by her. . . .

Thursday, 25th [October 1832]

. . . A Mr, Mrs, and young Mr Biddle, called upon us: they are the only inhabitants of this good city who have done us that honour. . . .

---

* Not filled in by Fanny.

Saturday, 27th [October 1832]

The poor sick lady, whose pretty children I met running about the stairs, sent to say she should be very glad if I would go in and see her: I had had sundry inward promptings to this effect before, but was withheld by the real English dread of intruding. At eleven, went to rehearsal: on my return, called on Mrs Dulaney*. . . .

Began practising, when in walked that interesting youth, Mr Biddle, with a nosegay, as big as himself, in his hand. Flowers – sweet blooming, fresh, delicious flowers – in the last days of October; the very sackcloth season of the year. How they do rejoice my spirit. He sat some time, making most excessively fine speeches to me: while he was here, arrived another bouquet from my unknown friend; how nice, to be sure! all but not knowing who they come from.† . . .

Sunday, 28th [October 1832]

Had only time to swallow a mouthful of breakfast, and off to church. I must say it requires a deal of fortitude to go into an American church: there are no pew openers, and the people appear to rush indifferently into any seats that are vacant. We went into a pew where there were two women and a man, who did not take up one half of it; but who, nevertheless, looked most ungracious at our coming into it. They did not move to make way or accommodate us, but remained, with very discourteous, unchristian-like sulkiness, spread over twice as much space as they required.

The spirit of independence seems to preside paramount, even in the house of God. This congregation, by frequenting an Episcopalian temple, evidently professed the form of faith of the English church; yet they neither uttered the responses, nor observed any one of the directions in the Common Prayer-book. Thus, during portions of the worship where kneeling is enjoined, they sat or stood; and while the Creed was being read, half the auditors were reclining comfortable in their pews: the same thing with the Psalms, and all parts of the service. I suppose their love of freedom will not suffer them to be amenable to forms, or wear the exterior of humbleness and homage, even in the house of the Most High God. The whole appearance of the congregation was that of

---

* 'The poor sick lady.'
† They were, of course, from Pierce Butler.

indifference, indolence, and irreverence, and was highly displeasing to my eye.

After church, came home. . . . Mr Staley called. He sat some time mending pens for me; and at half-past one Dall, he, and I packed ourselves into a coach, and proceeded on to Fair Mount, where we got out, and left the coach to wait for us. The day was bright and bitter cold: the keen spirit-like wind came careering over the crisping waters of the broad river, and carried across the cloudless blue sky the golden showers from the shivering woods. . . .

On we went, Mr Staley and I moderating our strides to keep pace with Dall; and she, puffing, panting, and struggling on to keep pace with us; yet I was perished, and she was half melted: like all compromises, it was but a botched business.

The wind was deliciously fresh; and I think, as we buffeted along in its very face, we should have made an admirable subject for Bunbury,* I, with my bonnet off, my combs out, and all my hair flying about, hooked up to Staley, who, willow-like, bent over me, to facilitate my reaching his arm. Dall following in the rear, her cap and hair half over her face, her shawl and clothes fluttering in the blast, her cheeks the colour of crimson, which, relieved by her green bonnet, whose sides she grappled tightly down to balk the wind, had much the effect of a fine carnation bursting its verdant sheath. I never saw any thing half so absurd in my life, as we all looked. Yet it was very pleasant and wholesome, good for soul and body. . . .

Friday, November 2d [1832]
A bright sunny day; too hot for a fire; windows open, shutters closed, and the room full of flowers. How the sweet summer-time stays lingering here. . . .

Mrs Dulaney came in and sat with me: she played to me, and sang 'Should those fond hopes ever leave thee.' Her voice was as thin as her pale transparent hands. She appeared to me much better than when last I saw her; but presently told me she had just been swallowing eighty drops of laudanum, poor thing!

When she was gone, went on practising, and writing, till my father came home. Walked with him and Dall to call on old Lady Oldmison.

* Henry William Bunbury (1750–1811), English cartoonist.

The day was so hot that I could scarcely endure my boa. The election was going on; the streets full of rabblement, the air full of huzzaing, and the sky obscured with star-spangled banners, and villainous transparencies of 'Old Hickory'* hung out in all directions. We went round the Town House, and looked at the window out of which Jefferson† read the Act of Independence, that proclaimed the separation between England and America.

Called at a music-shop, tossed over heaps of music, bought some, and ordered some to be sent home for me to look over. Came home, put out things for the theatre.

Dined at three. Received another beautiful nosegay. . . . I played pretty well. The house was very good; but at the end I really was half dead. On our return home, met a procession of electioneerers carrying triangular paper lanterns upon poles, with 'sentiments' political scribbled thereon, which, however, I could not distinguish. Found a most exquisite nosegay waiting for me at home, so sweet, so brilliant, so fragrant, and fresh.

Found nothing for supper that I could fancy. Drank some tea, wrote journal. Colonel Sibell came in after supper, and wondered that I had played better to my father's Jaffier, than to Mr Keppel's. Heaven bless the world, for a conglomerated amalgamation of fools!

Monday, 5th [November 1832]
Guy Fawlk's [sic] day, and no squibs, no firing of pistols, no bonfires, nor parading about of ferocious looking straw men. Ah! these poor people never had a king and two houses of parliament, and don't know what a mercy it is they weren't blown up before they passed the reform bill. Now if such an accident should occur to them, they'd all be sure to be blown straight into heaven, and hang there.

Rose at half-past five. Oh, I quite agree with the Scotch song,

> Up in the morning's na for me,
> Up in the morning early;
> I'd rather watch a winter's night,
> Than rise in the morning early.

* General Andrew Jackson (1767–1845), seventh President of the United States.
† Thomas Jefferson (1743–1826), third President of the United States.

Dressed myself by candle light. . . . Started from the Mansion House (which is a very nice inn, kept by the civilest of people) at six, and reached the quay just in time to meet the first rosy breaking of the clouds over the Delaware.

I am sorry to leave Philadelphia. I like the town, and the little I have seen of its inhabitants, very much; I mean in private, for they are intolerable audiences. There is an air of stability, of well to do, and occasionally of age, in the town, that reminds me of England. Then, as far as my yesterday's dinner will allow me to judge, I should say, that not only the style of living, but the society was superior to that which I saw in New York. Certainly both the entertainment itself, and the guests, were irreproachable; the first was in very good taste, the latter appeared to me well-informed, and very agreeable.

The morning . . . was beautiful beyond description. The river like the smoothest glass. . . . The tints of the woods were what no words can convey the slightest idea of. Now, a whole track of withered oaks, of a red brick hue, like a forest scorched with fire; now, a fresh thicket of cedars, of the brightest green; then, wide screens of mingled trees, where the foliage was one gorgeous mixture of vermilion, dark maroon, tender green, golden yellow, and deep geranium. . . . It was very beautiful.

I did not, however, see much of it, for I was overcome with fatigue, and slept, both in the steam-boat, and in the stage-coach. When we embarked on the Raritan, I had intended lying down in the cabin, and taking my sleep fairly out, but the jolting of those bitter roads had made every one of the women sick, and the cabin was horrible beyond expression.

Came up on deck, and worked till within a quarter of a mile of New York, when I went on the upper deck, and walked about with Colonel Sibell. I asked Captain Seymour how often the engine would strike in a minute; he told me thirty-six times. By the by, we had a race coming down the Raritan, with the *Union* steam-boat. The *Water Witch* beat her hollow; but she came so near as to make our water rough, and so impede our progress, that I thought we should have had a concussion; there is something very exciting in emulation, certainly. . . .

Our second landing at New York was rather melancholy: shall I ever forget the first? Came up to our comfortless quarters at the American; dressed, and dined, and began finishing my letter to dear Harriet, when they brought me in another from her, by the packet that has just come in. . . .

Wednesday, 7th [November 1832]
Our breakfast was so bad, none of us could eat any thing. . . . Practised for an hour – sketched for an hour. . . . Worked at the ornaments of my Bianca dress, finished one, and wrote journal. . . .

Thursday, 8th [November 1832]
Came to my own room – refurbished my green velvet bonnet. 'T is a worthy old thing that, and looks amazingly well. The cold weather is setting in very bitterly today; we were obliged to have a fire. Heard my father his part. . . .

At a quarter to six, went to the theatre. Play, *Fazio*; house very fine; dress like a bonfire. I played well, but then my father was the Fazio. The people cried abundantly. . . . Received a nosegay, as big as myself, of dahlias and other autumnal flowers.

The moon is resplendent! the earth is flooded with her cold light – beautiful! By the by, last night, at three o'clock this morning, I was awakened by music. It was a military band playing Yankee Doodle, the national anthem of the Americans, accompanied by the tramp of a considerable body of men. They took the direction of the Park, and there halted, when I heard a single voice haranguing for a length of time, with occasional interruptions of vehement huzzas, and rolling of drums. And anon, the march struck up again, grew faint, and died into the stillness of the night. . . .

Saturday, 10th [November 1832]
Skipped yesterday: so much the better, for though it began, like May, with flowers and sunshine, it ended, like December, with the sulks, and a fit of crying. The former were furnished me by my friends and Heaven, the latter, by myself and the devil.

At six o'clock, Dall roused me; and grumpily enough I arose. I dressed myself by candlelight in a hurry. Really, by way of a party of pleasure, 't is too abominable to get up in the middle of the night this fashion.

At half-past six, Colonel Sibell came; and as soon as I could persuade myself into my clothes, we set off to walk to the quay. Just as we were nearing the bottom of Barclay Street, the bell rang from the steam-boat, to summon all loiterers on board; and forthwith we rushed, because in this country steam and paddles, like wind and tide in others, wait for no man. We got on board in plenty time, but Dall was nearly killed with the pace at which we had walked, in order to do so. . . .

As far as regards the speed, safety, and convenience with which these vessels enable one to perform what would be in any other conveyance most fatiguing journeys, they are admirable inventions. The way in which they are conducted, too, deserves the highest commendation. Nothing can exceed the comfort with which they are fitted up, the skill with which they are managed, and the order and alacrity with which passengers are taken up from, or landed at, the various points along the river. . . .

Doubtless all this has many and great advantages; but to an English person, the mere circumstance of being the whole day in a crowd is a nuisance. As to privacy at any time, or under any circumstances, 't is a thing that enters not into the imagination of an American. They do not seem to comprehend that to be from sunrise to sunset one of a hundred and fifty people confined in a steam-boat is in itself a great misery, or that to be left by one's self can ever be desirable. They live all the days of their lives in a throng, eat at ordinaries of two or three hundred, sleep five or six in a room, take pleasure in droves, and travel by swarms. In spite, therefore, of all its advantages, this mode of journeying has its drawbacks. And the greatest of all, to me, is the being *companioned* by so many strangers, who crowd about you, pursue their conversation in your very ears, or, if they like it better, listen to yours, stare you out of all countenance, and squeeze you out of all comfort.

It is perfectly intolerable to me; but then I have more than even the national English abhorrence of coming in contact with strangers. There is no moment of my life when I would not rather be alone, than in company; and feeling, as I often do, the society of even those I love a burden, the being eternally surrounded by indifferent persons is a positive suffering that interferes with every enjoyment, and makes pleasure three parts endurance. I think this constant living in public is one reason why the young women here are much less retiring and shy than English girls. . . .

To return to our progress. . . . While despatching breakfast, the reflection of the sun's rays on the water flickered to and fro upon the cabin ceiling; and through the loop-hole windows we saw the bright foam round the paddles sparkling like frothed gold in the morning light. On our return to the deck, the face of the world had become resplendent with the glorious sunshine that now poured from the east; and rock and river, earth and sky, shone in intense and dazzling brilliancy. The broad Hudson curled into a thousand crisp billows under the fresh north-wester that blew over it. The vaporous exhalations of night had melted from the horizon, and the bold, rocky range of one shore, and exquisite rolling outline of the other, stood out in fair relief against the deep serene of the blue heavens. I remained on deck without my bonnet, walking to and fro, and enjoying the delicious wind that was as bracing as a shower-bath. . . .

At about a quarter to eleven, the buildings of West Point were seen, perched upon the rock side, overhanging the water; above, the woody rise, upon whose summit stands the large hotel, the favourite resort of visitors during the summer season; rising again above this, the ruins of Fort Putnam, poor André's* prison-house, overlooking the Hudson and its shores; and towering high beyond them all, the giant hills, upon whose brown shoulders the trees looked like bristles standing up against the sky.

We left the boat, or rather she left us, and presently we saw her holding her course far up the bright water, and between the hills; where, framed by the dark mountains with the sapphire stream below and the sapphire sky above, lay the bright little town of Newburgh, with its white buildings glittering in the sunshine.

We toiled up the ascent, which, though by comparison with its overpeering fellows inconsiderable, was a sufficiently fatiguing undertaking under the unclouded weather and over the unshaded downs that form the parade ground for the cadets.

West Point is a military establishment containing some two hundred and fifty pupils; who are here educated for the army under the superintendence of experienced officers. The buildings, in which they reside and pursue their various studies, stand upon a grassy knoll holding the top of the rocky bank of the river, and commanding a most enchanting view of its course. They are not particularly extensive; but commodious and well-ordered. I am

---

* John André (1751–80) was an English soldier condemned to death as a spy during the American War of Independence and executed.

told they have a good library; but on reaching the dwelling of Mr Cozzens (proprietor of the hotel, which being at this season shut, he received us most hospitably and courteously in his own house) I felt so weary, that I thought it impossible I should stir again for the whole day, and declined seeing it.

I had walked on the deck at an amazing pace, and without once sitting down from eight o'clock till eleven; and I think must nearly have killed Colonel Sibell, who was my companion during this march. However, upon finding that it wanted full an hour till dinner-time, it was agreed that we should go up to the fort, and we set off under the guidance of one of Mr Cozzens' servants, who had orders not to go too fast with us. . . .

I had thought that I was tired, and could not stir, even to follow the leisurely footsteps of our cicerone; but tangled brake and woodland path, and rocky height, soon roused my curiosity, and my legs following therewith, I presently outstripped our party, guide and all, and began pursuing my upward path; through close growing trees and shrubs, over pale, shining ledges of granite, over which the trickling mountain springs had taken their silvery course; through swampy grounds, where the fallen leaves lay like gems under the still pools that here and there shone dimly in little hollow glens; over the soft starry moss that told where the moist earth retained the freshening waters, over sharp, hard splinters of rock, and rough masses of stone.

Alone, alone, I was alone and happy, and went on my way rejoicing, climbing and climbing still, till the green mound of thick turf, and ruined rampart of the fort arrested my progress. I coasted the broken wall; and lighting down on a broad, smooth table of granite fringed with young cedar bushes, I looked down, and for a moment my breath seemed to stop, the pulsation of my heart to cease – I was filled with awe. The beauty and wild sublimity of what I beheld seemed almost to crush my faculties – I felt dizzy as though my senses were drowning – I felt as though I had been carried into the immediate presence of God. Though I were to live a thousand years, I never can forget it.

The first thing that I distinctly saw was the shadow of a large cloud, which rolled slowly down the side of a huge mountain, frowning over the height where I stood. The shadow moved down its steep sunny side, threw a deep blackness over the sparkling river, and then passed off and climbed the opposite mountain on the other shore, leaving the world in the full blaze of noon. I could have stretched out my arms, and shouted aloud – I could have fallen on my knees and worshipped – I could have committed any extravagance that ecstasy could suggest. I stood filled with amazement and delight, till the footsteps and voices of my companions roused me.*

We came down from the mountain at about half-past one: our party had been joined by Colonel —,† Governor of the College, who very courteously came toiling up to Fort Putnam, to pay his compliments to us. I lingered far behind them, returning; and, when they were out of sight, turned back, and once more ascended the ruin, to look my last of admiration and delight, and then down, down, every step bringing me out of the clouds, farther from heaven, and nearer this work i' day world. I loitered, and loitered, looking back at every step; but at last the hills were shut out by a bend in the road, and I came into the house to throw myself down on the floor, and sleep most seriously for half an hour; at the end of which time, we were called to dinner. . . .

We had scarce finished our dinner, when in rushed a waiter to tell us that the boat was in sight. Away we trotted, trailing cloaks, and shawls, anyhow fashion, down the hill. The steamer came puffing up the gorge between the mountains, and in a moment we were bundled into the boat, hauled alongside, and landed on the deck; and presently the glorious highlands, all glowing in the rosy sunset, began to recede from us. . . .

As the day fell, the volumes of smoke from our steam-boat chimneys became streams of fiery sparks, which glittered over the water with a strange unearthly effect. I sat on deck watching the world grow dark, till my father, afraid of the night air, bade me go down; and there, in spite of the chattering of a score of women, and the squalling of half as many children, I slept profoundly till we reached New York, at a quarter to seven. . . .

Wednesday 21st [November 1832]
. . . Gave Dall her muff and tippet, which are exceedingly magnificent. After dinner, pottered about, and dressed at once. Played

* This quasi-mystical experience places Fanny firmly among the romantics, and in company with William Beckford, Wordsworth, Shelley.

† Not filled in by Fanny.

on the piano till nine, when we adjourned to the Hones's. A complete 'small party, my dear'.

Dr Wainwright* was there, whom I was glad to see; also Mrs —:†
also Mr and Miss Bell; also that Mrs Charles David, who is utter horror and perturbation of spirit to me; also —;† also —;† all our riding party, and a world besides. After a little time, dancing was proposed; and I stood up to waltz with Mr Robert Emmet, who observed that Dr Wainwright was gone, as he never chose to be present while waltzing was going on.

I felt shocked to death that unconsciously I should have been instrumental in driving him away, and much surprised that those who knew his disapprobation of waltzing should have proposed it. However, he was gone, and did not return. Therefore I waltzed myself out of my conscientious remorse. Sang them 'Fanny Gray', and 'Ye Mariners of Spain'. Danced sundry quadrilles; and, finally, what they called a Kentucky reel – which is nothing more than Sir Roger de Coverly turned Backwoodsman – and afterwards a 'foursome reel'. Played magic music; and, finally, at one o'clock, came home, having danced myself fairly off my legs.

Thursday, 22nd [November 1832]
It poured with rain all day. Dr Wainwright called, and gave me a sermon about waltzing. As it was perfectly good sense, to which I could reply nothing whatever in the shape of objection, I promised him never to waltz again, except with a woman, or my brother. After all, 't is not fitting that a man should put his arm round one's waist, whether one belongs to any one but one's self or not. 'T is much against what I have always thought most sacred – the dignity of a woman in her own eyes and those of others.

I like Dr Wainwright most exceedingly. He spoke every way to my feelings of what was right, to-day. After saying that he felt convinced, from conversations which he had heard amongst men, that waltzing was immoral in its tendency, he added, 'I am married, and have been in love, and cannot imagine any thing more destructive of the deep and devoted respect which love is calculated to excite in every honourable man's heart, not only for the individual object of his affections, but for her whole sex, than to

* A distinguished New York divine.
† Not filled in by Fanny.

see any and every impertinent coxcomb in a ball-room come up to her, and, without remorse or hesitation, clasp her waist, imprison her hand, and absolutely whirl her round in his arms.' So spake the Doctor; and my sense of propriety and conviction of right bore testimony to the truth of his saying. So, farewell sweet German waltz – next to hock, the most intoxicating growth of the Rheinland. I shall never keep time to your pleasant measure again! . . .

We dined at three. After dinner, received a pretty anonymous nosegay, with sundry very flattering doggrel. The play was *The Stranger*. It poured cats and dogs, and the streets were all grey pudding. I did not expect to see six people in the house; instead of which, 't was crowded: a satisfactory proof of our attraction.

Sunday, 25th [November 1832]
My dear father's birth-day! also, by the by, a grand occasion here – the anniversary of the evacuation of the island by the British troops, which circumstance the worthy burghers have celebrated ever since with due devotion and thankfulness.

Went to church: Dr Wainwright did not preach, which was a disappoinment to me. The music was exquisite; and there was a beautiful graceful willow branch, with its long delicate fibres and golden leaves, waving against the blue sky and the church window, that seemed to me like a magical branch in a fairy tale.

It struck me as strange to-day, as I looked from the crowded gloomy church to the bright unbounded sky, to think that we call the one the house of God; to be sure, we have other authority for calling the blue heavens his throne; and oh, how glorious they did look! The day was bright, but bitter cold. . . .

Monday, 26th [November 1832]
Yesterday was evacuation day; but as yesterday was the Lord's day also, the American militia army postponed their yearly exhibition, and, instead of rushing about the streets in token of their thankfulness at the departure of the British, they quietly went to church, and praised God for that same.

To-day, however, we have had firing of pop-guns, waving of star-spangled banners (some of them rather the worse for wear), infantry marching through the streets, cavalry (oh, Lord, what delicious objects they were!) and artillery prancing along them, to the infinite ecstasy and peril of a dense mob.

Went to rehearsal at half-past ten. Was detained full ten minutes on the way thither, by the de-filing of troops, who were progressing down Broadway.

After rehearsal, came home – put out things for the theatre. . . . Spent a delightful half hour at the window, which, overlooking the park, commanded a full view of the magnanimous military marshalled there. O, pomp and circumstance of glorious war!

They were certainly not quite so bad as Falstaff's men, of ragged memory; for, for aught I know to the contrary, they perhaps all of them had shirts to their backs. But some had gloves, and some had none; some carried their guns one way, and some another; some had caps of one fashion, and some of another; some had no caps at all, but 'shocking bad hats,' with feathers in them. . . .

But the cavalry! Oh, the cavalry! what gems without price they were! Apparently extremely frightened at the shambling tituppy chargers upon whose backs they clung, straggling in all directions, putting the admiring crowd in fear of their lives, and proving beyond a doubt how formidable they must appear to the enemy, when, with the most peaceable intentions in the world, they thus jeopardied the safety of their enthusiastic fellow-citizens. . . .

Some wore boots, and some wore shoes, and one independent hero had got on grey stockings and slippers! Some had bright yellow feathers, and some red and black feathers! I remembered, particularly, a doctor, in a black suit, Hessian boots, a cocked hat, and bright yellow gauntlets; another fellow was dressed in the costume of one of the Der Freyschutz's corps: it looked for all the world like a fancy parade. The officers fulfilled completely my idea of Macheath's company of gentlemen of the road; only, I strongly suspect the latter would have been heartily ashamed of the unhappy hacks the evacuation heroes had gotten up upon. The parade terminated with a full half hour's *feu de joie*. . . .

Wednesday, 28th [November 1832]
. . . After breakfsat, sat reading the poems of Willis,* a young man, whose works, young as they evidently are, would have won him some consideration in any but such a thorough work-day world as this. I cried a good deal over some of this man's verses. I thought some of them beautiful; and 't is the property of beauty to stir the wells of my soul sadly rather than cast sunshine over them.

* Nathaniel Parker Willis (1806–67), American author of plays, essays and poems.

I think all things are sad. 'T is sad to hear sweet music; 't is sad to read fine poetry; 't is sad to look upon the beautiful face of a fair woman; 't is sad to behold the unclouded glory of a summer's sky. There is a deep and lingering tone in the harmony of all beauty that resounds in our souls with too full and solemn a vibration for pleasure alone. In fact, intensity, even of joy and delight, is in itself serious; 't is impossible to be fulfilled with emotion of any sort and not feel as though we were within the shadow of a cloud.

I remember when first I recited Juliet to my mother, she said I spoke the balcony scene almost sadly. Was not such deep, deep love too strong, too passionate, too pervading, to be uttered with the light laughing voice of pleasure? Was not that love, even in its fullness of joy, sad – awful? However, perhaps, I do but see through my own medium, and fancy it the universal one. My eyes are dark, and most things look darkly through them. . . .

After dinner, sat making blonde tippet, and strumming on the piano till eight. Drank tea, dressed, and off to Mrs Bell's 'small party, my dear'.

The people here have no conscience about the questions they ask; and, as I have one in answering, and always give them 'the truth, the whole truth, and nothing but the truth,' it follows that nothing can be more disagreeable than their queries, except my replies. . . .

We stood up to dance a couple of quadrilles; but as they had not one distinct idea of what the figures were, the whole was a mess of running about, explaining, jostling, and awkward blundering. I took greatly to the governess of the family, a German woman, with a right German face, a nice person, with quiet simple manners. The women's voices here distract me; so loud, so rapid, and with such a twang! What a pity, for they are, almost without an exception, lovely-looking creatures, with an air of refinement in their appearance, which would be very attractive, but for their style of dress, and those said tremendous shrill loud voices.

Came home at twelve o'clock. . . .

Thursday, 29th [November 1832]
My birth-day. After breakfast sat writing to dear Harriet for some time. Put out things for the theatre, and went to rehearsal.

My father has received a most comical note from one Grant Thorburn, a Scotch gardener, florist, and seedsman; the original, by the by, of Galt's Lawrie Todd* – and original enough he must be. The note expresses a great desire that my father and myself will call upon him, for that he wishes very much to look at us – that the hours of the theatre are too late for him, and that besides, he wants to see us as ourselves, and not as 'kings and princesses'. I have entreated my father to go: this man must be worth knowing. I shall certainly keep his note. . . .

Friday, 30th [November 1832]
How the time goes! Bless the old traveller, how he posts along! . . . The day was grey, and cold, and damp – a real November day, such as we know them. We held the good man's note, and steered our course by it, and in process of time entered a garden, passed through a green-house, and arrived in an immense and most singularly arranged seed-shop, with galleries running round it, and the voice of a hundred canaries resounding through it. I don't know why, but it reminded me of a place in the *Arabian Nights*.

'Is Mr Thorburn within?' shouted forth my father, seeing no one in this strange-looking abode. 'Yes, he is,' was replied from somewhere, by somebody. We looked about, and presently, with his little grey bullet head, and shrewd piercing eyes, just appearing above the counter, we detected the master of the house. My father stepped up to him and returning his coarse, curiously folded note to him, said, 'I presume I am addressing Mr Thorburn: this, sir,' drawing me forward, 'is Miss Fanny Kemble.'

The little man snatched off his spectacles, rushed round the counter, rubbed his enormous hand upon his blue stuff apron, and held it out to us with a most hearty welcome. He looked at us for some time, and then exclaimed, 'Ha! ye're her father. Well, ye'll have married pretty early – ye look very young: I should not have been sae much surprised if ye had called her ye're wife!'

I laughed, and my father smiled at this compliment, which was recommended by a broad Scotch twang, which always sounds sweetly in my ears.

The little man, whose appearance is that of a dwarf in some fairy tale, then went on to tell us how Galt had written a book all about him; how it was, almost word for word, his own story; how he had come to this country in early life, with three halfpence in his

* John Galt (1779–1839), novelist.

pocket, and a nail and hammer in his hand, for all worldly substance; how he had earned his bread by making nails, which was his business in Scotland; how, one day, passing by some flowers exposed for sale, he had touched a geranium leaf by accident, and, charmed with its fragrance, bought it, having never seen one before; how, with fifteen dollars in his pocket, he commenced the business of a florist and gardener; and how he had refused as many thousand dollars for his present prosperous concern; how, when he first came to New York, the place opposite his garden, where now stands a handsome modern dwelling-house, was the site of a shed where he did his first bit of work; how, after six-and-twenty years' absence from Scotland, he returned home; how he came to his father's house – "T was on a bright morning in August – the eighth of August, just, it was – when I went through the door. I knew all the old passages so well: I opened the parlour door, and there, according to the good old Scottish custom, the family were going to prayers afore breakfast. There was the old Bible on the table, and the old clock ticking in the corner of the room: there was my father in his own old chair, exactly just where I had left him six-and-twenty years gone by. The very shovel and tongs by the fire were the same; I knew them all. I just sat down, and cried as sweetly as ever a man did in his life.'

These were, as nearly as I can recollect, his words; and oh, what a story! His manner, too, was indescribably vivid and graphic. My father's eyes filled with tears. He stretched out his hand, and grasped and shook the Scotchman's hand repeatedly without speaking; I never saw him more excited. I never was more struck myself with the wonderful strangeness of this bewildering life.

He showed us the foot of a rude rustic-looking table. 'That,' he said, 'was cut from out the hawthorn hedge that grows by my father's house; and this,' showing us a wooden bowl, 'is what I take my parritch in!'

I asked him if he never meant to leave this country, and return to bonny Scotland. He said, No, never: he might return, but he never meant to settle any where but here. 'For,' added he, 'I have grown what I am in it, madam, and 't is a fine country for the poor.' . . .

His father, by the by, is still alive, and residing within six miles of Edinburgh, a man of ninety years and upwards.

We walked about the shop, visited the birds, who are taken most admirable care of, and are extremely beautiful. I saw several mocking birds: they should sing well, for they are not pretty. Their plumage is of a dull grey colour, and they are clumsy-looking birds.

Saw two beautiful African widow birds, with their jet black hoods and trains. Saw an English blackbird, and thrush, in cages. They made my heart ache. I wonder if they ever think of the red ripe cracking cherries, the rich orchard lands, and the hawthorn-hedged lanes in the summer sunsets of dear England? I did for them.

We then went and looked at a tank full of beautiful gold fish, as they indiscriminately called them. But though the greater number were the glittering scarlet creatures usually so denominated, some were of the richest purple, with a soft dark bloom playing over their sides; others, again, were perfectly brown, with a glancing golden light shining through their scales; others were palest silver; others, again, mingled the dazzling scarlet with spots of the most beautiful gloomy violet, like dark-coloured jewels set in fire. Their tank was planted with the roots of aquatic vegetables, which, in summer, spread their cool leaves over the water, which is perpetually renewed by means of an escape, and a little silvery fountain which keeps bubbling up in the midst. They seemed very happy, and devoured sundry pieces of wafer paper, while we admired them at our leisure. . . .

After dawdling about very satisfactorily for some time, we departed from the dwelling of Lawrie Todd. Of a verity, 'truth is strange, stranger than fiction.' . . .

Saturday, December 1st, 1832
First day of the last month of the year – go it, old fellow! I'm sick of the road, and would be at my journey's end.

Got two hundred dollars from my father, and immediately after breakfast sallied forth: paid bills and visits, and came home. . . . persuaded my father to come down and take a breathing on the Battery with me.

And a breathing it was with a vengeance. The wind blew tempestuously, the waters, all troubled and rough, were of a yellow green colour, breaking into short, strong, angry waves. . . . The wind was so powerful, we could scarcely keep our legs. My sleeves and skirts fluttered in the blast, my bonnet was turned front part behind, my nose was blue, my cheeks were crimson, my hair was all tangled, my breath was gone, my blood was in a glow: what a walk!

Sunday, 2d [December 1832]
While dressing, received a 'sweet note' from Mrs Bell, accompanied with a volume of Bryant's poetry, which, as I like very much, I am her obliged.

Swallowed two mouthfuls of bread, and away to church. It was very crowded, and a worthy woman had taken possession of the corner seat in Mr Hone's pew, with a fidgeting little child, which she kept dancing up and down every two minutes; though in church I wished for the days of King Herod.*

What strange thoughts did occur to me to-day during service! 'T is the first Sunday in Advent. The lesson for the day contained the history of the Annunciation. What a mystery our belief is! How seldom it is that we consider and, as it were, take hold of what we say we believe, and when we do so, how bewildered and lost we become, – how lost among a thousand wild imaginations, – how driven to and fro by a thousand doubts, – how wrecked amidst a thousand fears! Surely we should be humble: we should indeed remember that we cannot know, and not strive for that knowledge which our souls will lose themselves in seeking for, and our overstrained minds crack in reaching at. . . .

The Kembles now moved on to their second appearance in Philadelphia. It was to prove an engagement with dramatic consequences. . . .

Monday, 3d [December 1832]
Rose at half-past four. The sky was black as death, but in the night winter had dropped his mantle on the earth, and there it lay, cold, and purely white, against the inky sky.

Dressed: crammed away all the gleanings of the packing, and in thaw, and sleet, and rain, drove down to the steam-boat. Went directly to the cabin. On my way thither, managed to fall down half-a-dozen steep steps, and give myself as many bruises. I was picked up and led to a bed, where I slept profoundly till breakfast time. . . .

After breakfast, returned to my crib. As I was removing *Contarini*

---

* Who slaughtered the 'innocents'!

*Fleming,** in order to lie down, a lady said to me, 'Let me look at one of those books;' and without further word of question or acknowledgement, took it from my hand, and began reading. I was a little surprised, but said nothing, and went to sleep. Presently I was roused by a pull on the shoulder, and another lady, rather more civil, and particularly considerate, asked me to do her the favour of lending her the other. I said by all manner of means, wished her at the devil, and turned round to sleep once more.

Arrived at Amboy, we disembarked and bundled ourselves into our coach. . . .

Arrived at the Delaware, we took boat again; and, as I was sitting very quietly reading *Contarini Fleming*, with the second volume lying on the stool at my feet, the same unceremonious lady who had borrowed it before, snatched it up without addressing a single syllable to me, read as long as she pleased, and threw it down again in the same style when she went to dinner. . . .

. . . The mixture of the republican feeling of equality peculiar to this country, and the usual want of refinement common to the lower classes of most countries, forms a singularly felicitous union of impudence and vulgarity to be met with no where but in America.

Arrived at the Mansion House,† which I was quite glad to see again. Installed myself in a room, and while they brought in the packages, finished *Contarini Fleming*. Mr Butler came in while we were at dinner.

After dinner, came up to my room, continued unpacking and putting away my things till near nine o'clock.

When we went down to tea, my father was lying on the sofa asleep, and a man was sitting with his back to the door, reading the newspaper. He looked up as we came in: it was Mr Staley, whom I greatly rejoiced to see again.

During tea, he told us all the Philadelphia gossip. So the ladies are all getting up upon horses, and wearing the 'Kemble cap', as they call Lady Ellesmere's device. How she would laugh if she could hear it; how I did laugh when I did hear it. The Kemble cap, forsooth! thus it is that great originators too often lose the fame of their inventions, and that the glory of a new idea passes by the

* A novel by Benjamin Disraeli (1804–81), published 1832.

† Their hotel.

head that conceived it, to encircle, as with a halo, that of some mere imitator; thus it is that this very big world comes to be called America, and not Columbia, as it ought to; thus it is – &c. &c. &c. He sat for some time. . . .

On this first evening of their return to Philadelphia Pierce Butler had at last admitted to being the nosegay-sending 'Friend'. From now on Fanny was to see him almost every day. . . .

Wednesday, 5th [December 1832]
After breakfast, practised. . . . Went and saw poor Mrs Dulaney for a little time; she interests me most extremely – I like her very, very much.

Came up to my own room; read a canto of Dante. Was called down to see folk, and found the drawing-room literally thronged. . . . Two ladies, a whole load of men, and Mr Biddle, who had brought me a curious piece of machinery, in the shape of a musical box, to look at. It contained a little bird, no larger than a large fly, with golden and purple wings, and a tiny white beak. On the box being wound up, this little creature flew out, and perching itself on the brink of a gold basin, began fluttering its wings, opening its beak, and uttering sundry very melodious warblings, in the midst of which, it sank suddenly down, and disappeared, the lid closed, and there was an end.

What a pity 't is that we can only realize fairy-land through the means of machinery. One reason why there is no such thing left as the believing faculty among men, is because they have themselves learnt to make magic, and perform miracles.

When the coast was once more clear, I returned to my room, got out things for the theatre, dined tête-à-tête with Dall. . . .

At half-past five, went to the theatre. The play was *Romeo and Juliet*; the house not good. . . . I acted like a wretch, of course; how could I do otherwise? . . .

How I do loathe the stage! these wretched, tawdry, glittering rags, flung over the breathing forms of ideal loveliness; these miserable, poor, and pitiful substitutes for the glories with which poetry has invested her magnificent and fair creations – the glories with which our imagination reflects them back again. What a mass of wretched mumming mimicry acting is! Pasteboard and paint, for the thick breathing orange groves of the south; green silk and oiled parchment, for the solemn splendour of her noon of night; wooden platforms and canvass [*sic*] curtains, for the solid marble balconies, and rich dark draperies of Juliet's sleeping chamber, that shrine of love and beauty; rouge, for the startled life-blood in the cheek of that young passionate woman; an actress, a mimicker, a sham creature, me, in fact, or any other one, for that loveliest and most wonderful conception, in which all that is true in nature, and all that is exquisite in fancy, are moulded into a living form. To act this! To act *Romeo and Juliet*! Horror! horror! How I do loathe my most impotent and unpoetical craft! . . .

In the last scene of the play, I was so mad with the mode in which all the preceding ones had been perpetrated, that, lying over Romeo's corpse, and fumbling for his dagger, which I could not find, I, Juliet, thus apostrophized him – Romeo being dead – 'Why, where the devil is your dagger, Mr __?'*

What a disgusting travesty. On my return home, I expressed my entire determination to my father to perform the farce of *Romeo and Juliet* no more. Why, it's an absolute shame that one of Shakespeare's plays should be thus turned into a mockery.

I received a note from young Mr Biddle, accompanied by a very curious nosegay in shells; a poor substitute for the breathing fresh, rosy flowers he used to furnish me with, when I was last here.

Thursday, 6th [December 1832]
. . . Dined at five: my father dined out. After dinner, sat writing journal till ten, when he returned. The moon was shining soft and full, and he asked me if I would take a walk.

I bonneted and booted, and we sallied forth to the Schuylkill. The moon withdrew herself behind a veil of thin white clouds, but left a grey clear light over the earth, and through the sky. We reached the Fair Mount bridge at about eleven. The turnpike was fast, and every body asleep, so we climbed over the gate, and very deliberately pursued our way through the strange dark-looking covered bridge, where the glimmering lamps, at distant intervals, threw the crossing beams and rafters into momentary brightness, that had a strange effect contrasted with the surrounding gloom. . . .

My father steered for the grassy knoll just opposite Fair Mount;

* Not filled in by Fanny.

and there, screened by a thicket of young cedar bushes, with the river breaking over the broad dam far below us, and the shadowy banks on the other side melting away in the soft grey light, we sat down on a tree trunk. Here we remained for upwards of a quarter of an hour without uttering a syllable; indeed, we had not spoken three words since we set out. My father was thinking, I presume, of . . . something; I, of the day of judgement – when these thick forests, and wide strong waters, like a shrivelled scroll, are to burn to ashes before the coming of God's justice.

We were disturbed by a large white spaniel dog, who, coming down from among the cedar bushes, reminded me of the old witch stories, and *Faust*. We arose to depart, and took our way towards the Market Street bridge, along the banks of the river. . . . We did not reach home till half-past twelve. As we walked down Market Street, through the long ranges of casks, the only creatures stirring, except some melancholy night-loving cat, my father said very calmly, 'How I do wish I had a gimlet.'

'What for?'

'What fun it would be to pierce every one of these barrels.'

For a gentleman of his years, this appeared to me rather a juvenile prompting of Satan; and as I laughingly expostulated on the wickedness of such a proceeding, he replied with much innocence, 'I don't think they'd ever suspect me of having done it'; and truly I don't think they would.

Came home, and to bed. That was a curious fancy of my father's. . . .

Friday, 7th [December 1832]
A break. Found Pierce Butler in the breakfast room.

The morning was very unpropitious; but I settled to ride at one, if it was tolerably fine then. He remained pottering a long time: when he was gone, practised, habited, went in, for a few minutes, to Mrs Dulaney.

At one the horses came; but mine was brought without a stirrup, so we had to wait, Lord knows how long, till the blundering groom had ridden back for it. At length we mounted. 'Handsome is that handsome does,' is verity; and, therefore, pretty as was my steed, I wished its good looks and itself at the devil, before I was half way down Chestnut Street. It pranced, and danced, and backed me once right upon the pavement.

We took the Laurel Hill road. The day was the perfection of gloom – the road six inches deep in heavy mud. We walked the whole way out: my father got the cramp, and lost his temper. At Laurel Hill we dismounted, and walked down to the river side. How melancholy it all looked: the turbid rhubarby water, the skeleton woods, the grey sky, and far winding away of the dark rocky shores; yet it was fine even in this gloom, and wonderfully still. The clouds did not move, – the water had not the faintest ripple, – the trees did not stir a branch; the most perfect and profound trance seemed to have fallen upon every thing.

Pierce Butler and I scrambled down the rocks towards the water, expatiating on the capabilities of this place, which was once a country-seat, and with very little expense might be made a very enchanting as well as a very comfortable residence. . . .

I was horrified at Dr Charles Mifflin's account of the state of the negroes in the south. To teach a slave to read or write is to incur a penalty either of fine or imprisonment. They form the larger proportion of the population, by far; and so great is the dread of insurrection on the part of the white inhabitants, that they are kept in the most brutish ignorance, and too often treated with the most brutal barbarity, in order to insure their subjection.

Oh! what a breaking asunder of old manacles there will be, some of these fine days; what a fearful rising of the black flood; what a sweeping away, as by a torrent, of oppressions and tyrannies; what a fierce and horrible retaliation and revenge for wrong so long endured – so wickedly inflicted.

When I came in to tea, at half-past eight, found Dr Mifflin there. When he was gone, sang a song or two like a crow in the quinsy. . . .

Thursday, 13th [December 1832]
While dressing, had the pleasure of witnessing from my window a satisfactory sample of the innate benevolence, gentleness, and humanity of our nature: a child of about five years old, dragging a cat by a string tied to its throat round and round a yard, till the poor beast ceased to use its paws, and suffered itself to be trailed along the ground, after which the little fiend set his feet upon it, and stamped and kicked it most brutally.

The blood came into my face; and, though almost too far for hearing, I threw up the sash, and at the top of my voice apostrophized the little wretch with 'Hollo there! wicked, naughty boy!'

He seemed much puzzled to discover whence this appeal proceeded, but not at all at a loss to apply it; for, after looking about with a very conscience-stricken visage, he rushed into the house, dragging his victim with him.

I came down, fairly sick, to breakfast. After despatching it, I put on my bonnet and walked round to the house where this scene had taken place. I enquired for the child, describing his appearance, and he was presently brought to me; when I sat down at the foot of the stairs in the hall, and spent some time in expatiating on the enormity of such proceedings to the little ruffian, who, it seems, has frequently been corrected for similar ferocities before. I fear my preachment will not avail much.

Came home, put room to rights, practised for an hour; got ready, and dawdled about most dreadfully, waiting for Dall, who had gone out with my father.

At half-past twelve, set off with her to the riding school. It was full of women in long calico skirts, and gay bonnets with flaunting feathers, riding like wretches; some cantering, some trotting, some walking – crossing one another, passing one another in a way that would have filled the soul of Fossard* with grief and amazement.

I put on a skirt and my riding-cap, and mounted a rough, rugged, besweated white–brown beast, that looked like an old trunk more than any thing else, its coat standing literally on end, like 'quills upon the fretful porcupine,' with heat and ill condition. 'T is vain attempting to ride like a Christian on these heathen horses, which are neither broken, bitted, nor bridled properly; and poor *dum creturs* have no more idea of what a horse ought to be, or how a horse ought to behave, than so many cows.

My hair, presently, with the damp and the shaking, became perfectly straight. As I raised my head, after putting it up under my cap, I beheld Pierce Butler earnestly discoursing to Dall.

I asked for Tuesday's charger; and the school having by degrees got empty, I managed to become a little better acquainted with its ways and means. 'T is a pretty little creature, but 't is not half broken, is horribly ill ridden, and will never be good for any thing – what a pity!

* Captain Fossard, Fanny's London riding instructor.

At two o'clock I dismounted: Pierce Butler walked home with us. Went in to see Mrs Dulaney: she seemed a good deal better, I thought; sat some time with her. . . .

Wednesday, 19th [December 1832]
. . . Went to rehearsal – afterwards to the riding school. The school was quite empty, and I alone. The boy brought me my horse, and I mounted by means of a chair. As I was cantering along, amusing myself with cogitations various, Pierce Butler came in. He stayed the whole time I rode.

I settled with him about riding tomorrow, and came home to dinner. After dinner, went in to see Mrs Dulaney. . . . She is a very delightful person, with a great deal of intellect and a wonderful quantity of fortitude and piety, and a total absence of knowledge of the world, except through books. . . .

Her children enchant me, and her care of them enchants me too. She is an excellent person, with a heart overflowing with the very best affections our nature is capable of, fulfilled, I think, to the uttermost. Stayed with her till time to go to the theatre.

The house was very full: the play was *The Wonder* – my first time of acting Violante. My dress was not finished till the very last moment – and then, oh, horror! was so small that I could not get into it. It had to be pinned upon me; and thus bebundled, with the dread of cracking my bodice from top to bottom every time I moved, and the utter impossibility of drawing my breath, from the narrow dimensions into which it squeezed me, I went on to play a new part. The consequence was, that I acted infamously, and for the first time in my life was horribly imperfect – out myself and putting every body else out. Between every scene my unlucky gown had to be pinned together; and in the laughing scene, it took the hint from my admirable performance, and facetiously grinned in an ecstasy of amusement till it was fairly open behind, displaying, I suppose, the lacing of my stays, like so many teeth, to the admiring gaze of the audience; for, as I was perfectly ignorant of the circumstance, with my usual easy nonchalance, I persisted in turning my back to the folk, in spite of all my father's pulls and pushes, which, as I did not comprehend, I did not by any means second either. . . .

Thursday, 20th [December 1832]

The day was beautifully brilliant, clear, and cold – winter, but winter in dazzling array of sunshine and crystal; blue skies, with light feathery streaks of white clouds running through them; dry, crisp, hard roads, with the delicate rime tipping all the ruts with sparkling jewellery; and the waters fresh, and bright, and curling under the keen breath of the arrow-like wind.

After breakfast, Mr Staley called. Walked out with him to get a cap and whip for Dall. The latter he insisted on making her a present of, and a very pretty one indeed it was, with a delicate ivory handle, and a charming persuading lash.

Went in for a short time to Mrs Dulaney, who entertained herself with letting all my hair down about my ears, and pulling it all manner of ways. At twelve habited, and helped to equip dear Dall, who really looked exceedingly nice in her jockey habiliments. Went to the school, where we found Mr Staley waiting for us. Mounted and set forth.

We rode out to Laurel Hill. . . . When we reached Laurel Hill, we dismounted, tied up the horses, slacked their girths, and walked first up to that interesting wooden monument, where I inscribed my initials on our first ride thither. Afterwards, Mr Staley and I scrambled down the rocks to the river side, which Dall declined doing, 'cause vy? – she'd have had to climb up again. The water was like a broad dazzling river of light and had a beautiful effect, winding away in brightness that the eye could scarce endure, between its banks, which, contrasted by the sunny stream, and blue transparent sky, appeared perfectly black.

As I bent over a fine bluff (as they here call any mass of rock standing isolated), I espied below me a natural rocky arch, overhanging the river, all glittering with pure long diamond icicles. Thither Mr Staley convoyed [*sic*] me, and broke off one of these wintry gems for me. It measured about two feet long, and was as thick at the root as my wrist. I never saw any thing so beautiful as these pendant adornments of the silver-fingered ice god.

Toiled up to the house again, where, after brushing our habits, we remounted our chargers, and came home. . . .

While we were at tea, young Biddle and Dr Mifflin came in. They put me down to the piano, and I continued to sing until past eleven o'clock, when, somebody looking at a watch, there was a universal

71

exclamation of surprise, the piano was shut down, the candles put out, the gentlemen vanished, and I came to bed. . . .

Sunday, 23d [December 1832]
Was only dressed in time to swallow two mouthfuls of breakfast, and get ready for church. Edward Biddle came to know at what time we would ride, and walked with us to the church door.

After church, came home, – habited; went and sat with Mrs Dulaney till half-past one. The villanous [*sic*] servants did not think fit to announce the horses till they had been at the door full half an hour, so that when we started it was near two o'clock. Dall seemed quite at her ease upon her gangling charger, and I had gotten up upon Mr Becket's big horse to see what I could make of him.

The day was beautifully bright and clear, with a warm blessed sunshine causing the wintry world to smile. We had proceeded more than half way to Laurel Hill without event, when, driving my heavy-shouldered brute at a bank, instead of lifting up his feet, he thought fit to stumble, fall, and fling me very comfortably off upon the mound. I sprang up neither hurt nor frightened, shook my habit, tightened my girths, and mounted again; when we set off, much refreshed by this little incident, which occasioned a world of mirth and many saucy speeches from my companions to me.

At Laurel Hill the master of the house came bowing forth. . . . Had the horses taken to the stable, and their girths slackened. Dall kept the heights, and Edward Biddle and I ran, slipped, slid, and scrambled down to the water's edge. The river was frozen over, not, however, strongly enough to bear much, and every jutting rock was hung with pure glittering icicles that shone like jewels in the bright sunshine. Far down the river all was still and lonely, and bright, yet wintry-looking. The flow of the water and its plashing music were still; there was no breath of wind stirring the leafless boughs; the sunlight came down, warm and dazzling upon the silent sparkling world, all clad in its shimmering ice robe: the air was transparent and clear, and the whole scene was perfectly lovely.

Turning to re-ascend the rocks, I called aloud to Dall, and the distinctest, loudest echo answered me. So perfect was the reflection of the sound, that at first I thought some one was mocking me. I ran up a scale as loud, and high, and rapid as I could; and from among the sunny fields, a voice repeated the threaded notes as clearly, as rapidly, only more softly, with a distinctness that was startling. I never heard an echo that repeated so much of what was sung or said.

I stood in perfect enchantment exercising my voice, and provoking the hidden voice of the air, who answered me with a far off tone, that seemed as though the mocking spirit fled along the hill tops, repeating my notes with a sweet gleeful tone that filled me with delight. Oh, what must savages think an echo is? How many, many lovely and wild imaginations are suggested by that which natural philosophers analyse into mere conformations of earth and undulations of air.

At length we joined Dall, and walked to the house, where presently appeared the master of the mansion, with cakes, wine, cordial, preserves, or, as *Comus* hath it, 'a table covered with all manner of deliciousness.' . . .

We did not reach Philadelphia till it it was perfectly dark. To add to my consternation, too, when we asked Edward Biddle to dine with us, he said that he had an engagement, for which I began to fear this . . . ride would have kept him too late. . . .

I came up to my own room, changed my clothes, and went in to see Mrs Dulaney. She was completely overpowered with laudanum. Her head was declined upon a chair. She looked very lovely, with her beautiful head bowed, and her dark eyelashes lying on her wan cheeks. Her features were contracted with suffering.

I sat watching her with much heartfelt sadness and interest. I was summoned away, however, to see some gentlemen who were in the drawing-room, whither I adjourned, and where I found Mr Butler, and Dr Charles Mifflin. I was stupid and sleepy: and the gentlemen had the charity not to keep me up, or make me sing.

Monday 24th, Christmas-eve [December 1832]
. . . After dinner, went and sat with my poor invalid, whom, in spite of her republicanism, I am greatly inclined to like and admire. Remained with her till coffee-time.

Went to the theatre: the play was *The Merchant of Venice* – my favourite part, Portia. The house was very full: I played so-soish.

Tuesday, 25th, Christmas-day [December 1832]
I wish you a merry Christmas, poor child! away from home and

friends. Truly, the curse of the old Scriptures has come upon me; my lovers and my acquaintance are far off from me. After breakfast, practised for an hour; went and saw Mrs Dulaney; drove out shopping; saw Pierce Butler walking with my father. Came home and wrote journal: went out with Dall; bought a rocking-horse for Mrs Dulaney's chicks, whose merry voices I shall miss most horribly by and by. Dragged it in to them in the midst of their dinner.

Dined at three. After dinner, went and sat with her till coffee-time. When I came into the drawing-room, found a beautiful work-box sent me by that very youthful admirer of mine, Mr Biddle. I was a little annoyed at this, but still more so at my father's desiring me to return it to him, which I know will be a terrible mortification to him.

Went to the theatre: the house was crammed with men, and very noisy – a Christmas audience. Play, *Macbeth*: I only played so-so. . . .

Wednesday, 26th [December 1832]
After breakfast, put out things for theatre. When I came down to the drawing-room, I found a middle-aged gentleman of very respectable appearance sitting with my father. He rose on my coming in, and, after bowing to me, continued his discourse to my father thus: 'Yes, sir, yes; you will find as I tell you, sir, the winter is our profitable theatrical season, sir; so that if any thing should take you to England, you can return again at the beginning of next fall.'

I modestly withdrew to another end of the room, supposing they were engaged upon business. But my curiosity was presently attracted by the continuation of his discourse. 'And recollect, sir, and this lady, your daughter, too, if you please; that what I have said must not on any account be repeated out of this room. I am myself going immediately to England, and from thence direct to Jerusalem!'

I stared.

'There, sir, is my real name, __: the card I sent up to you is not my real name. You see, sir, I am an Irishman, that is to say, in fact, I am really a Jew. *I am one of those of the tribe of Ephraim who refused to cross the Red Sea: we were not to be humbugged by that damned fellow, Moses – no, sir, we were not!*'

Here my heart jumped into my throat, and my eyes nearly out of my head with fright and amazement.

'Well,' continued the poor madman, 'I suppose I may deliver this to the young lady herself;' giving me a small parcel, which I took from him as if I thought it would explode and blow me up.

'And now, sir, farewell. Remember, remember my words – in three years, perhaps, but *certainly* in ten, *He* that will come, will come, and it's all up with the world, and the children of men!'

This most awful announcement was accompanied with a snap of his fingers, and a demi-pirouette. . . . At last I bethought me of opening the little packet the madman had left me. It was a small box, on the cover of which was written, To Miss Kemble, with the compliments of St George.

I then recollected, that some time past I had received some verses, in which love and religion were very crazily blended, signed St George. But, as I am abundantly furnished with epistles of this sort, I had flung them aside, merely concluding the writer to be gone a short way from his wits. The box contained a most beautiful and curious ornament, something like a Sevigné, highly wrought in gold and enamel, and evidently very costly. I was more confounded than ever, and did not recover from my amazement and fright for a long time. . . .

Practised for a short time, and then went to the riding school. It was quite empty; I put on my cap and skirt, and was sitting thinking of many things, in the little dressing room, when I heard the school door open, and Mr Pierce Butler walked straight up to me. . . .

Went to the theatre at half-past five. The house was very fair, considering the weather, which was very foul. Play, *School for Scandal.* They none of them knew their parts, or remembered their business – delightful people, indeed! I played only so-so.

Pierce Butler supped with us. He is a very gentlemanly, nice person, and I am told he is extremely amiable. He told me sundry steam-boat stories that made my blood curdle; such as, a public brush, a public comb, and a public tooth-brush. Also, of a gentleman who was using his own tooth-brush – a man who was standing near him said, 'I'll trouble you for that article when you've done with it.' When he had done with it, the gentleman presented it to him, and on receiving it again, immediately threw it into the river, to the infinite amazement of the borrower, who only exclaimed, 'Well, however, you're a queer fellow.'

Friday, 28th [December 1832]
After breakfast, Pierce Butler called. Settled to ride, if possible, tomorrow. I would give the world for a good shaking. I'm dying of the blue devils; I have no power to rouse myself.

Fanny was – perhaps in spite of herself – falling in love. They were shortly due to move on to Baltimore for their next engagement, leaving Philadelphia, where she had been so happy – leaving Pierce.

When Pierce Butler was gone, sat down to practise. Tried Mrs Hemans's 'Messenger Bird,'* but the words were too solemn, and too sad: I sobbed instead of singing, and was a little relieved.

Went in to see Mrs Dulaney. She seemed better; she was *en toilette*, in a delicate white wrapper, with her fine hair twisted up round her classical head. She is a beautiful person; she is better – an amiable, a sensible, and a pious one; I am very deeply interested by her; I like her extremely. . . . I am sorry to leave Philadelphia on Mrs Dulaney's account. I am growing to her. Oh, Lord! how soon, how soon we do this! – How we do cling to every thing in spite of the pitiless wrenches of time and chance! Her dear babies are delightful to me; their laughing voices have power to excite and make me happy – and when they come dancing to meet me, my heart warms very fondly towards them.

She amuses me much by her intense anxiety that I should be married. First, she wishes Pierce Butler would propose to me; then she thinks Mr Shelton's estates in Cuba would be highly acceptable; in short, my single blessedness seems greatly to annoy her, and I believe she attributes every thing evil in life to that same.

She seemed surprised, and a little shocked, when I said I would accept death most thankfully in preference to the happiest lot in life – and so I would – I would.

Even so it is strange to find Fanny addressing a poem to Harriet St Leger in the following melancholy vein, the second verse going:

---

* Felicia Dorothea Hemans (1793–1835) was the author of various sentimental works which were highly popular in the United States.

Oh, friend! my heart is sad: 't is strange,
As I sit musing on the change
That has come o'er my fate, and cast
A longing look upon the past,
That pleasant time comes back again
So freshly to my heart and brain,
That I half think the things I see
Are but a dream, and I shall be
Lying beside you when I wake,
Upon the lawn beneath the brake,
With the hazel copse behind my head,
And the new-mown fields before me spread . . .

Saturday, 29th [December 1832]
When I came down to breakfast, found a very pretty diamond ring
and some Scotch rhymes. . . . I wish my hand wasn't abominably
ugly – I hate to put a ring upon it.

Pierce Butler called to see if we would ride; but Dall had too
much to do; and, after sitting pottering for some time, I sang him
the 'Messenger Bird', and sent him away. . . .

At half-past five, went to the theatre: play, *The Wonder*. I acted
only so-so: my father was a leetle *dans les vignes du seigneur*.* When
the play was over, the folk called for us, and we went on: he made
them a neat speech, and I nothing but a cross face and three
courtesies. How I do hate this! 'T is quite enough to exhibit myself
to a gaping crowd, when my profession requires that I should do so
in a feigned semblance; but to come bobbing and genuflectioning
on, as me myself, to be clapped and shouted at, and say, 'Thank ye
kindly,' is odious.

After the play, dressed, and off to Mrs Biddle, with my father
and Mr Bancroft. On our way thither, the spring of our coach
broke, and we had to go halting along for half an hour, with a
graceful inclination towards the pavement on one side, which was
very pleasant.

There was quite a brilliant party at Mrs Biddle's. . . . Saw and
spoke to all Philadelphia. . . .

Came home, and supped. I had eaten nothing since four o'clock,

* Tipsy!

and was famished; for I do not like stewed oysters and terrapins, which are the refreshments invariably handed round at an American evening party.

Did not get to bed till two o'clock. How beautifully bright the heavens are here. The sky has an earnest colour that is lovely and solemn to look at; and the moon, instead of being 'the maiden with white fire laden,' has a rich, mellow, golden light, than which nothing can be more beautiful. The stars, too, are more vivid than in our skies, and there is a variety of hues in their light which I never observed before – some reddish, some violet, and again others of the palest silver. . . .

Sunday, 30th [December 1832]

. . . Spent my Sunday morning on my knees, indeed, but packing, not praying. The horses did not come till half-past twelve; so that, instead of avoiding, we encountered the pious multitude. I'm sure when we mounted there were not less than a hundred and fifty beholders round the Mansion House.

Rode out to Laurel Hill. . . . While Dall put up her hair, Pierce Butler and I ran down to the water side. The ice had melted from the river, in whose still waters the shores, and trees, and bridge lay mirrored with beautiful and fairy-like distinctness. The long icicles under the rocky brow beneath which we stood had not melted away, though the warm sun was shining brilliantly on them, and making the granite slab on which we stood sparkle like a pavement of diamonds.

I called to the echo, and sang to it scales up, and scales down, and every manner of musical discourse I could think of, during which interesting amusement I as nearly as possible slipped from my footing into the river, which caused both Pierce Butler and myself to gulp.

We left our pleasant sunny stand at last, to rejoin Dall and the lunch, and having eaten and drunken, we remounted and proceeded on to Manayunk. . . .

We reached Philadelphia at half-past four, and had again to canter down Chestnut Street just as the folks were all coming from church, which caused no little staring, and turning of heads. My father asked Pierce Butler to dine with us, but he refused. . . .

After dinner, went in to pay my last visit to my poor sick friend. I sat with her until summoned to see some gentlemen in the drawing-room. It pained me to part from her; for though she exerted herself bravely, she was very much overcome. I fear she will miss me, poor thing; I had become very much attached to her. . . .

31 December 1832 – 30 June 1833

The lovers were not to be parted after all. Pierce Butler met Fanny and her father on the Delaware river steamboat, and accompanied them to Baltimore, and afterwards to Washington, playing the flute in the theatre orchestra.

Monday, 31st [December 1832]
The river being yet open, thank Heaven, we arose at half-past four o'clock. Dressed sans dawdling for once and came down.

Dall and I were bundled into a coach, and rumbled and tumbled over the stones, through the blackness of darkness down to the steam-boat. Pierce Butler was waiting for us, and convoyed us safely to the cabin, where I laid myself down, and slept till breakfast-time. . . . After breakfast, walked up and down deck with Pierce Butler. . . .

This boat – the *Charles Carroll* – is one of the finest they have. 'T is neither so swift nor so large, I think, as some of the North river boats, but it is a beautiful vessel, roomy and comfortable in its arrangements. I went below for a few minutes, but found, as usual, the atmosphere of the cabin perfectly intolerable.

The ladies' cabin, in winter, on board one of these large steamers, is a right curious sight. 'T is generally crammed to suffocation with women, strewn in every direction. The greater number cuddle round a stove, the heat of which alone would make the atmosphere unbreathable. Others sit lazily in a species of rocking-chair – which is found wherever Americans sit down – cradling themselves backwards and forwards, with a lazy, lounging, sleepy air, that makes me long to make them get up and walk. Others again manage, even upon fresh water, to be very sick. There are generally a dozen young human beings, some naughty, sick, and squalling, others happy, romping, and riotous; and what with the vibratory motion of the rocking-chairs and their contents, the women's shrill jabber, the children's shriller wailing and shouting, the heat and closeness of the air, a ladies' cabin on board an American steam-boat is one of the most over-powering things to sense and soul that can well be imagined.

There was a poor sick woman with three children, among our company, two of which were noisy, unruly boys, of from eight to ten years old. One of them set up a howl as soon as he came on board, which he prolonged, to our utter dismay, for upwards of half an hour sans intermission, except to draw breath. I bore it as long as I could; but threats, entreaties, and bribes having been resorted to in vain, by all the women in the cabin, to silence him, I at length very composedly took him up in my arms, and deposited him on his back in one of the upper berths; whereupon his brother flew at his mother, kicking, thumping, screaming, and yelling. The cabin was in an uproar; the little wretch I held in my arms struggled like a young giant, and though I succeeded in lodging him upon the upper shelf, presently slid down from it like an eel. However, this effort had a salutary effect, for it obtained silence – the crying gave way to terror, which produced silence, of which I availed myself sleep till dinner-time. . . .

We reached Baltimore at about half-past four. . . . The day was more lovely than a fine day in early September, in England – bright, soft, and sunny, with the blue in the sky of the delicate colour one sees in the Sèvres porcelain. As we entered the Patapsco, and neared Baltimore, North Point and Fort M'Henry were pointed out to me. My spirits always sink when I come to a strange place; and as we came along the wharf sides, under the red dingy-looking warehouses, between which the water ran in narrow, dark-looking canals, I felt terribly gloomy. We drove up to Barnham's, the best house in the town; and having found out where to lay my head, I had my fill of crying. . . .

Tuesday, January, 1st, New-Year's Day, 1833
. . . After breakfast, began writing journal. 'T was not until dating it that I discovered it was New-year's day. When I did so, and looked at my strange surroundings, at the gloomy wintry sky, and thought of the heathenish disregard with which I was passing over, in this far land, the season of home-gathering and congregating of kin in my own country, I could not refrain from crying bitterly. . . . Sat diligently crying the whole morning.

The afternoon cleared up, and became soft and sunny. My father insisted on my taking a walk; so I bonneted and set out with him. What I saw of the town appeared to me extremely like the outskirts of Birmingham or Manchester. Bright-red brick houses, in rows of

81

three and five, with interesting gaps of gravel pits, patches of meadow, and open spaces between, which give it an untidy, straggling appearance. They are building in every direction, however, and in less than two years, these little pauses being filled up, Baltimore will be a very considerable place; for it covers, in its present state, a large extent of ground, and contains a vast population. . . .

Sunday, 6th [January 1833]
At about half-past ten . . . we walked up to the cathedral, which is a large unfinished stone building, standing on the brow of a hill, which is to be the fashionable quarter of the town, and where there are already some very nice-looking houses. The interior of the church is large and handsome, and has more the look of a church than any thing I have been inside of in this country yet. 'T is full eight years since I was in a Catholic church; and the sensation with which I approached the high altar, with its golden crucifix, its marble entablatures, and its glimmering starry lights, savoured fully as much of sadness as devotion. I have not been in a Catholic place of worship since I was at school. . . . They sang that exquisitely mournful and beautiful *Et incarnatus est* of Haydn's, which made my blood all run backwards.

One thing disgusted me dreadfully, though the priests who were officiating never passed or approached the altar without bending the knee to it, they kept spitting all over the carpet that surrounded and covered the steps to it, interrupting themselves in the middle of the service to do so, without the slightest hesitation. We had a very indifferent sermon: the service was of course in Latin. . . .

Mrs Caton amused me very much by her account of the slaves on their estates, whom, she said, she found the best and most faithful servants in the world. Being born upon the land, there exists among them something of the old spirit of clanship, and 'our house,' 'our family,' are the terms by which they designate their owners. In the south, there are no servants but blacks; for the greater proportion of domestics being slaves, all species of servitude whatever is looked upon as a degradation; and the slaves themselves entertain the very highest contempt for white servants, whom they designate as 'poor white trash.'

Monday, 7th [January 1833]

. . . At half-past five, took coffee, and off to the theatre. The play was *Romeo and Juliet*; the house was extremely full: they are a delightful audience. My Romeo had gotten on a pair of trunk breeches, that looked as if he had borrowed them from some worthy Dutchman of a hundred years ago. Had he worn them in New York, I could have understood it as a compliment to the ancestry of that good city; but here, to adopt such a costume in *Romeo*, was really perfectly unaccountable. They were of a most unhappy choice of colours, too – dull, heavy-looking blue cloth, and offensive crimson satin, all be-puckered, and be-plaited, and be-puffed, till the young man looked like a magical figure growing out of a monstrous, strange-coloured melon, beneath which descended his unfortunate legs, thrust into a pair of red slippers, for all the world like Grimaldi's legs *en costume* for clown.

The play went off pretty smoothly, except that they broke one man's collar-bone, and nearly dislocated a woman's shoulder by flinging the scenery about. My bed was not made in time, and when the scene drew, half a dozen carpenters in patched trowsers and tattered shirt sleeves were discovered smoothing down my pillows, and adjusting my draperies. The last scene is too good not to be given verbatim:

> *Romeo*   Rise, rise, my Juliet,
> And from this cave of death, this house of horror,
> Quick let me snatch thee to thy Romeo's arms.

Here he pounced upon me, plucked me up in his arms like an uncomfortable bundle, and staggered down the stage with me.

> *Juliet*   (aside) Oh, you've got me up horridly! – that'll never do; let me down, pray let me down.
> *Romeo*   There, breathe a vital spirit on thy lips,
> And call thee back, my soul, to life and love!
> *Juliet*   (aside) Pray put me down; you'll certainly throw me down if you don't set me on the ground, directly.

In the midst of 'cruel, cursed fate,' his dagger fell out of his dress; I, embracing him tenderly, crammed it back again, because I knew I should want it at the end.

> *Romeo*   Tear not our heart-strings thus!
> They crack! they break! – Juliet! Juliet! (Dies.)

Juliet	(to corpse) Am I smothering you?
Corpse	(to Juliet) Not at all; could you be so kind, do you think, as to put my wig on again for me? – It has fallen off.
Juliet	(to corpse) I'm afraid I can't, but I'll throw my muslin veil over it. You've broken the phial, haven't you? (Corpse nodded.)
Juliet	(to corpse) Where's your dagger?
Corpse	(to Juliet) 'Pon my soul, I don't know.

Sunday, 13th [January 1833]

By half-past ten we were packed in what in this country is termed an exclusive extra, i.e. a stage-coach to ourselves, and progressing towards Washington. . . .

As for the road, we had been assured it was exceedingly good; but mercy on us! I can't think of it without aching. Here we went up, up, up, and there we went down, down, down – now, I was in my father's lap, and now I was half out of window. The utter impossibility of holding one's self in any position for two minutes is absolutely ridiculous. Sometimes we laughed, and at other times we groaned, at our helpless and hopeless condition; but at last we arrived, with no bones broken, at about three o'clock, at the capital and seat of government of the United States. . . .

Monday, 14th [January 1833]

. . . The theatre is the tiniest little box that ever was seen – not much bigger, I verily think, than the baby's play-house at Versailles. When I came to perceive who the company were, and that sundry of our Baltimore comrades were come on hither, I begged to be excused from rehearsing, as they had all done their parts but a few days before with me. . . .

We walked up to the Capitol: the day was most beautifully bright and sunny, and the mass of white building, with its terraces and columns, stood out in fine relief against the cloudless blue sky. We went first into the senate, or upper house, because Webster* was speaking, whom I especially wished to hear. The room itself is neither large nor lofty; the senators sit in two semi-circular rows, turned towards the President, in comfortable arm-chairs. On the same ground, and literally sitting among the senators, were a whole regiment of ladies, whispering, talking, laughing, and

* Daniel Webster (1782–1852), American statesman.

fidgeting. A gallery, level with the floor, and only divided by a low partition from the main room, ran round the apartment: this, too, was filled with pink, and blue, and yellow bonnets; and every now and then, while the business of the house was going on, and Webster speaking, a tremendous bustle, and waving of feathers, and rustling of silks, would be heard, and in came streaming a reinforcement of political beauties, and then would commence a jumping up, a sitting down, a squeezing through, and a how-d'ye-doing, and a shaking of hands. The senators would turn round; even Webster would hesitate, as if bothered by the row, and, in short, the whole thing was more irregular, and unbusiness-like, than any one could have imagined. . . .

The heat of the room was intolerable; and after sitting till I was nearly suffocated, we adjourned to the House of Representatives. . . . The room itself is lofty and large, and very handsome, but extremely ill constructed for the voice, which is completely lost among the columns, and only reaches the gallery, where listeners are admitted, in indistinct and very unedifying murmurs. The members not infrequently sit with their feet upon their desks.

At half-past five, we went to the theatre. We walked out upon the terrace, and looked at the view of the Potomac, and the town, which, in spite of the enlivening effect of an almost summer's sky, looked dreary and desolate in the extreme. We then returned home.

We were a long time before we could discover, among the intricate, dark little passages, our own private entrance, and were as nearly as possible being carried into the pit by a sudden rush of spectators making their way thither: I wish we had been; I think I should like to have seen myself very much.

The theatre is absolutely like a doll's play-house: it was completely crammed with people. I played ill; I cannot act tragedy within half a yard of the people in the boxes. . . .

Wednesday, 16th [January 1833]
After breakfast, went to rehearsal. . . . At half-past five, went to the theatre. The play was the *Hunchback*: the house was crowded. . . .

We had a discussion as to how far real feeling enters into our scenic performances. 'T is hard to say: the general question it would be impossible to answer, for acting is altogether a monstrous anomaly. John Kemble and Mrs Siddons were always in earnest in what they were about; Miss O'Neill used to cry bitterly in all her tragedy parts; whilst Garrick could be making faces and playing tricks in the middle of his finest points, and Kean would talk gibberish while the people were in an uproar of applause at him.

In my own individual instance, I know that sometimes I could turn every word I am saying into burlesque (never Shakespeare, by the by) and at others my heart aches, and I cry real, bitter, warm tears, as earnestly as if I was in earnest.

Thursday, 17th [January 1833]

Sat writing journal till twelve o'clock, when we went to Mr Bancroft's. Took him up, and thence proceeded to the Presidency to be presented in due form.

His Excellency Andrew Jackson is very tall and thin, but erect and dignified in his carriage – a good specimen of a fine old well-battered soldier. His hair is very thick and grey: his manners are perfectly simple and quiet, therefore very good; so are those of his niece, Mrs Andrew Darelson, who is a very pretty person, and lady of the house, Mrs Jackson having been dead some time. He talked about South Carolina, and entered his protest against scribbling ladies, assuring us that the whole of the present southern disturbances* had their origin in no larger a source than the nib of the pen of a lady. Truly, if this be true, the lady must have scribbled to some purpose. . . .

Saturday, 19th [January 1833]

. . . At half-past twelve, Captain Martin came for me; just as we were going, Mr Fulton called. He was on horseback, and asked leave to join us, which I agreed to very readily. He was pilot, and led us round and about through the woods, and across the waters; all of which, as Captain Martin observed, was in the day's work. We returned at half-past three. Directly after dinner, I set out to pay sundry cards. . . .

By 30 January 1833 Fanny and her father were back in Philadelphia, but tailed by an unpleasant rumour. A joke cracked by Fanny with one of

* Presumably to do with South Carolina nullifying the Tariff Act of 1832.

the many Washington young men eager to escort her on her rides had misfired. It was subsequently alleged that, in the course of the particular ride, she 'had spoken most derogatorily of America and Americans . . .' The peccadillo was to have unpleasant consequences on their return to Philadelphia.

Wednesday, 30th [January 1833] Philadelphia
. . . Went to the theatre at half-past five. It poured with rain, in spite of which the house was very good: the play was *Fazio*. When I came on in my fine dress, at the beginning of the second act, the people hailed me with such a tremendous burst of applause, and prolonged it so much, that I was greatly puzzled to imagine what on earth possessed them. I concluded they were pleased with my dress, but could not help being rather amused at their vehement and continued clapping, considering they had seen it several times before. However, they ceased at last, and I thought no more about it.

Towards the time for the beginning of the third act, which opens with my being discovered waiting for Fazio's return, as I was sitting in my dressing-room working, Dall suddenly exclaimed, 'Hark! – what is that?' – opened the door, and we heard a tremendous noise of shouts and of applause.

'They are waiting for you, certainly,' said Dall. She ran out, and returned, saying, 'The stage is certainly waiting for you, Fanny, for the curtain is up.'

I rushed out of the room; but on opening the door leading to the stage, I distinctly heard my father's voice addressing the audience. I turned sick with a sort of indefinite apprehension, and on enquiry found that at the beginning of the play a number of handbills had been thrown into the pit, professing to quote my conversation with Mr Fulton at Washington, and calling upon the people to resent my conduct in the grossest and most vulgar terms. This precious document had, it seems, been brought round by somebody to my father, who immediately went on with it in his hand, and assured the audience that the whole thing was a falsehood.

I scarce heard what he said, though I stood at the side scene: I was crying dreadfully with fright and indignation. How I wished I was a caterpillar under a green gooseberry-bush!

Oh, how I did wince to think of going on again after this scene, though the feeling of the audience was most evident; for all the applause I had fancied they bestowed upon my dress, was, in fact, an unsolicited testimony of their disbelief in the accusation brought against me.

They received my father's words with acclamations; and when the curtain drew up, and I was discovered, the pit rose and waved their hats, and the applause was tremendous. I was crying dreadfully, and could hardly speak; however, I mastered myself and went on with my part – though, what with the dreadful exertion that it is in itself, and the painful excitement I had just undergone, I thought I should have fainted before I got through with it.

They now returned to fulfil engagements in New York.

Monday, 18th [February 1833]
After breakfast, went to rehearsal; came home and stitched at my *Françoise de Foix* head-dress. My father is extremely unwell; I scarce think he will be able to get through his part tonight.

After dinner, practised, and read a canto in Dante. It pleases me when I refer to Biagioli's notes, to find that the very lines Alfieri* has noted, are those under which I have drawn my emphatic pencil marks.

At half-past five, went to the theatre. The play was *Macbeth*, for my benefit: the house was very full, and I played very ill. My father was dreadfully exhausted by his work.

I had an interesting discussion about the costume and acting of the witches in this awful play. I should like to see them acted and dressed a little more like what they should be, than they generally are. It has been always customary – heaven only knows why – to make low comedians act the witches, and to dress them like old fish-women. Instead of the wild unearthly appearance which Banquo describes, and which belongs to their most terrible and grotesquely poetical existence and surroundings, we have three jolly-faced fellows – whom we are accustomed to laugh at, night after night, in every farce on the stage, – with as due a proportion of petticoats as any woman, letting alone witch, might desire, jocose red faces, peaked hats, and broomsticks. . . .

If I had the casting of *Macbeth*, I would give the witches to the first

---

* Vittorio Alfieri (1749–1803), Italian dramatist.

melo-dramatic actors on the stage . . . – and give them such dresses, as, without ceasing to be grotesque, should be a little more fanciful, and less ridiculous than the established livery; something that would accord a little better with the blasted heath, the dark, fungus-grown wood, the desolate, misty hillside, and the flickering light of the cauldron cave. . . .

Saturday, 23d [February 1833]
We came home at two. Pierce Butler and the horses were waiting for me: we mounted and rode down to the Hoboken ferry, where we crossed.

The day was like an early day in spring in England; a day when the almond trees would all have been in flower, the hawthorn hedges putting forth their tender green and brown shoots, and the primroses gemming the mossy roots of the trees by the watercourses. . . .

On our way, discussing the difference between religion as felt by men and women, Pierce Butler agreed with me, that hardly one man out of five thousand held any distinct and definite religious belief. He said that religion was a sentiment, and that as regarded all creeds, there was no midway with them; that entire faith or utter disbelief were the only alternatives; for that displacing one jot of any of them made the whole totter – which last is, in some measure, true, but I do not think it is true that religion is only a sentiment.

There are many reasons why women are more religious than men. Our minds are not generally naturally analytical – our educations tend to render them still less so: 't is seldom in a woman's desire (because seldom in her capacity) to investigate the abstract bearings of any metaphysical subject. Our imaginations are exceedingly sensitive, our subservience to early impressions, and exterior forms, proportionate; and our habits of thought, little enlarged by experience, observation, or proper culture, render us utterly incapable of almost any logical train of reasonings.

With us, I think, therefore, faith is the only secure hold; for disbelief, acting upon mental constructions so faulty and weak, would probably engender insanity, or a thousand species of vague, wild, and mischievous enthusiasms. I believe, too, that women are more religious than men, because they have warmer and deeper affections. There is nothing surely on earth that can satisfy and utterly fulfil the capacity for loving which exists in every woman's nature. . . .

They were now due to leave New York for their engagement in Boston.

Saturday, April 13th [1833]

At a quarter after four, drove down to the boat. . . . Owing to the yesterday's boat not having sailed, it was crowded today, and freighted most heavily, so as to draw an unusual quantity of water, and proceed at a much slower rate than common. At a few minutes after five, the huge brazen bell on deck began to toll; the mingled crowd justled [*sic*], and pushed, and rolled about; the loiterers on shore rushed on board; the bidders-farewell on board rushed on shore.

Dall and I took a quiet, sunny stand, away from all the confusion, and watched, from our floating palace, New York glide away like a glittering dream from before us. . . .

Sunday, 14th [April 1833]

The morning was beautifully bright and clear. While dressing, heard the breakfast bell, and received sundry intimations to descend and eat; however, I declined leaving my cabin until I had done dressing, which I achieved very comfortably at leisure, during which time the ship weathered Point Judith, where the Atlantic comes in to the shore between the termination of Long Island and the southern extremity of Rhode Island. The water is generally rough here, and I had been prophesied an agreeable little fit of sea sickness; but no such matter – we passed it very smoothly, and presently stopped at Newport, on Rhode Island, to leave and take up passengers. . . .

We entered Providence river in a few moments, and steamed along between Rhode Island and the main land, until we reached Providence, a town on the shore of Rhode Island, where we were to leave the boat, and pursue our route by coach to Boston. . . . The distance from Providence to Boston is forty miles; but we were six hours and a half doing it over an excellent road. . . .

As we approached Boston, the country assumed a more culti-vated aspect – the houses in the road-side villages were remarkably neat, and pretty, and cottage-like – the land was well farmed; and the careful cultivation, and stone walls which perform the part of hedges here, together with the bleak look of the distances on each side, made me think of Scotland. We entered Boston through a long road with houses on each side, making one fancy one's self in the town long before one reaches it. We did not arrive until half-past six. Went to my own room and dressed for dinner. . . . Here we are in a new place! – How desolate and cheerless this constant changing of homes is: the Scripture saith, 'There is no rest to the wicked;' and truly I never felt so convinced of my own wickedness as I have done since I have been in this country.

Monday, 15th [April 1833]
Went over to the theatre to rehearse *Fazio*. The manager met us at the door, and assured me there was no necessity for my doing so till to-morrow. Pierce Butler came early to see me, and stayed all the morning. . . . At about half-past four, the horses came to the door.

'He rides with her, walks with her, and waits on her most devotedly,'[12]
wrote a friend of Fanny's of Pierce at this time. On this particular ride William Hodgkinson took them to Auburn, where soon the lovers would be riding together, as at New York, unchaperoned. . . .

. . . The afternoon was lovely, and the roads remarkably good: I had a fine, handsome, spirited horse, who pulled my hands to pieces for want of being properly curbed. We rode out to Cambridge, the University of Massachusetts, about three miles distant from Boston. The village round it, with its white cottages, and meeting roads, and the green lawns and trees round the college, reminded me of England.

We rode on to a place called Mount Auburn, a burial-ground which the Bostonians take great pride in, and which is one of the lions of the place. . . . The enclosure is of considerable extent – about one hundred acres – and contains several high hills and deep ravines, in the bottom of which are dark, still, melancholy-looking meres. The whole is cut, with much skill and good taste, by roads for carriages, and small, narrow footpaths. The various avenues are distinguished by the names of trees, as, Linden walk, Pine walk, Beech walk; and already two or three white monuments are seen glimmering palely through the woods, reminding one of the solemn use to which this ground is consecrated, which, for its beauty, might seem a pleasure-garden instead of a place of graves. . . .

Our time was limited; so, after lingering for a short space along the narrow pathways that wind among the dwellings of the dead, we rode home. We reached Boston at a quarter to seven.

My father and Dall were already gone to the theatre. I dressed, and went over myself immediately. The play was begun: the house was not very full. The managers have committed the greatest piece of mismanagement imaginable – they advertise my father alone in *Hamlet* tonight, and instead of making me play alone tomorrow night, and so securing our attraction singly before we act together, we are *both* to act tomorrow in *Fazio*, which circumstance, of course, kept the house thin tonight. . . .

The following account of Fanny's performance in Fazio *was written by Anna Quincey, then in her early twenties. It has special interest in showing how Fanny, now passionately in love, played the part of heroine in this torrid melodrama.*

'Her grace, the expression of her countenance, her shrieks, her starts are admirable,' wrote Anna. 'Her voice has rather too much stage tone, but there are tones of it which went to my heart. Her great power, however, is in her attitudes and her expression, and her laugh of agony and insanity was truly horrific.

When Fazio is led off to execution she stands for five minutes 'a perfect statue' – deathlike stillness in the audience, everyone seeming to hold their breath, she gave a start which everyone seemed to feel, and with one of her thrilling screams of agony, rushed from the stage.'

Miss Quincey and her friend were still sobbing when they arrived at the party to meet Fanny. They saw a 'delicate, gentle, subdued shadowy creature. . .' They agreed she was not handsome off stage, but had very fine eyes with very black lashes and eyebrows, fine teeth, though her complexion was coarse and her features unremarkable, in spite of a highly intelligent expression. . . .[13]

Saturday, 20th [April 1833]
. . . At about twelve, we rode to Mount Auburn. The few days of sunshine since we were last there have clothed the whole earth with delicate purple and white blossoms, a little resembling the wood anemone, but growing close to the soil, and making one think of violets with their pale purple colour: they have no fragrance whatever. . . . By the by, on our way out to Mount Auburn we took the Charleston road, and rode over

Bunker Hill.* . . . And this is where so much English blood was shed, thought I; for after all, 't was all English blood – do as they can, they can never get rid of their stock. . . .

England and America ought not to be enemies, 't is unnatural while the same language is spoken in both lands. Until Americans have found a tongue for themselves, they must still be the children of old England, for they speak the words her children speak by the fireside of her homes. Oh, England! noble, noble land! . . .

Wednesday, 27th [24th April 1833]
. . . At half-past five, off to the theatre. The house was crammed: the play, *The Stranger*. It is quite comical to see the people in the morning at the box-office: our window is opposite to it, and 't is a matter of the greatest amusement to me to watch them. They collect in crowds for upwards of an hour before the doors open, and when the bolts are withdrawn, there is a yelling and shouting as though the town were on fire. In they rush, thumping and pummelling one another, and not one comes out without rubbing his head, or his back, or showing a piteous rent in his clothes. I was surprised to see men of a very low order pressing foremost to obtain boxes, but I find that they sell them again at an enormous increase to others who have not been able to obtain any; and the better to carry on their traffic, these worthies smear their clothes with molasses, and sugar, &c., in order to prevent any person of more decent appearance, or whose clothes are worth a cent, from coming near the box-office: this is ingenious, and deserves a reward. . . .

Tuesday, 30th [April 1833]
We rode down to the 'Chelsea Ferry,' and crossed over the Charles river, where the shore opposite Boston bears the name of that refuge for damaged marine stores. The breath of the sea was delicious, as we crossed the water in one of the steam-boats constantly plying to and fro, and on the other side, as we rode towards the beach, it came greeting us delightfully from the wide waters. . . .

How happy I was to see the beautiful sea once more – to be once

* On 17 June 1775 it was the site of the first major engagement of the American War of Independence.

more galloping over the golden sands, – to be once more wondering at and worshipping the grandeur and loveliness of this greatest of God's marvellous works. How I do love the sea! – my very soul seems to gather energy, and life, and light, from its power, its vastness, its bold, bright beauty, its fresh, invigorating airs, its glorious, triumphant, rushing sound. The thin, thin rippling waves came like silver leaves spreading themselves over the glittering sand with just a little, sparkling, pearly edge, like the cream of a bright glass of champagne. . . .

For a short time my spirits seemed like uncaged birds; I rejoiced with all my might – I could have shouted aloud for delight; I galloped far along the sand, as close in to the water's restless edge as my horse would bear to go. But the excitement died away, and then came vividly back the time when last I stood upon the sea beach at Cramond,* and lost myself in listening to that delicious sound of the chiming waters – I was many years younger then. . . .

Thursday, 2d [May 1833]
After breakfast, went over to rehearsal; at half-past eleven, went out to ride: the day was heavenly, bright, and mild, with a full, soft, sweet spring breeze blowing life and health over one. The golden willow trees were all in flower, and the air, as we rode by them, was rich with their fragrance. The sky was as glorious as the sky of Paradise: the whole world was full of loveliness; and my spirits were in most harmonious tune with all its beauty. We rode along the chiming beach, talking gravely of many matters, temporal and spiritual. . . .

At about this time, following persistent wooing among the memorials of Boston's Mount Auburn cemetery, Fanny and Pierce at last became engaged. She was twenty-four, he twenty-six.†

Some years later Pierce had his phrenological 'bumps' interpreted by a mutual friend. These were pronounced impressive on Amativeness, Philoprogenitiveness, Concentration, Self-Esteem and Love of Approbation; rather impressive on Adhesiveness (Persistence), Combativeness, Destructiveness, Sensitiveness and Firmness.

---

* On the outskirts of Edinburgh, by the Firth of Forth.

† Fanny's descendant, Wister, puts Pierce's year of birth as 1807, the scholar A. J. Scott as 1808!

Of Pierce at this time Fanny remarked that though a person of little cultivation, he had strong natural sense, an extreme love of truth, and much straightforwardness of character.

'Do let me know dearest Fan, when this terrible affair of marriage is to be . . .' wrote her elder brother when the news broke, 'they say . . . that when you have a house and a nursery to look after, you will leave off writing.'[14]

This, she had no doubt already foreseen; more worrying was her friend Charles Hodgkinson's attempt to warn her of Pierce's 'early career of profligacy'. But as Fanny herself said, 'I was in love, and paid little heed to . . . cautions at second-hand.'[15]

The engagement was no more popular with Fanny's father. Not only would he have preferred Fanny to marry an Englishman, but the Kemble finances still needed a further successful season to establish them on a firm footing. It was finally agreed, however, that he and Fanny would exploit their popularity in the North-East, winter in New Orleans, and return to the North-East in the spring of 1834, when Fanny might possibly be allowed to marry. Meanwhile, the 1832–3 Season being all but over, they would take time off to visit the Niagara Falls, holding brief engagements en route *at Albany, Montreal and Quebec.*

By June they were back in New York.

Thursday [early June 1833]
At a little after ten, Pierce Butler came to take us to see the savages. We drove down, Dall, my father, he and I, to their hotel. We found, even at that early hour, the portico, passage, and staircase, thronged with gazers upon the same errand as ourselves. We made our way, at length, into the presence chamber; a little narrow dark room, with all the windows shut, crowded with people, come to stare at their fellow wild beasts.

Upon a sofa sat Black Hawk, a diminutive, shrivelled looking old man, with an appearance of much activity in his shrunk limbs, and a calmness and dignified self-composure in his manner, which, in spite of his want of size and comeliness, was very striking. Next to him sat a young man, the adopted son of his brother the prophet; whose height and breadth, and peculiar gravity of face and deportment, were those of a man nearly forty, whereas he is little more than half that age.

The undisturbed seriousness of his countenance was explained to me by their keeper, thus: he had, it seems, the day before, indulged rather too freely in the delights of champagne, and was suffering just retribution in the shape of a head-ache – unjust retribution I should say, for in his savage experience no such sweet bright poison had ever before been recorded, I guess, by the after pain it causes.

Next to him sat Black Hawk's son, a noble, big young creature, like a fine Newfoundland puppy, with a handsome, scornful face, which yet exhibited more familiarity and good-humoured amusement at what was going on than any of the rest. His hair was powdered on the top, and round the ears with a bright vermilion-coloured powder, and knots of scarlet berries or beads, I don't know which, hung like ear-rings on each side of his face. A string of glass beads was tied round his naked throat; he was wrapped in a large blanket, which completely concealed his form, except his legs and feet, which were clothed in common leather shoes, and a species of deerskin gaiter. He seemed much alive to what was going on, conversed freely in his own language with his neighbour, and laughed once or twice aloud, which rather surprised me, as I had heard so much of their immovable gravity. The costume of the other young man was much the same, except that his hair was not adorned.

Black Hawk himself had on a blue cloth surtout, scarlet leggings, a black silk neck handkerchief, and ear-rings. His appearance altogether was not unlike that of an old French gentleman. Beside him, on a chair, sat one of his warriors, wrapped in a blanket, with a cotton handkerchief whisped [sic] round his head. At one of the windows, apart from their companions, with less courtesy in their demeanour, and a great deal of sullen savageness in their serious aspects, sat the great warrior, and the prophet of the tribe – the latter is Black Hawk's brother.

I cannot express the feeling of commiseration and disgust which the whole scene gave me. That men such as ourselves, creatures with like feelings, like perceptions should be brought, as strange animals at a show, to be gazed at the livelong day by succeeding shoals of gaping folk, struck me as totally unfitting. The cold dignity of the old chief, and the malignant scowl of the prophet, expressed the indecency and the irksomeness of such a situation. Then, to look at those two young savages, with their fine muscular proportions, and think of them cooped up the whole horrible day long, in this hot prison-house full of people, made my heart ache.

How they must loathe the sight of these narrow walls, and the sound of these strange voices; how they must sicken for their unmeasured range of wilderness!

The gentleman who seemed to have the charge of them pressed me to go up and shake hands with them, as every body else in the room did; but I refused to do so from literal compassion, and unwillingness to add to the wearisome toil they were made to undergo. As we were departing, however, they reiterated their entreaties that we would go up and shake hands with them – so I did.

Black Hawk and the young men received our courtesy with great complaisance; but when we went to the great warrior and the prophet, they seemed exceedingly loath to receive our hands, the latter particularly, who had, moreover, one of the very worst expressions I think I ever saw upon a human countenance. I instinctively withdrew my hand; but when my father offered his, the savage's face relaxed into a smile, and he met his greeting readily. I wonder what pleased him about my father's appearance, whether it was his large size or not. I had a silver vinaigrette in my pouch, which I gave Black Hawk's son, by way of keepsake: it will make a charming present for his squaw.

30 June – 17 July 1833

On Sunday 30 June 1833 the Niagara trip began, Pierce returning to Philadelphia to complete some unfinished business before rejoining them at Utica.

Fanny was so excited she woke at four, went back to sleep until six, and almost missed the steamboat that was to take them up the Hudson river. She had no sooner set foot on board than she found herself standing next to that notorious traveller and adventurer (not to say bounder), Edward Trelawny, friend of Byron and Shelley. He was to accompany Fanny, Aunt Dall and her father for the remainder of the journey.

On reaching West Point they stopped off for two days to visit a distant kinsman, Governor Kemble, whose estate, Cold Springs, lay across the river.

Here, with the Governor's two sons, Fanny inspected an iron works, viewed a precipitous and highly satisfactory cascade, and an even more satisfactory 'proving' of two yet unfired West Point cannon. The experience fulfilled her craving for the martial.

'The sound was glorious; the first heavy peal, and then echo after echo, as they rimbombavano among the answering hills, who growled aloud at the stern voice waking their still and noonday's deep repose.'[16]

On then to meet the boat. Once safely on board, she sat down, took out some sewing, and found Trelawny once more beside her. '. . . We cannot like those who force themselves upon us,' she wrote apropos in her journal, though on publication it was artfully changed to 'As a nuisance, which all unsought-for companionship is, he is quite the most endurable possible . . .'[17]

In fact Trelawny would prove excellent company, reminiscing freely about the fascinating people he had known, even reading Don Quixote aloud to them as they glided up the canal to Utica where they were to rendezvous with Pierce.

At this time Trelawny was forty-one, almost twenty years older than Fanny, but years later, Fanny's friend Mrs Jameson gave it as her opinion that if Trelawny had ever loved anyone, it had been Fanny Kemble 'who appears to be his ideal of womankind'.[18] One certainly wonders what Pierce Butler thought about the persistent presence of this attractive man

98

('sun-burnt enough to warm one through with a look,' according to Fanny), who was to write to his bride-to-be that she reminded him of no one so much as Shelley.

'From some real or imagined resemblance in person or mind, or both,' he later wrote to Fanny from the Gulf of Mexico, 'you recalled his image so vividly to my mind that I was forced to admire you on the instant – and every day my admiration augmented.'[19]

Saturday, 6th [July 1833]

. . . We reached Albany in very good time for dinner. Mr Trelawny dined with us: what a savage he is, in some respects! He's a curious being: a description of him would puzzle any one who had never seen him. A man with the proportions of a giant for strength and agility; taller, straighter, and broader than most men; yet with the most listless, indolent carelessness of gait; and an uncertain, wandering way of dropping his feet to the ground, as if he didn't know where he was going, and didn't much wish to go any where. His face is as dark as a Moor's; with a wild, strange look about the eyes and forehead, and a mark like a scar upon his cheek: his whole appearance giving one an idea of toil, hardship, peril, and wild adventure. The expression of his mouth is remarkably mild and sweet; and his voice is extremely low and gentle. His hands are as brown as a labourer's: he never profanes them with gloves, but wears two strange magical-looking rings: one of them, which he showed me, is made of elephant's hair. . . .

Tuesday, 9th [July 1833]

. . . Mr Trelawny killed us with laughing with an account he gave us of some of Byron's sayings and doings, which were just as whimsical and eccentric as un-amiable, but very funny. To-morrow we start for Utica: Mr Trelawny comes with us: I am glad of it – I like him. . . .

Wednesday, 10th [July 1833]

. . . We proceeded by canal to Utica, which distance we performed in a day and a night, starting at two from Schenectady, and reaching Utica the next day at about noon.

I like travelling by the canal boats very much. Ours was not crowded; and the country through which we passed being delightful, the placid, moderate gliding through it, at about four miles and a half an hour, seemed to me infinitely preferable to the noise of wheels, the rumble of a coach, and the jerking of bad roads, for the gain of a mile an hour. The only nuisances are the bridges over the canal, which are so very low, that one is obliged to prostrate one's self on the deck of the boat, to avoid being scraped off it; and this humiliation occurs, upon an average, once every quarter of an hour.

Mr Trelawny read *Don Quixote* to us: he reads very peculiarly; slowly, and with very marked emphasis. He has a strong feeling of humour, as well as of poetry: in fact, they belong to each other; for humour is but fancy laughing, and poetry but fancy sad.

The valley of the Mohawk, through which we crept the whole sunshining day, is beautiful from beginning to end: fertile, soft, rich, and occasionally approaching sublimity and grandeur in its rocks and hanging woods. . . . The sun had scarce been down ten minutes from the horizon, when the deck was perfectly wet with the heaviest dew possible, which drove us down to the cabin. Here I fell fast asleep, till awakened by the cabin girl's putting her arms affectionately round me, and telling me that I might come and have the first choice of a berth for the night, in the horrible hen-coop allotted to the female passengers. I was too sleepy to acknowledge or avail myself of the courtesy; but the girl's manner was singularly gentle and kind.

We sat in the men's cabin until they began making preparations for bed, and then withdrew into a room about twelve feet square, where a whole tribe of women were getting to their beds. Some half undressed, some brushing, some curling, some washing, some already asleep in their narrow cribs, but all within a quarter of an inch of each other: it made one shudder. As I stood cowering in a corner, half asleep, half crying, the cabin girl came to me again, and entreated me to let her make a bed for me. However, upon my refusing to undress before so much good company, or lie down in such narrow neighbourhood, she put Dall and myself in a small closet, where were four empty berths, where I presently fell fast asleep, where she established herself for the night, and where Dall, wrapped up in a shawl, sat till morning under the half-open hatchway, breathing damp starlight.

Thursday, 11th [July 1833]
. . . When we arrived at Utica, I gave the nice cabin girl my silver

needle-case: her tenderness and care of me the night before made it impossible for me to offer her money. She took my gift, and, throwing her arms round my neck, kissed me very fervently for it. . . .

Pierce met them at Utica, thoughtfully bringing a case of silver forks for their use.

At Utica we dined; and after dinner I slept profoundly. . . . Passed the evening in writing journal. Mr Trelawny showed me his of Sunday last.

Friday, 12th [July 1833]
We all breakfasted early together, and immediately after breakfast got into an open carriage and set off for Trenton. Dall and my father sat beside each other, Pierce Butler and I opposite them; Mr Trelawny on the box; and so we progressed.

The day was bright and breezy: the country was all smiling round us in rich beauty. . . . About seven miles from Utica, we stopped to water the horses at a lonely road-side house: we alighted, and without ceremony strolled into the garden – a mere wilderness of overgrown sweet-briar, faint breathing dog-roses, and flaunting red poppies, overshadowed by some orchard trees, from which we stole sundry half-ripe cherries. The place was desolate, I believe; yet we lingered in it, and did not think it so.

We got into the carriage again: the remaining eight miles of our journey were as beautiful and as bad as the preceding ones had been. I thought of our dark drive back through these miry and uneven ways. At last we reached the house at which visitors to the Falls put up: a large, comfortable dwelling enough, kept by a couple of nice young people, who live in this solitude all the year round, and maintain themselves and a beautiful big baby by the profits they derive from the pilgrims to Trenton. We ordered dinner, and set forth to the Falls, with our host for guide.

We crossed a small wood immediately adjoining the house, and, descending several flights of steps connected by paths in the rocky bank, we presently stood on the brink of the channel, where the water was boiling along, deep, and black, and passing away like time. . . . We walked on steadily, warning each other at every step, and presently we arrived at the first fall, where the rest of our party were halting. I can't describe it: I don't know either its height or width; I only know it was extremely beautiful, and came pouring down like a great rolling heap of amber. . . . After standing before the tumbling mass of water for a length of time, we climbed to the brink above, and went on.

Mr Trelawny flung himself down under a roof of rock by the waterfall. My father, Dall, and the guide went on out of sight, and Pierce Butler and I loitered by the rapid waters, flinging light branches and flowers upon the blood-coloured torrent, that whirled, and dragged, and tossed them down to the plunge beneath. When we came to the beautiful circular fall, we crept down to a narrow ridge, and sat with our feet hanging over the black cauldron, just opposite a vivid rainbow that was clasping the waterfall. We sat here till I began to grow dizzy with the sound and motion of the churning darkness beneath us, and begged to move, which we did very cautiously. I was in an agony lest we should slip from the narrow dripping ledges along which we crawled.

We wandered on, and stopped again at another fall, upon a rocky shelf overhanging the torrent, beside the blasted and prostrate trunk of a large tree. I was tired with walking, and Pierce Butler was lifting me up to seat me on the fallen tree, when we saw Mr Trelawny coming slowly towards us. He stopped and spoke to us, and presently passed on; we remained behind, talking and dipping our hands into the fresh water. At length we rejoined the whole party, sitting by a narrow channel, where the water looked like ink. Beyond this our guide said it was impossible to go: I was for ascertaining this by myself; but my father forbade me to attempt the passage further.

I was thirsty; and the guide having given me a beautiful strawberry and a pale blue-bell, that he had found, like a couple of jewels in some dark crevice of the rocks, I devoured the one, and then going down to the black water's edge, we dipped the fairy cup in, and drank the cold clear water, with which abundant draught I relieved my father's thirst also. . . .

We returned to the house, and dined. After dinner, had a gossip with Mrs Moore, and a romp with her beautiful baby. . . .

At about sunset, I wandered into the wood, to the top of the steps leading to the waterfall; where I could hear, far below, its sweet voice singing as it passed away. I remained standing here till the carriage was announced. . . .

It grew dark long before we reached Utica: half the way, I sang; the other half, I slept, in spite of ruts five fathoms deep, and all the joltings of these evil ways. Tomorrow we start on our way to Niagara; which, Mr Trelawny says, is to sweep Trenton clean from our memories. I do not think it.

Saturday, 13th [July 1833]
Left Utica at six o'clock, in our exclusive extra: we were to go on as far as Auburn, a distance of seventy-six miles. The day was very beautiful, but extremely hot. . . . The country was very rich and beautiful; and, at every knoll, backed by woodlands, and skirted by golden grain fields.

Mr Trelawny exclaimed, 'Come, we will have a farm here.' He and my father were to smoke, reflect, and enjoy life; I was to sing, whenever I happened to please, and enjoy life too; Dall was to brew, to bake, wash, iron, plough, manage the house, look after the cattle, take care of the poultry, mind the dairy; in short, do every thing on earth that was to be done, and enjoy life too: all which arrangements afforded us matter of converse on the way, and much amusement. . . .

At about half-past three, we arrived at a place called *Syracuse*!!! – where, stopping to change horses, my father observed that here there were two different routes to our point of destination; and desired our driver to take that which passes through Skaneateles, a very beautiful village, situated on a lake so called. However, to this the master of the inn, who was also, I believe, proprietor of the coach, seemed to have some private objection; and while my father was yet speaking, very coolly shut the coach-door in his face, and desired the driver to go on in the contrary direction. The insolence of the fellow enraged my father extremely; and it was rather astonishing, that's the fact: but the deuce is in't [*sic*] if, in a free country, a man may not choose which way his own coach shall go, in spite of the folk who pay him for the use of it. We had to pocket the affront; and, what was much more disagreeable, to travel an ugly, uninteresting road, instead of a picturesque and pretty one.

We had not proceeded many miles after this occurrence, and were just recovering our equanimities, when the said vehicle broke down. We were not overturned or hurt, only tilted a little on one side. The driver, however, did not seem to think it safe to proceed in this condition: the gentlemen got out, and searched the hedges and thickets for a piece of oak sufficiently strong and stout to repair, at least for the moment, the damage: we were not at the time within reach of any house. At last, they procured what they wanted; and, having propped up the carriage after the best fashion they could, we proceeded at a foot pace to the next village.

Here, while they were putting our conveyance into something like better order, Pierce Butler and I wandered away to a pretty bright watercourse, which, like all water in this country, was made to turn a mill. The coach being made sound once more, we packed ourselves into it, and progressed.

The evening was perfectly sultry. I never shall forget, at a place where we stopped to water the horses, a cart-full of wretched sheep and calves, who were, I suppose, on their way to the slaughter-house, but who, in the mean time, seemed enduring the most horrible torture that creatures can suffer. They were jammed into the cart so as to be utterly incapable of moving a single limb; the pitiless sun shone fiercely upon their wretched heads, and their poor eyes were full of dust and flies. I never saw so miserable a spectacle of suffering. I looked at the brutal-looking man that was driving them, and wondered whether he would go to hell, for tormenting these helpless beasts in this fashion.

The sun set gloriously. Mr Trelawny began talking about Greece, and getting a good deal excited, presently burst forth into 'The isles of Greece! the isles of Greece!' which he recited with amazing vehemence and earnestness. He reminded me of Kean several times: while he was declaiming, he looked like a tiger. . . .

Towards evening the heat became more and more oppressive. Our coach was but ill cobbled, and leaned awfully to one side. I fell asleep lying in my father's lap; and when we reached Auburn, which was not until nine o'clock, I was so tired, so miserably sleepy, and so tortured with the side-ache, from the cramped position in which I had been lying, that I just crawled into the first room in the inn where we alighted, and dropped down on the floor fast asleep.

They roused me for supper; and very soon after I betook myself to bed. The heat was intolerable; the pale feet of the summer lightning ran along the black edges of the leaden clouds – the world was alight with it. I could not sleep: I never endured such suffocating heat.

Sunday, 14th [July 1833]

Rose at eight: the morning was already sultry as the hottest noon in England. After breakfast, I wandered about the house in search of shade; went into an empty room, opened the shutters, and got out upon a large piazza, or, rather, colonnade, which surrounded it. The side I had chosen was defended by the house from the fierce sunlight; and I walked up and down in quiet and loneliness for some time. . . .

At about ten, our exclusive extra having driven to the door, we packed ourselves into it, and proceeded towards Geneva, where we were to dine. The sky, however, presently became overcast; and, towards noon, the world was absolutely shrouded in a lead-coloured pall. The air was stifling: it was impossible to draw one's breath; and a quarter of a degree more of heat would certainly have occasioned suffocation. We were all gasping. Suddenly the red lightning tore open the heavy clouds, the thunder rolled round the heavens, the rain came down in torrents: we were away from all shelter, and obliged to proceed through the storm. The leather curtains of our coach were speedily unrolled and buttoned down; but this formed but a miserable shelter against the furious rain. Our carpet-bags, which were on the outside of the carriage, were soaked through; and we ourselves were soon in nearly as bad a plight. The rain came in rivulets through the crevices of our insufficient shelter, and the seats and bottom of the coach were presently standing pools.

We arrived between twelve and one o'clock at Cayuga; and here we drew up before the inn door, to await the end of the storm. . . . The storm having abated, we proceeded on our way; crossed a bridge a mile and some roods long, over the Cayuga lake; which, however, was still so veiled with scowling mist and clouds, that we could discern none of its features.

At about three o'clock we reached Geneva, a small town situated on a lake called Seneca Water. Here we dined. Pierce Butler had most providentially brought silver forks with him: for the wretched two-pronged iron implements furnished us by our host were any thing but clean or convenient. . . .

After resting ourselves for a short time, we again took to our coach, and pursued our route towards Canandaigua, where we were to pass the night. . . . As the evening began to come on, we reached Canandaigua Lake, a very beautiful sheet of water, of considerable extent; we coasted for some time close along its very margin. The opposite shore was high, clothed with wood, from amidst which here and there a white house looked peacefully down on the clear mirror below: the dead themselves can hardly inhabit regions more blessedly apart from the evil turmoil of the world, than the inhabitants of these beautiful solitudes. Leaving the water's edge, we proceeded about a quarter of a mile, and found ourselves at the door of the inn at Canandaigua. . . .

We came down to supper, which was served to us, as usual, in a large desolate-looking public room. After this, we came to the sitting-room they had provided for us, a small comfortable apartment, with a very finely-toned piano in it. To this I forthwith sat down, and played and sang for a length of time: late in the evening, I left the instrument, and my father, Mr Trelawny, and I took a delightful stroll under the colonnade, discussing Milton; many passages of which my father recited most beautifully, to my infinite delight and ecstasy. By and by they went in, and Pierce Butler came out to walk with me. . . .

Monday, 15th [July 1833]
. . . It was nine o'clock when we left Canandaigua: we were all a little done up with our two previous days; and it was unanimously settled that we should proceed only to Rochester, a distance of between thirty and forty miles, which we accomplished by two o'clock. . . .

The inn at which we alighted was large and comfortable: in the drawing-room I found a very tolerable piano-forte, to which I instantly betook myself. . . .

Tuesday, 16th [July 1833]
Had to get up before I'd half done my sleep. At six, started from Rochester for Murray, where we purposed breakfasting. Just as we were nearing the inn, at this same place, our driver took it into his head to give us a taste of his quality. We were all earnestly engaged in a discussion, when suddenly I felt a tremendous sort of stunning blow, and as soon as I opened my eyes, found that the coach was overturned, lying completely on its side. I was very comfortably curled up under my father, who, by Heaven's mercy, did not suffocate me; opposite sat Dall, as white as a ghost, with her forehead cut open, and an awful-looking stream of blood falling

from it; by her stood Mr Trelawny, also as pale as ashes; Pierce Butler was perched like a bird above us all, on the edge of the doorway, which was open.

The first thing I did, was to cry as loud as ever I could, 'I'm not hurt, I'm not hurt!' which assurance I shouted sufficiently lustily to remove all anxiety from their minds. The next thing was to get my father up; in accomplishing which, he trampled upon me most cruelly. As soon as I was relieved from his mountainous pressure, I got up, and saw, to my dismay, two men carrying Mr Trelawny into the house. We were all convinced that some of his limbs were broken: I ran after as quickly as I could, and presently the house was like a hospital.

They carried him into an upper room, and laid him on a bed; here, too, they brought Dall, all white and bleeding. Our hand-baskets and bags were ransacked for salts and eau de Cologne. Cold water, hot water, towels, and pocket handkerchiefs, were called into requisition; and I, with my clothes all torn, and one shoulder all bruised and cut, went from the one to the other in utter dismay.

Presently, to my great relief, Mr Trelawny revived; and gave ample testimony of having the use of his limbs, by getting up, and, in the most skilful manner, plastering poor Dall's broken brow up. Pierce Butler went in quest of my father, who had received a violent blow on his leg, and was halting about, looking after the baggage and the driver, who had escaped unhurt. . . . Poor Dall was the most deplorable of the party, with a bloody handkerchief bound over one half her face; I only ached a little, and I believe Pierce Butler escaped with a scratch on his finger; so, seeing it was no worse, we thanked God, and devoured. After breakfast, we packed ourselves again in our vehicle, and progressed. . . .

We reached Lockport at about four o'clock. . . . The house where we stopped appeared to be hardly finished. We ordered dinner, and I forthwith began kindling a fire, which was extremely welcome to us all. I was very much bruised with our morning's overturn, and went and lay down in my bed-room, where I presently slept profoundly.

Wednesday, 17th [July 1833]
At nine o'clock, we started from Lockport. . . . The road between Lockport and Lewistown is very pretty; and we got out and walked

whenever the horses were changed. At one place where we stopped, I saw a meek-eyed, yellowish-white cart-horse, standing with a man's saddle on his back. The opportunity was irresistible, and the desire too – I had not backed a horse for so long. So I got up upon the amazed quadruped woman's fashion, and took a gallop through the fields, with infinite risk of falling off, and proportionate satisfaction.

We reached Lewistown at about noon, and anxious enquiries were instituted as to how our luggage was to be forwarded, when on the other side; for we were exclusive extras; and for creatures so above common fellowship there is no accommodation in this levelling land. A ferry and a ferry-boat, however, it appeared, there were, and thither we made our way.

While we were waiting for the boat, I climbed out on the branches of a huge oak, which grew over the banks of the river, which here rise nearly a hundred feet high. Thus comfortably perched, like a bird, 'twixt heaven and earth, I copied off some verses which I had scrawled just before leaving Lockport. The ferry-boat being at length procured, we got into it. The day was sultry; the heat intolerable.

The water of this said river Niagara is of a most peculiar colour, like a turquoise when it turns green. It was like a thick stream of verdigris, full of pale, milky streaks, whirls, eddies, and counter currents, and looked as if it were running up by one bank, and down by the other. I sat in the sun, on the floor of the boat, revising my verses. Arrived on the other side, i.e. Canada, there was a second pause, as to how we were to get conveyed to the Falls. . . .

An uneasy-looking, rickety cart without springs was the sole conveyance we could obtain, and into this we packed ourselves. Trelawny brought me some beautiful roses, which he had been stealing for me, and Pierce Butler gave me a glass of milk; with which restoratives I comforted myself, and we set forth. As we squeaked and creaked (I mean our vehicle) up the hill, I thought either my father's or Trelawny's weight quite enough to have broken the whole down; but it did not happen. My mind was eagerly dwelling on what we were going to see: that sight which Trelawny said was the only one in the world which had not disappointed him. I felt absolutely nervous with expectation.

The sound of the cataract is, they say, heard within fifteen miles when the wind sets favourably: to-day, however, there was no wind; the whole air was breathless with the heat of midsummer, and, though we stopped our waggon once or twice to listen as we approached, all was profoundest silence. There was no motion in the leaves of the trees, not a cloud sailing in the sky; every thing was as though in a bright, warm death. When we were within about three miles of the Falls, just before entering the village of Niagara, Pierce Butler stopped the waggon; and then we heard distinctly, though far off, the voice of the mighty cataract. Looking over the woods, which appeared to overhang the course of the river, we beheld one silver cloud rising slowly into the sky – the ever-lasting incense of the waters.

A perfect frenzy of impatience seized upon me: I could have set off and run the whole way; and when at length the carriage stopped at the door of the Niagara house, waiting neither for my father, Dall, nor Pierce Butler, I rushed through the hall, and the garden, down the steep footpath cut in the rocks. I heard steps behind me; Trelawny was following me: down, down I sprang, and along the narrow footpath, divided only by a thicket from the tumultuous rapids. I saw through the boughs the white glimmer of that sea of foam.

'Go on, go on; don't stop,' shouted Trelawny; and in another minute the thicket was passed: I stood upon Table Rock. Trelawny seized me by the arm, and, without speaking a word, dragged me to the edge of the rapids, to the brink of the abyss. I saw Niagara. – Oh, God! who can describe that sight?

It is of the greatest interest that Fanny chose to excise from her published Journal *the powerful evocation of the Falls which follows. Perhaps it was too private, because too revealing, for in it she was not only revealing something of the nature of the artistic spirit, but unconsciously expressing unspeakable forebodings about her impending marriage.*

Curiously, Pierce was to play very little part in the extraordinary psychic drama of her visit to Niagara. It was Edward Trelawny, the familiar of poets, who was the catalyst, and from Fanny's account, 'Go on, go on; don't stop!' as she reports Trelawny shouting, he knew it too.

It is significant that on the Hudson steamboat she had met a woman who had impressed her with her 'long stories, like fairy tales, of caverns lately discovered in the bosom of these mountains; of pits, black and fathomless; of subterranean lakes in gloomy chambers of the earth; and tumbling waters, which fall down in the dark, where men heard, but none had dared to go . . .' Like the young Beckford of Fonthill before her, Fanny had expressed a passion to visit these unearthly regions, and as Beckford himself might have written, asked 'Oh, who will lead me into the secret parts of the earth; who will guide me to the deep hiding places where spirits are – where the air of this upper world is not breathed, and its sounds are unknown – where the light of the sun is unseen, and the voice of human creatures unheard? How I should like to go there!'[20]

Trelawny was to take her.

What is one to make of what follows? Although her spiritual perceptions are timeless, her personal dilemma strikes one as extraordinarily modern – whether to dare live free as an artist or be committed (equally daring) to love and duty. Then, perhaps, it was more of a man's choice, but its implications Fanny certainly understood. It was her inability to decide completely either way that was to ruin her.

The Niagara experience continues as it was published many years later, in her Records of a Girlhood:

'. . . there was a broad flashing sea of furious foam, a deafening rush and roar, through which I heard Mr Trelawny who was following me, shout, 'Go on, go on: don't stop!'

I reached an open floor of broad flat rock, over which the water was pouring. Trelawny seized me by the arm and all but carried me to the very brink; my feet were in the water and on the edge of the precipice, and then I looked down.

I could not speak, and I could hardly breathe; I felt as if I had an iron band across my breast.

I watched the green, glassy, swollen heaps go plunging down, down, down; each mountainous mass of water, as it reached the dreadful brink, recoiling as in horror from the abyss; and after rearing backward in helpless terror, as it were, hurling itself down to be shattered in the inevitable doom over which eternal clouds of foam and spray spread in an impenetrable curtain. The mysterious chasm, with its uproar of voices, seemed like the watery mouth of hell.

I looked and listened till the wild excitement of the scene took such possession of me that, but for the strong arm that held me back, I really think I should have let myself slide down into the gulf.

It was long before I could utter, and as I began to draw my breath I could only gasp out, 'Oh God! Oh God!'

No words can describe either the scene itself, or its effect upon me.[21]

3

After Niagara

17 July 1833 – December 1838

The engagement had dominated much of 1833. Marriage over-shadowed 1834. Pierce was impatient, pressing Fanny to marry him – and soon. They appeared to be passionately in love. Yet dread as well as passion seems continuously to have possessed her at this time, manifesting itself, if only subconsciously, in her writing. This is evident in her account of a wild night ride she and Pierce took together, in which there is more than a foretaste of the Brontës.

> The thermometer stood at 17 degrees below zero. It was the middle of a Massachusetts winter, and the cold was intense, the moon was at the full, and the night as bright as day. Not a stone but was visible on the iron-hard road that ran under our horses' hoofs. The whole country was sheeted with snow, over which the moon threw great floods of yellow light, while here and there a broken ridge in the smooth, white expanse turned a sparkling crystalline edge up to the lovely splendour.
>
> It was wonderfully beautiful and exhilarating, though so cold that my veil was all frozen over my lips, and we literally hardly dared utter a word for fear of swallowing scizzors [*sic*] and knives in the piercing air, which however was perfectly still and without the slightest breath of wind.
>
> So we rode hard and fast and silently, side by side, through the bright, profound stillness of the night, and never drew rein till we reached Dedham.

At Dedham they found the town asleep, but seeing light streaming through the chink in a shutter, asked if they could wait in the house until the coach arrived that was to take them on to New York.

> I found myself in a miserable little low room, heated almost to suffocation by an iron stove, and stifling with the peculiar smell of black dyestuffs. Here, by the light of two wretched bits of candle, two women were working with the utmost dispatch at mourning garments for a funeral, which was to take place that day in a few hours. They did not speak to me after making room for me near the stove, and the only words they exchanged with each other were laconic demands for scissors, thread etc. and so they rapidly plied their needles in silence. . . .[1]

There is no knowing the extent of the psychic struggle now taking place within that tense triangle of Charles, Fanny and Pierce Butler, though it can be guessed at. Equilibrium had probably been maintained by the ever sensible and realistic Aunt Dall, but by the spring of 1834 she was dying. The coach accident at the time of the Niagara trip had permanently damaged her spine, and, towards the end of their second Boston engagement, she had become paralysed from the waist down, and was suffering from convulsions. By April all further bookings had to be cancelled so that Fanny could nurse her. On the 24th of the month Fanny sadly took up her pen: 'Dear Dall has gone from us. She is dead; she died in my arms, and I closed her eyes . . .'[2]

They buried her at Mount Auburn where Fanny and Pierce had so often met as sweethearts during the previous spring. 'I wished her to lie there,' wrote Fanny, 'for life and love and youth and death have their trysting place at the grave.'[3]

Aunt Dall's death seems to have been the signal for Pierce to press his suit with renewed vigour. Until now it had been understood that he would wait for a year to marry Fanny while she returned to England with her father for one last season. Plans were now to be altered yet again. 'A ray of sunshine is parting my stormy sky,' she wrote to a friend, 'Pierce has behaved *most* nobly, and my father most kindly . . . before sailing for New York, we shall *be married* . . . Pierce has promised me that this shall not interfere with my departure or the discharge of my duties to my father . . . he implored me so that I do not believe I had much power of thought . . .' she added.[4]

'On June 7th 1834 I became the wife of Pierce Butler,' writes

Fanny in conclusion to the autobiography of her girlhood. 'Poor girl,' her friend, Catharine Sedgwick commented to Mary Russell Mitford, 'she makes a dangerous experiment, I have a thousand fears for the result.'[5]

At the ceremony, which took place in Philadelphia, the *Atlas* reported the bride bursting into tears, then fainting. Afterwards, a large crowd congregated outside the hotel to serenade the happy couple. What happened that night in the privacy of their bedroom will never be known, but all can hardly have been well since on the steamer to New York the following morning fellow passengers reported that the poor bride wept all the way to Burlington.

Fanny was booked to play for the last time at the Park Theatre. Title and content of the piece were alike ominous – *The Day After The Wedding*, in which a fractious bride is brought to heel by a clever husband. This turned out to be precisely the case. Determined to exert the rights of the husband over those of the father, Pierce now persuaded his new wife to go back on her word to her father and allow him to return to England alone. As a sweetener Charles was to be allowed to retain the life interest on the 35,000 dollars his daughter had earned on their American tour. He nevertheless parted from her 'wronged and deceived', and neither he nor her mother was to contact their daughter for many long months.

Years before, with one of the flashes of insight that sometimes came to her, Fanny had written that she did not consider herself fit to marry or to make an obedient wife and affectionate mother. 'My imagination is paramount with me and would disqualify me, I think, from the everyday matter of fact cares and duties of the mistress of a household . . .'[6] Such misgivings were to be realized all too soon.

The newly married couple had as yet no home of their own, and for the time being went to live with Pierce's brother, John, and his wife. This inauspicious beginning was only partly relieved by their spending most of this first summer in a succession of watering places. Meanwhile, Fanny, who hated being idle for a moment, had begun to prepare her *American Journal* for publication. Pierce detested the *Journal*, the very thought of publication was anathema, and in his new role of husband he forbade it. Fanny, unused to frustration of this kind, rebelled instantly. There was a terrifying row, and Pierce beat a tactical retreat. The *Journal* might be published, but only if he edited it.

It was November. Already three months pregnant, Fanny impetuously walked out of her brother-in-law's house, leaving Pierce a note. She was returning home to England. After wandering aimlessly round Philadelphia for several hours she thought better of this decision, and returned. But a pattern of behaviour had been established that would last a decade.

The controversial *Journal* was published the following year and was a sensational success: '. . . like herself,' wrote her friend, Catharine Sedgwick, 'glorious faculties, delightful accomplishments, unmeasurable sensibility . . . and half a hundred little faults.'[7]

Much to John Butler's relief, no doubt, Fanny and Pierce had by now moved to Butler Place, six miles west of Philadelphia. The house had been lent them by Pierce's aunt, but was nothing like an English mansion or estate according to one visitor, 'more like a second rate English farm'.[8]

For a time Fanny tried her hand at playing Lady Bountiful to their tenants, but with so little appreciation on their part that she soon lapsed into self-pity. 'I live alone,' she wrote to a friend, 'much alone bodily, more alone mentally. I have no intimates, no society, no intellectual intercourse whatever, and I give myself up, as I never did in my life before, to mere musing . . .'[9]

They had not been married a year. Later, Pierce recalled that Fanny frequently expressed regret at this time for having married him. She also began to insist that he release her from her promises. He comforted himself with the thought that the imminent birth of their child would resolve matters, but he was to be disappointed. Their first daughter, Sarah, was born towards the end of 1835. Far from enjoying motherhood, Fanny was only a few weeks into her new rôle when she was suggesting that Pierce procure a healthy nurse for the baby and let her go free: 'provided she is fed, she will not fret after me'.[10]

She was already revealing the partial cause for her discontent in letters to friends: 'Persuade your lover to embrace a profession,' she wrote to one of these who was about to marry. 'To be idle, objectless, useless, becomes neither man nor woman.'[11] She was referring to Pierce.

Along with growing disappointment in her husband, and certainly implicated, was a developing interest – perhaps self-identifying – in the abolition of slavery. It was in many ways unfortunate that the projected Kemble tour of New Orleans two years before had been abandoned, for to have seen a slave state and to have studied its workings, might have cautioned her against marrying a man set to become a large slave-owner. 'The white population of the slave states are, I should think, almost the most depraved of their species,'[12] she wrote to a cousin at the very time the unfortunate Pierce was at last succeeding to his family estate in Georgia.

Towards the end of 1836 he and his brother, leaving Fanny behind, travelled south to view their new property. 'I am not going to Georgia,' wrote Fanny bitterly, 'I am not to accompany my husband on his expedition, I am not to open his mind to the evils of slavery, I am not to ameliorate the condition and enlighten the minds of those whose labour feeds me . . .'[13] Instead November 1st 1836 saw her and the new baby boarding the *South America* for England.

The voyage was exceedingly rough. The ship sprang her mainmast, and the cabin skylight, claustrophobically, had to be battened down for the entire voyage. Notwithstanding, as soon as they landed, Fanny resumed life with all her old energy. A play was begun. There were dinner parties in the old style, visits to the Miss Berrys, to Lord and Lady Landsdowne, and vivacious skirmishes with Lady Holland. In short, she might never have been away. Indeed she might never have returned to the States at all, had not Pierce, battling with delays and contrary winds, sailed over to England to fetch her.

Reconciliation of a kind must have followed since, nine months after her return, Frances, their second child, was born. But no doubt the taste of freedom had been too much. Pierce and Fanny had been home only two months before they were quarrelling again, and communicating only by written notes. 'You will oblige me by taking immediate means for my return to my own family . . .' ran one of these, written in November. 'I will never be subject to rudeness and ill manners from anyone . . . I have my watch and gold chain,' she threatened the mystified Pierce, 'which will give me sufficient money to go home in some manner or other.'[14]

Nothing came of this threat, but the birth of their second daughter the following May was followed by the familiar symptoms – low spirits, nervous prostration, raging discontent and further passionate demands for a separation.

Five months later their relationship seems to have taken a turn for the better. They were now preparing to visit the Butler plantation in Georgia. 'I am about to depart into slavery,' wrote Fanny in buoyant mood, shortly before their departure, 'though whether I shall die of yellow fever or the jaundice, or whether I shall be shot at from behind a tree for my Abolitionism, or swallowed horse and all by an Altamaha alligator are matters yet folded within the unopened chambers of time.'[15]

The plantation they were about to visit had long fallen into neglect. None of the family had lived there for years, and its mansion was ruinous. Its heyday had been under old Major Butler, Pierce's grandfather. At that time the estate had been totally self-supporting, growing its own food, forging its own tools and building the cotton-bailing machinery in its own blacksmith's shop. The cotton crop had moreover been shipped direct to Liverpool in the Major's own schooners.

As far as plantations went, Butler Place, unlike the hideously termed 'nigger-killing' sugar plantations of Louisiana, was considered exceptionally humane. Butler slaves were seldom sold off the place. Parents and children were not split up, and, once their work was done, the slaves were allowed to sell the small produce of their gardens for money. Moreover, the women's required field-tasks had already been reduced below those of the men, 'even when they were not pregnant'. Seventy years after Abolition a former slave of the family was able to say that they had been treated 'very nicely'!

They were due to leave on 20th November: Pierce, Fanny, who was still nursing the nine-month-old baby, the elder little girl and her nurse, Margery. Owing to Pierce's compulsive dawdling they finally got away a month later.

The journey, upwards of a thousand miles by rail and steamboat, was appalling. It took eight days and was to acquire an almost nightmare quality. Fanny recalled '. . . endless pools of black water, where the melancholy cypress and juniper trees alone overshadowed the thick-looking surface, their roots globular like huge bulbous plants, and their dark branches woven together with a hideous matting of giant creepers . . . like a drapery of withered snakes . . .'[16] As if to highlight the despairing horror of it, 'a monstrous awkward-looking woman, who at first struck me as a man in disguise', shared their cabin on the steamboat from Savannah to Darien.

At long last the SS *Ocmulpec*, steaming through 'reeds like Lillipution [*sic*] forests rattling their brittle canes in the morning breeze', grazed the side of the wharf at Darien.

'Oh, massa! How you do massa? Oh missis! Oh! lilly missis! Me too glad to see you!' cried the crew of the plantation-boat sent to fetch them.

Not long after, as the low reedy banks of Butler's island rose into view, the steersman blew his conch-shell to sound their approach. Until now no member of the Butler family had lived on the plantation for seventeen years. '. . . it seemed,' wrote Fanny, 'as if we had touched the outer bound of civilized creation.'[17]

4

The Georgia Journal

Butler Island: early – mid January 1839

Darien, Georgia
. . . I purpose, while I reside here, keeping a sort of journal, such as Monk Lewis* wrote during his visit to his West India plantations. I wish I had any prospect of rendering my diary as interesting and amusing to you† as his was to me. . . .

My walks are rather circumscribed, inasmuch as the dykes are the only promenades. On all sides of these lie either the marshy rice-fields, the brimming river, or the swampy patches of yet unreclaimed forest, where the huge cypress-trees and exquisite evergreen undergrowth spring up from a stagnant sweltering pool, that effectually forbids the foot of the explorer. . . .

The profusion of birds here is one thing that strikes me as curious, coming from the vicinity of Philadelphia, where even the robin redbreast, held sacred by the humanity of all other Christian people, is not safe from the gunning prowess of the unlicensed sportsmen of your free country.

The negroes (of course) are not allowed the use of fire-arms, and their very simply constructed traps do not do much havoc among the feathered hordes that haunt their rice-fields. Their case is rather a hard one, as partridges, snipes, and the most delicious wild ducks abound here, and their allowance of rice and Indian meal would not be the worse for such additions.

No day passes that I do not, in the course of my walk, put up a number of the land birds, and startle from among the gigantic sedges the long-necked water-fowl by dozens. It arouses the

---

* Matthew Gregory Lewis (1775–1818), *Journal of a West Indian Proprietor*, 1834.
† Her close friend, Elizabeth Sedgwick.

killing propensity in me most dreadfully, and I really entertain serious thoughts of learning to use a gun, for the mere pleasure of destroying these pretty birds as they whirr from their secret coverts close beside my path.

How strong an instinct of animal humanity this is, and how strange if one be more strange than another. Reflection rebukes it almost instantaneously, and yet for the life of me I can not help wishing I had a fowling-piece whenever I put up a covey of these creatures; though I suppose, if one were brought bleeding and maimed to me, I should begin to cry, and be very pathetic, after the fashion of Jacques. However, one must live, you know; and here our living consists very mainly of wild ducks, wild geese, wild turkeys, and venison. . . .

I must inform you of a curious conversation which took place between my little girl and the woman who performs for us the offices of chambermaid here – of course one of Mr Butler's slaves. What suggested it to the child, or whence indeed she gathered her information, I know not; but children are made of eyes and ears, and nothing, however minute, escapes their microscopic observation. She suddenly began addressing this woman.

'Mary, some persons are free and some are not.' The woman made no reply. 'I am a free person [of a little more than three years old]. I say, I am a free person, Mary – do you know that?'

'Yes, missis.'

'Some persons are free and some are not – do you know that, Mary?'

'Yes, missis, here,' was the reply; 'I know it is so here, in this world.'

Here my child's white nurse, my dear Margery, who had hitherto been silent, interfered, saying, 'Oh, then you think it will not always be so?'

'Me hope not, missis.'

I am afraid, E, this woman actually imagines that there will be no slaves in heaven; isn't that preposterous, now, when, by the account of most of the Southerners, slavery itself must be heaven, or something uncommonly like it?

Oh, if you could imagine how this title 'Missis', addressed to me and to my children, shocks all my feelings! Several times I have exclaimed, 'For God's sake do not call me that!' and only been awakened, by the stupid amazement of the poor creatures I was addressing, to the perfect uselessness of my thus expostulating with them; once or twice, indeed, I have done more – I have explained to them, and they appeared to comprehend me well, that I had no ownership over them, for that I held such ownership sinful, and that, though I was the wife of the man who pretends to own them, I was, in truth, no more their mistress than they were mine. Some of them I know understood me, more of them did not.

Our servants – those who have been selected to wait upon us in the house – consist of a man, who is quite a tolerable cook (I believe this is a natural gift with them, as with Frenchmen); a dairy-woman, who churns for us; a laundry-woman; her daughter, our housemaid, the aforesaid Mary; and two young lads of from fifteen to twenty, who wait upon us in the capacity of footmen. As, however, the latter are perfectly filthy in their persons and clothes – their faces, hands, and naked feet being literally incrusted with dirt – their attendance at our meals is not, as you may suppose, particularly agreeable to me, and I dispense with it as often as possible. Mary, too, is so intolerably offensive in her person that it is impossible to endure her proximity, and the consequence is that, among Mr Butler's slaves, I wait upon myself more than I have ever done in my life before.

About this same personal offensiveness, the Southerners, you know, insist that it is inherent with the race, and it is one of their most cogent reasons for keeping them as slaves. But, as this very disagreeable peculiarity does not prevent Southern women from hanging their infants at the breasts of negresses, nor almost every planter's wife and daughter from having one or more little pet blacks sleeping like puppy-dogs in their very bedchamber, nor almost every planter from admitting one or several of his female slaves to the still closer intimacy of his bed, it seems to me that this objection to doing them right is not very valid.

I can not imagine that they would smell much worse if they were free, or come in much closer contact with the delicate organs of their white fellow-countrymen; indeed, inasmuch as good deeds are spoken of as having a sweet savour before God, it might be supposed that the freeing of the blacks might prove rather an odoriferous process than the contrary. . . .

And here it may be well to inform you that the slaves on this plantation are divided into field-hands and mechanics or artisans. The former, the great majority, are the more stupid and brutish of the tribe; the others, who are regularly taught their trades, are not only exceedingly expert at them, but exhibit a greater general activity of intellect, which must necessarily result from even a partial degree of cultivation. There are here a gang (for that is the honourable term) of coopers, of blacksmiths, of brick-layers, of carpenters, all well acquainted with their peculiar trades.

The latter constructed the wash-hand stands, clothes-presses, sofas, tables, etc., with which our house is furnished, and they are very neat pieces of workmanship – neither veneered or polished indeed, nor of very costly materials, but of the white pine wood planed as smooth as marble – a species of furniture not very luxurious perhaps, but all the better adapted therefore to the house itself, which is certainly rather more devoid of the conveniences and adornments of modern existence than any thing I ever took up my abode in before. . . .

Of our three apartments, one is our sitting, eating, and living room, and is sixteen feet by fifteen. The walls are plastered indeed, but neither painted nor papered; it is divided from our bedroom (a similarly elegant and comfortable chamber) by a dingy wooden partition covered all over with hooks, pegs, and nails, to which hats, caps, keys, etc., etc., are suspended in graceful irregularity. The doors open by wooden latches, raised by means of small bits of pack-thread – I imagine, the same primitive order of fastening celebrated in the touching chronicle of Red Riding Hood; how they shut I will not attempt to describe, as the shutting of a door is a process of extremely rare occurrence throughout the whole Southern country.

The third room, a chamber with sloping ceiling, immediately over our sitting-room and under the roof, is appropriated to the nurse and my two babies. Of the closets, one is the overseer's bedroom, the other his office or place of business; and the third, adjoining our bedroom, and opening immediately out of doors, is Mr Butler's dressing-room and cabinet d'affaires, where he gives audiences to the negroes, redresses grievances, distributes red woollen caps (a singular gratification to a slave), shaves himself, and performs the other offices of his toilet.

Such being our abode, I think you will allow there is little danger of my being dazzled by the luxurious splendours of a Southern slave residence. Our sole mode of summoning our attendants is by a pack-thread bell-rope suspended in the sitting-room. From the bedrooms we have to raise the windows and our voices, and bring them by power of lungs, or help ourselves – which, I thank God, was never yet a hardship to me. . . .

I had a most ludicrous visit this morning from the midwife of the estate – rather an important personage both to master and slave, as to her unassisted skill and science the ushering of all the young negroes into their existence of bondage is intrusted.

I heard a great deal of conversation in the dressing-room adjoining mine while performing my own toilet, and presently Mr Butler opened my room door, ushering in a dirty, fat, good-humoured looking old negress, saying, 'The midwife, Rose, wants to make your acquaintance.'

'Oh massa!' shrieked out the old creature, in a paroxysm of admiration, 'where you get this lilly alabaster baby!'

For a moment I looked round to see if she was speaking of my baby; but no, my dear, this superlative apostrophe was elicited by the fairness of my skin: so much for degrees of comparison. . . .

Soon after this visit, I was summoned into the wooden porch or piazza of the house, to see a poor woman who desired to speak to me. This was none other than the tall, emaciated-looking negress who, on the day of our arrival, had embraced me and my nurse with such irresistible zeal. She appeared very ill today, and presently unfolded to me a most distressing history of bodily afflictions. She was the mother of a very large family, and complained to me that, what with childbearing and hard field labour, her back was almost broken in two. With an almost savage vehemence of gesticulation, she suddenly tore up her scanty clothing, and exhibited a spectacle with which I was inconceivably shocked and sickened. The facts, without any of her corroborating statements, bore tolerable witness to the hardships of her existence.

I promised to attend to her ailments and give her proper remedies; but these are natural results, inevitable and irremediable ones, of improper treatment of the female frame; and, though there may be alleviation, there can not be any cure when once the beautiful and wonderful structure has been thus made the victim of ignorance, folly, and wickedness.

After the departure of this poor woman, I walked down the settlement toward the Infirmary or hospital. . . .

The Infirmary is a large two-storey building, terminating the broad orange-planted space between the two rows of houses which form the first settlement; it is built of whitewashed wood, and contains four large-sized rooms.

But how shall I describe to you the spectacle which was presented to me on entering the first of these? But half the casements, of which there were six, were glazed, and these were obscured with dirt, almost as much as the other windowless ones were darkened by the dingy shutters, which the shivering inmates had fastened to in order to protect themselves from the cold.

In the enormous chimney glimmered the powerless embers of a few sticks of wood, round which, however, as many of the sick women as could approach were cowering, some on wooden settles, most of them on the ground, excluding those who were too ill to rise; and these last poor wretches lay prostrate on the floor, without bed, mattress, or pillow, buried in tattered and filthy blankets, which, huddled round them as they lay strewed about, left hardly space to move upon the floor.

And here, in their hour of sickness and suffering, lay those whose health and strength are spent in unrequited labour for us – those who, perhaps even yesterday, were being urged on to their unpaid task – those whose husbands, fathers, brothers, and sons were even at that hour sweating over the earth, whose produce was to buy for us all the luxuries which health can revel in, all the comforts which can alleviate sickness.

I stood in the midst of them, perfectly unable to speak, the tears pouring from my eyes at this sad spectacle of their misery, myself and my emotion alike strange and incomprehensible to them.

Here lay women expecting every hour the terrors and agonies of childbirth, others who had just brought their doomed offspring into the world, others who were groaning over the anguish and bitter disappointment of miscarriages – here lay some burning with fever, others chilled with cold and aching with rheumatism, upon the hard cold ground, the draughts and dampness of the atmosphere increasing their sufferings, and dirt, noise, and stench, and every aggravation of which sickness is capable, combined in their condition – here they lay like brute beasts, absorbed in physical suffering; unvisited by any of those Divine influences which may ennoble the dispensations of pain and illness, forsaken, as it seemed to me, of all good; and yet, O God, Thou surely hadst not forsaken them!

Now pray take notice that this is the hospital of an estate where the owners are supposed to be humane, the overseer efficient and kind, and the negroes remarkably well cared for and comfortable.

As soon as I recovered from my dismay, I addressed old Rose the midwife, who had charge of this room, bidding her open the shutters of such windows as were glazed, and let in the light. I next proceeded to make up the fire; but, upon my lifting a log for that purpose, there was one universal outcry of horror, and old Rose, attempting to snatch it from me, exclaimed, 'Let alone, missis – let be; what for you lift wood? You have nigger enough, missis, to do it!'

I hereupon had to explain to them my view of the purposes for which hands and arms were appended to our bodies, and forthwith began making Rose tidy up the miserable apartment, removing all the filth and rubbish from the floor that could be removed, folding up in piles the blankets of the patients who were not using them, and placing, in rather more sheltered and comfortable positions, those who were unable to rise.

It was all that I could do, and having enforced upon them all my earnest desire that they should keep their room swept, and as tidy as possible, I passed on to the other room on the ground floor, and to the two above, one of which is appropriated to the use of the men who are ill.

They were all in the same deplorable condition, the upper rooms being rather the more miserable, inasmuch as none of the windows were glazed at all, and they had, therefore, only the alternative of utter darkness, or killing draughts of air from the unsheltered casements. In all, filth, disorder, and misery abounded; the floor was the only bed, and scanty begrimed rags of blankets the only covering. I left this refuge for Mr Butler's sick dependants with my clothes covered with dust, and full of vermin, and with a heart heavy enough, as you will well believe.

My morning's work had fatigued me not a little, and I was glad to return to the house, where I gave vent to my indignation and regret at the scene I had just witnessed to Mr Butler and his overseer, who, here, is a member of our family. The latter told me that the condition of the hospital had appeared to him, from his first entering upon his situation (only within the last year), to require a reform, and that he had proposed it to the former manager, Mr King, and Mr Butler's brother, who is part proprietor of the estate, but, receiving no encouragement from them, had supposed that it was a matter of indifference to the owners, and had left it in the condition in which he had found it, in which condition it has been for the last nineteen years and upward. . . .

With regard to the indifference of our former manager upon the subject of the accommodation for the sick, he was an excellent overseer, *videlicet** the estate returned a full income under his management, and such men have nothing to do with sick slaves: they are tools, to be mended only if they can be made available again; if not, to be flung by as useless, without farther expense of money, time, or trouble.

I am learning to row here, for circumscribed as my walks necessarily are, impossible as it is to resort to my favourite exercise on horseback upon these narrow dykes, I must do something to prevent my blood from stagnating; and this broad brimming river, and the beautiful light canoes which lie moored at the steps, are very inviting persuaders to this species of exercise. My first attempt was confined to pulling an oar across the stream, for which I rejoiced in sundry aches and pains altogether novel, letting alone a delightful row of blisters on each of my hands.

I forgot to tell you that in the hospital were several sick babies, whose mothers were permitted to suspend their field labour in order to nurse them. Upon addressing some remonstrances to one of these, who, besides having a sick child, was ill herself, about the horribly dirty condition of her baby, she assured me that it was impossible for them to keep their children clean; that they went out to work at daybreak, and did not get their tasks done till evening, and that then they were too tired and worn out to do any thing but throw themselves down and sleep.

This statement of hers I mentioned on my return from the hospital, and the overseer appeared extremely annoyed by it, and assured me repeatedly that it was not true. . . .

[January 1839]
Dear E, – This morning I paid my second visit to the Infirmary, and found there had been some faint attempt at sweeping and cleaning, in compliance with my entreaties. The poor woman

---

* That is to say.

Harriet, however, whose statement with regard to the impossibility of their attending properly to their children had been so vehemently denied by the overseer, was crying bitterly. I asked her what ailed her, when, more by signs and dumb show than words, she and old Rose informed me that the overseer had flogged her that morning for having told me that the women had not time to keep their children clean.

It is part of the regular duty of every overseer to visit the Infirmary at least once a day, which he generally does in the morning, and the overseer's visit had preceded mine but a short time only, or I might have been edified by seeing a man horsewhip a woman.

I again made her repeat her story, and she again and again affirmed that she had been flogged for what she told me, none of the whole company in the room denying it or contradicting her. I left the room because I was so disgusted and indignant that I could hardly restrain my feelings, and to express them could have produced no single good result. . . .

I have ingeniously contrived to introduce bribery, corruption, and pauperism, all in a breath, upon this island, which, until my advent, was as innocent of these pollutions, I suppose, as Prospero's isle of refuge.

Wishing, however, to appeal to some perception, perhaps a little less dim in their minds than the abstract loveliness of cleanliness, I have proclaimed to all the little baby nurses that I will give a cent to every little boy or girl whose baby's face shall be clean, and one to every individual with clean face and hands of their own.

My appeal was fully comprehended by the majority, it seems, for this morning I was surrounded, as soon as I came out, by a swarm of children carrying their little charges on their backs and in their arms, the shining, and in many instances, wet faces and hands of the latter bearing ample testimony to the ablutions which had been inflicted upon them. How they will curse me and the copper cause of all their woes in their baby bosoms! . . .

At the upper end of the row of houses, and nearest to our overseer's residence, is the hut of the head driver. Let me explain, by the way, his office. The negroes, as I before told you, are divided into troops or gangs, as they are called; at the head of each gang is a driver, who stands over them, whip in hand, while they perform their daily task, who renders an account of each individual slave and his work every evening to the overseer, and receives from him directions for their next day's tasks.

Each driver is allowed to inflict a dozen lashes upon any refractory slave in the field, and at the time of the offence; they may not, however, extend the chastisement, and if it is found ineffectual, their remedy lies in reporting the unmanageable individual either to the head driver or the overseer, the former of whom has power to inflict three dozen lashes at his own discretion, and the latter as many as he himself sees fit, within the number of fifty; which limit, however, I must tell you, is an arbitrary one on this plantation, appointed by the founder of the estate, Major Butler, Mr Butler's grandfather, many of whose regulations, indeed I believe most of them, are still observed in the government of the plantation. . . .

To return to our head driver, or, as he is familiarly called, head man, Frank – he is second in authority only to the overseer, and exercises rule alike over the drivers and the gangs in the absence of the sovereign white man from the estate, which happens whenever the overseer visits the other two plantations at Woodville and St Simon's.

He is sole master and governor of the island, appoints the work, pronounces punishments, gives permission to the men to leave the island (without it they never may do so), and exercises all functions of undisputed mastery over his fellow-slaves, for you will observe that all this while he is just as much a slave as any of the rest. Trustworthy, upright, intelligent, he may be flogged tomorrow if the overseer or Mr Butler so please it, and sold the next day, like a cart-horse, at the will of the latter.

Besides his various other responsibilities, he has the key of all the stores, and gives out the people's rations weekly; nor is it only the people's provisions that are put under his charge – meat, which is only given out to them occasionally, and provisions for the use of the family, are also intrusted to his care.

Thus you see, among these inferior creatures, their own masters yet look to find, surviving all their best efforts to destroy them, good sense, honesty, self-denial, and all the qualities, mental and moral, that make one man worthy to be trusted by another. . . .

As I was returning toward the house after my long morning's lounge, a man rushed out of the blacksmith's shop, and, catching me by the skirt of my gown, poured forth a torrent of self-gratulations on having at length found the 'right missis'.

They have no idea, of course, of a white person performing any of the offices of a servant, and as throughout the whole Southern country the owner's children are nursed and tended, and sometimes suckled by their slaves (I wonder how this inferior milk agrees with the lordly white babies?), the appearance of Margery with my two children had immediately suggested the idea that she must be the missis.

Many of the poor negroes flocked to her, paying their profound homage under this impression; and when she explained to them that she was not their owner's wife, the confusion in their minds seemed very great – Heaven only knows whether they did not conclude that they had two mistresses, and Mr Butler two wives; for the privileged race must seem, in their eyes, to have such absolute masterdom on earth, that perhaps they thought polygamy might be one of the sovereign white men's numerous indulgences.

The ecstasy of the blacksmith on discovering the 'right missis' at last was very funny, and was expressed with such extraordinary grimaces, contortions and gesticulations, that I thought I should have died of laughing at this rapturous identification of my most melancholy relation to the poor fellow. . . .

I had a conversation that interested me a good deal, during my walk to-day, with my peculiar slave Jack. This lad, whom Mr Butler has appointed to attend me in my roamings about the island, and rowing expeditions on the river, is the son of the last head driver, a man of very extraordinary intelligence and faithfulness – such, at least, is the account given of him by his employers (in the burial-ground of the negroes is a stone dedicated to his memory, a mark of distinction accorded by his masters, which his son never failed to point out to me when we passed that way).

Jack appears to inherit his quickness of apprehension; his questions, like those of an intelligent child, are absolutely inexhaustible; his curiosity about all things beyond this island, the prison-house of his existence, is perfectly intense; his countenance is very pleasing, mild, and not otherwise than thoughtful; he is, in common with the rest of them, a stupendous flatterer, and, like the rest of them, also seems devoid of physical and moral courage.

To-day, in the midst of his torrent of inquiries about places and things, I suddenly asked him if he would like to be free. A gleam of light absolutely shot over his whole countenance, like the vivid and instantaneous lightning; he stammered, hesitated, became excessively confused, and at length replied, 'Free, missis! What for me wish to be free? Oh no, missis, me no wish to be free, if massa only let we keep pig!'

The fear of offending by uttering that forbidden wish – the dread of admitting, by its expression, the slightest discontent with his present situation – the desire to conciliate my favour, even at the expense of strangling the intense natural longing that absolutely glowed in his every feature – it was a sad spectacle, and I repented my question.

As for the pitiful request, which he reiterated several times, adding, 'No, missis, me no want to be free; me work till me die for missis and massa,' with increased emphasis; it amounted only to this, that negroes once were, but no longer are, permitted to keep pigs. . . . 'T was a sad passage between us, and sent me home full of the most painful thoughts.

I told Mr Butler, with much indignation, of poor Harriet's flogging, and represented that if the people were to be chastized for any thing they said to me, I must leave the place, as I could not but hear their complaints, and endeavour, by all my miserable limited means, to better their condition while I was here.

He said he would ask the overseer about it, assuring me, at the same time, that it was impossible to believe a single word any of these people said.

At dinner, accordingly, the inquiry was made as to the cause of her punishment, and the overseer then said it was not at all for what she had told me that he had flogged her, but for having answered him impertinently; that he had ordered her into the field, whereupon she had said she was ill and could not work; that he retorted he knew better, and bade her get up and go to work; she replied, 'Very well, I'll go, but I shall just come back again!' meaning that when in the field she would be unable to work, and obliged to return to the hospital.

'For this reply,' the overseer said, 'I gave her a good lashing; it was her business to have gone into the field without answering me, and then we should have soon seen whether she could work or not; I gave it to Chloe too for some such impudence.'

I give you the words of the conversation, which was prolonged to a great length, the overseer complaining of the sham sicknesses of the slaves, and detailing the most disgusting struggle which is going on the whole time, on the one hand to inflict, and on the other to evade oppression and injustice. With this sauce I ate my dinner, and truly it tasted bitter.

Toward sunset I went on the river to take my rowing lesson. A darling little canoe, which carries two oars and a steersman, and rejoices in the appropriate title of the *Dolphin*, is my especial vessel; and with Jack's help and instructions, I contrived this evening to row upward of half a mile, coasting the reed-crowned edge of the island to another very large rice mill, the enormous wheel of which is turned by the tide.

A small bank of mud and sand, covered with reedy coarse grass, divides the river into two arms on this side of the island; the deep channel is on the outside of this bank, and as we rowed home this evening, the tide having fallen, we scraped sand almost the whole way. Mr Butler's domain, it seems to me, will presently fill up this shallow stream, and join itself to the above-mentioned mud-bank.

The whole course of this most noble river is full of shoals, banks, mud, and sand-bars, and the navigation, which is difficult to those who know it well, is utterly baffling to the inexperienced. . . . Amphibious creatures, alligators, serpents, and wild-fowl haunt these yet but half-formed regions, where land and water are of the consistency of hasty-pudding – the one seeming too unstable to walk on, the other almost too thick to float in.

But then the sky – if no human chisel ever yet cut breath, neither did any human pen ever write light; if it did, mine should spread out before you the unspeakable glories of these Southern heavens, the saffron brightness of morning, the blue intense brilliancy of noon, the golden splendour and the rosy softness of sunset. Italy and Claude Lorraine may go hang themselves together!

Heaven itself does not seem brighter or more beautiful to the imagination than these surpassing pageants of fiery rays, and piled-up beds of orange, golden clouds, with edges too bright to look on, scattered wreaths of faintest rosy bloom, amber streaks and pale green lakes between, and amid sky all mingled blue and rose tints, a spectacle to make one fall over the side of the boat, with one's head broken off with looking adoringly upward, but which, on paper, means nothing. . . .

[January 1839]
Dear E, – We had a species of fish this morning for our breakfast

which deserves more glory than I can bestow upon it. Had I been the ingenious man who wrote a poem upon fish, the white mullet of the Altamaha should have been at least my heroine's cousin. 'Tis the heavenliest creature that goes upon fins.

I took a long walk this morning to Settlement No. 3, the third village on the island. My way lay along the side of the canal, beyond which, and only divided from it by a raised narrow causeway, rolled the brimming river, with its girdle of glittering evergreens, while on my other hand a deep trench marked the line of the rice fields. It really seemed as if the increase of merely a shower of rain might join all these waters together, and lay the island under its original covering again. . . .

During the course of my walk, I startled from its repose in one of the rice fields a huge blue heron. You must have seen, as I often have, these creatures stuffed in museums; but 't is another matter, and far more curious, to see them stalking on their stilts of legs over a rice field, and then, on your near approach, see them spread their wide heavy wings, and throw themselves upon the air, with their long shanks flying after them in a most grotesque and laughable manner. They fly as if they did not know how to do it very well; but standing still, their height (between four and five feet) and peculiar colour, a dusky, greyish blue, with black about the head, render their appearance very beautiful and striking. . . .

I do not think that a residence on a slave plantation is likely to be peculiarly advantageous to a child like my eldest. I was observing her to-day among her swarthy worshippers, for they follow her as such, and saw, with dismay, the universal eagerness with which they sprang to obey her little gestures of command. She said something about a swing, and in less than five minutes head man Frank had erected it for her, and a dozen young slaves were ready to swing little 'missis'.

Elizabeth, think of learning to rule despotically your fellow-creatures before the first lesson of self-government has been well spelt over! It makes me tremble; but I shall find a remedy, or remove myself and the child from this misery and ruin. . . .

I have let this letter lie for a day or two, dear E, from press of more immediate avocations. I have nothing very particular to add to it. On Monday evening I rowed over to Darien with Mr Butler to fetch over the doctor, who was coming to visit some of our people. As I sat waiting in the boat for the return of the gentlemen, the sun went down, or rather seemed to dissolve bodily into the glowing clouds, which appeared but a fusion of the great orb of light; the stars twinkled out in the rose-coloured sky, and the evening air, as it fanned the earth to sleep, was as soft as a summer's evening breeze in the north. A sort of dreamy stillness seemed creeping over the world and into my spirit as the canoe just tilted against the steps that led to the wharf, raised by the scarce perceptible heaving of the water. A melancholy, monotonous boat-horn sounded from a distance up the stream, and presently, floating slowly down with the current, huge, shapeless, black, relieved against the sky, came one of those rough barges piled with cotton, called, hereabouts, Ocone boxes.

The vessel itself is really nothing but a monstrous square box, made of rough planks, put together in the roughest manner possible to attain the necessary object of keeping the cotton dry. Upon this great tray are piled the swollen, apoplectic-looking cotton-bags, to the height of ten, twelve, and fourteen feet. This huge water-wagon floats lazily down the river, from the upper country to Darien. They are flat-bottomed, and, of course, draw little water. The stream from whence they are named is an up-country river, which, by its junction with the Ocmulgee, forms the Altamaha.

Here at least, you perceive, the Indian names remain, and long may they do so, for they seem to me to become the very character of the streams and mountains they indicate, and are indeed significant to the learned in savage tongues, which is more than can be said of such titles as Jones's Creek, Onion Creek, etc. These Ocone boxes are broken up at Darien, where the cotton is shipped either for the Savannah, Charleston, or Liverpool markets, and the timber of which they are constructed sold. . . .

I went again to-day to the Infirmary, and was happy to perceive that there really was an evident desire to conform to my instructions, and keep the place in a better condition than formerly.

Among the sick I found a poor woman suffering dreadfully from the earache. She had done nothing to alleviate her pain but apply some leaves, of what tree or plant I could not ascertain, and tie up her head in a variety of dirty cloths, till it was as large as her whole body. I removed all these, and found one side of her face and neck very much swollen, but so begrimed with filth that it was really no very agreeable task to examine it.

The first process, of course, was washing, which, however, appeared to her so very unusual an operation, that I had to perform it for her myself. Sweet oil and laudanum, and raw cotton, being then applied to her ear and neck, she professed herself much relieved, but I believe in my heart that the warm water sponging had done her more good than any thing else. I was sorry not to ascertain what leaves she had applied to her ear. These simple remedies resorted to by savages, and people as ignorant, are generally approved by experience, and sometimes condescendingly adopted by science.

I remember once, when Mr Butler was suffering from a severe attack of inflammatory rheumatism, Dr Chapman* desired him to bind round his knee the leaves of the tulip-tree – poplar I believe you call it – saying that he had learned that remedy from the negroes in Virginia, and found it a most effectual one. . . .

Returning to the house, I passed up the 'street'. It was between eleven o'clock and noon, and the people were taking their first meal in the day. . . .

At one of the doors I saw three young girls standing, who might be between sixteen and seventeen years old; they had evidently done eating, and were rudely playing and romping with each other, laughing and shouting like wild things. I went into the house, and such another spectacle of filthy disorder I never beheld. I then addressed the girls most solemnly, showing them that they were wasting in idle riot the time in which they might be rendering their abode decent, and told them that it was a shame for any woman to live in so dirty a place and so beastly a condition.

They said they had seen buckree (white) women's houses just as dirty, and they could not be expected to be cleaner than white women. I then told them that the only difference between themselves and buckree women was, that the latter were generally better informed, and, for that reason alone, it was more disgraceful to them to be disorderly and dirty.

They seemed to listen to me attentively, and one of them exclaimed, with great satisfaction, that they saw I made no difference between them and white girls, and that they never had been so treated before. . . .

---

* A leading Philadelphia physician. His daughter, a reigning belle, had been supplanted by Fanny in Pierce's affections.

I must not forget to tell you of a magnificent bald-headed eagle which Mr Butler called me to look at early this morning. I had never before seen alive one of these national types of yours, and stood entranced as the noble creature swept, like a black cloud, over the river, his bald white head bent forward and shining in the sun, and his fierce eyes and beak directed toward one of the beautiful wild ducks on the water, which he had evidently marked for his prey.

The poor little duck, who was not ambitious of such a glorification, dived, and the eagle hovered above the spot. After a short interval, its victim rose to the surface several yards nearer shore. The great king of birds stooped nearer, and again the watery shield was interposed. This went on until the poor water-fowl, driven by excess of fear into unwonted boldness, rose, after repeatedly diving, within a short distance of where we stood.

The eagle, who, I presume, had read how we were to have dominion over the fowls of the air (bald-headed eagles included), hovered sulkily a while over the river, and then, sailing slowly toward the woods on the opposite shore, alighted and furled his great wings on a huge cypress limb, that stretched itself out against the blue sky, like the arm of a giant, for the giant bird to perch upon. . . .

[January 1839]
Dearest E, – After finishing my last letter to you, I went out into the clear starlight to breathe the delicious mildness of the air, and was surprised to hear rising from one of the houses of the settlement a hymn sung apparently by a number of voices.

The next morning I inquired the meaning of this, and was informed that those negroes on the plantation who were members of the Church were holding a prayer-meeting.

There is an immensely strong devotional feeling among these poor people. The worst of it is, that it is zeal without understanding, and profits them but little; yet light is light, even that poor portion that may stream through a keyhole, and I welcome this most ignorant profession of religion in Mr Butler's dependants as the herald of better and brighter things for them.

Some of the planters are entirely inimical to any such proceedings, and neither allow their negroes to attend worship, or to congregate together for religious purposes, and truly I think they are wise in their own generation. On other plantations, again, the same rigid discipline is not observed; and some planters and overseers go even farther than toleration, and encourage these devotional exercises and professions of religion, having actually discovered that a man may become more faithful and trustworthy, even as a slave, who acknowledges the higher influences of Christianity, no matter in how small a degree.

Slaveholding clergymen, and certain piously inclined planters, undertake, accordingly, to enlighten these poor creatures upon these matters, with a safe understanding, however, of what truth is to be given to them, and what is not; how much they may learn to become better slaves, and how much they may not learn, lest they cease to be slaves at all. . . .

I really never was so busy in all my life as I am here. I sit at the receipt of custom (involuntarily enough) from morning till night – no time, no place, affords me a respite from my innumerable petitioners; and whether I be asleep or awake, reading, eating, or walking – in the kitchen, my bedroom, or the parlour, they flock in with urgent entreaties and pitiful stories, and my conscience forbids my ever postponing their business for any other matter; for, with shame and grief of heart I say it, by their unpaid labour I live – their nakedness clothes me, and their heavy toil maintains me in luxurious idleness. Surely the least I can do is to hear these, my most injured benefactors. . . .

Mr Butler has been much gratified to-day by the arrival of Mr King, who, with his father, for nineteen years was the sole manager of these estates, and discharged his laborious task with great ability and fidelity toward his employers. How far he understood his duties to the slaves, or whether, indeed, an overseer can, in the nature of things, acknowledge any duty to them, is another question. . . .

My companions, when I do not request the attendance of my friend Jack, are a couple of little terriers, who are endowed to perfection with the ugliness and the intelligence of their race; they are of infinite service on the plantation, as, owing to the immense quantity of grain, and chaff, and such matters, rats and mice abound in the mills and store-houses.

I crossed the threshing-floor today – a very large square, perfectly level, raised by artificial means about half a foot from the ground, and covered equally all over, so as to lie quite smooth, with some preparation of tar. It lies immediately between the house and the steam mill, and on it much of the negroes' work is done – the first threshing is given to the rice, and other labours are carried on.

As I walked across it to-day, passing through the busy groups, chiefly of women, that covered it, I came opposite to one of the drivers, who held in his hand his whip, the odious insignia of his office. I took it from him; it was a short stick of moderate size, with a thick square leather thong attached to it. As I held it in my hand, I did not utter a word; but I conclude, as is often the case, my face spoke what my tongue did not, for the driver said, 'Oh, missis, me use it for measure; me seldom strike nigger with it.'

For one moment I thought I must carry the hateful implement into the house with me. An instant's reflection, however, served to show me how useless such a proceeding would be. The people are not mine, nor their drivers, nor their whips. I should but have impeded, for a few hours, the man's customary office, and a new scourge would have been easily provided, and I should have done nothing, perhaps worse than nothing. . . .

Mr Butler was called out this evening to listen to a complaint of overwork from a gang of pregnant women. I did not stay to listen to the details of their petition, for I am unable to command myself on such occasions, and Mr Butler seemed positively degraded in my eyes as he stood enforcing upon these women the necessity of their fulfilling their appointed tasks.

How honourable he would have appeared to me begrimed with the sweat and soil of the coarsest manual labour, to what he then seemed, setting forth to these wretched, ignorant women, as a duty, their unpaid exacted labour! I turned away in bitter disgust.

I hope this sojourn among Mr Butler's slaves may not lessen my respect for him, but I fear it; for the details of slaveholding are so unmanly, letting alone every other consideration, that I know not how any one with the spirit of a man can condescend to them. . . .

Mid – late January 1839

[January 1839]
Dearest E, – Since I last wrote to you I have been actually engaged in receiving and returning visits; for even to this *ultima thule** of all civilization do these polite usages extend. I have been called upon by several families residing in and about Darien, and rowed over in due form to acknowledge the honour.

How shall I describe Darien to you? The abomination of desolation is but a poor type of its forlorn appearance, as, half buried in sand, its straggling, tumble-down wooden houses peer over the muddy bank of the thick slimy river. The whole town lies in a bed of sand: side-walks, or mid-walks, there be none distinct from each other; at every step I took my feet were ankle deep in the soil, and I had cause to rejoice that I was booted for the occasion.

Our worthy doctor, whose lady I was going to visit, did nothing but regret that I had not allowed him to provide me a carriage, though the distance between his house and the landing is not a quarter of a mile. The magnitude of the exertion seemed to fill him with amazement, and he over and over again repeated how impossible it would be to prevail on any of the ladies there to take such a walk. The houses seemed scattered about here and there, apparently without any design, and looked, for the most part, either unfinished or ruinous. . . .

Our doctor's wife is a New England woman; how can she live here? She had the fair eyes and hair, and fresh complexion of your part of the country, and its dearly beloved snuffle, which seemed actually dearly beloved when I heard it down here. She gave me some violets and narcissus, already blossoming profusely – in January – and expressed, like her husband, a thousand regrets at my having walked so far. . . .

In his memoirs Dr James Holmes referred to Fanny as 'a hopeless monomaniac', but added, 'I liked her social companionability and even

---

* The most remote part.

*playful ways.' She exasperated most of the plantation owners, but the
slaves adored her. One of them, years later, remembered how Fanny used to
row herself about the waterways; she also recalled how Fanny 'used to stop
and pull up she stock'n's an' garters* anywhere!'[1]

I rowed over to Darien again, to make some purchases, yesterday,
and, inquiring the price of various articles, could not but wonder to
find them at least three times as dear as in your Northern villages.
The profits of these Southern shopkeepers (who for the most part
are thoroughbred Yankees, with the true Yankee propensity to
trade, no matter on how dirty a counter, or in what manner of
wares) are enormous. The prices they ask for every thing, from
coloured calicoes for negro dresses to piano-fortes (one of which,
for curiosity sake, I inquired the value of), are fabulous, and such
as none but the laziest and most reckless people in the world would
consent to afford.

On our return we found the water in the cut so extremely low
that we were obliged to push the boat through it, and did not
accomplish it without difficulty. . . .

On landing, I was seized hold of by a hideous old negress,
named Sinda, who had come to pay me a visit, and of whom Mr
Butler told me a strange anecdote. She passed at one time for a
prophetess among her fellow-slaves on the plantation, and had
acquired such an ascendancy over them that, having given out . . .
that the world was to come to an end at a certain time, and that not
a very remote one, the belief in her assertion took such possession
of the people on the estate that they refused to work, and the rice
and cotton fields were threatened with an indefinite fallow in
consequence of this strike on the part of the cultivators.

Mr King, who was then overseer of the property, perceived the
impossibility of arguing, remonstrating, or even flogging this
solemn panic out of the minds of the slaves. The great final
emancipation which they believed at hand had stripped even the
lash of its prevailing authority, and the terrors of an overseer for
once were as nothing, in the terrible expectation of the advent of
the universal Judge of men. They were utterly impracticable; so,
like a very shrewd man as he was, he acquiesced in their
determination not to work; but he expressed to them his belief that
Sinda was mistaken, and he warned her that if, at the appointed
time, it proved so, she would be severely punished.

I do not know whether he confided to the slaves what he thought likely to be the result if she was in the right; but poor Sinda was in the wrong. Her day of judgment came indeed, and a severe one it proved, for Mr King had her tremendously flogged . . . the spirit of false prophecy was mercilessly scourged out of her, and the faith of her people of course reverted from her to the omnipotent lash again.

Think what a dream that must have been while it lasted for those infinitely oppressed people – freedom without entering it by the grim gate of death, brought down to them at once by the second coming of Christ, whose first advent has left them yet so far from it! . . .

[January 1839]
. . . I was looking over this morning, with a most indescribable mixture of feelings, a pamphlet published in the South upon the subject of the religious instruction of the slaves, and the difficulty of the task undertaken by these reconcilers of God and Mammon really seems to me nothing short of piteous.

'We must give our involuntary servants' (they seldom call them slaves, for it is an ugly word in an American mouth, you know) 'Christian enlightenment,' say they; and where shall they begin? 'Whatsoever ye would that men should do unto you, do ye also unto them?' No; but 'Servants, obey your masters;' and there, I think, they naturally come to a full stop. This pamphlet forcibly suggested to me the necessity for a slave Church Catechism, and also, indeed, if it were possible, a slave Bible.

If these heaven-blinded negro enlighteners persist in their pernicious plan of making Christians of their cattle, something of the sort must be done, or they will infallibly cut their own throats with this two-edged sword of truth, to which they should in no wise have laid their hand, and would not, doubtless, but that it is now thrust at them so threateningly that they have no choice. Again and again, how much I do pity them!

I have been walking to another cluster of negro huts, known as Number Two, and here we took a boat and rowed across the broad brimming Altamaha to a place called Woodville, on a part of the estate named Hammersmith, though why that very thriving suburb of the great city of London should have been selected as the name of the lonely plank house in the midst of the pine woods which here enjoys that title I can not conceive, unless it was suggested by the contrast.

This settlement is on the main land, and consists apparently merely of this house (to which the overseer retires when the poisonous malaria of the rice plantations compels him to withdraw from it), and a few deplorably miserable hovels, which appeared to me to be chiefly occupied by the most decrepit and infirm samples of humanity it was ever my melancholy lot to behold. . . .

There were two very aged women, who had seen different, and, to their faded recollections, better times, who spoke to me of Mr Butler's grandfather, and of the early days of the plantation, when they were young and strong, and worked as their children and grandchildren were now working, neither for love nor yet for money.

One of these old crones, a hideous, withered, wrinkled piece of womanhood, said that she had worked as long as her strength had lasted, and that then she had still been worth her keep, for, said she, 'Missus, tho' we no able to work, we make little niggers for massa.' Her joy at seeing her present owner was unbounded, and she kept clapping her horny hands together and exclaiming, 'While there is life there is hope; we seen massa before we die.'

These demonstrations of regard were followed up by piteous complaints of hunger and rheumatism, and their usual requests for pittances of food and clothing, to which we responded by promises of additions in both kinds. . . .

We returned home certainly in the very strangest vehicle that ever civilized gentlewoman travelled in – a huge sort of cart, made only of some loose boards, on which I lay, supporting myself against one of the four posts which indicated the sides of my carriage; six horned creatures, cows or bulls, drew this singular equipage, and a yelping, howling, screaming, leaping company of half-naked negroes ran all round them, goading them with sharp sticks, frantically seizing hold of their tails, and inciting them by every conceivable and inconceivable encouragement to quick motion: thus, like one of the ancient Merovingian monarchs, I was dragged through the deep sand from the settlement back to the river, where we re-embarked for the island. . . .

At our own settlement (No. 1) I found every thing in a high fever of preparation for the ball. A huge boat had just arrived from the cotton plantation at St Simon's, laden with the youth and beauty of that portion of the estate who had been invited to join the party; and the greetings among the arrivers and welcomers, and the heaven-defying combinations of colour in the gala attire of both, surpass all my powers of description.

The ball, to which of course we went, took place in one of the rooms of the Infirmary. As the room had, fortunately, but few occupants, they were removed to another apartment, and, without any very tender consideration for their not very remote, though invisible sufferings, the dancing commenced, and was continued.

Oh, my dear E, I have seen Jim Crow – the veritable James: all the contortions, and springs, and flings, and kicks, and capers you have been beguiled into accepting as indicative of him are spurious, faint, feeble, impotent – in a word, pale Northern reproductions of that ineffable black conception.

It is impossible for words to describe the things these people did with their bodies, and, above all, with their faces, the whites of their eyes, and the whites of their teeth, and certain outlines which either naturally and by the grace of heaven, or by the practice of some peculiar artistic dexterity, they bring into prominent and most ludicrous display.

The languishing elegance of some – the painstaking laboriousness of others – above all, the feats of a certain enthusiastic banjo-player, who seemed to me to thump his instrument with every part of his body at once, at last so utterly overcame any attempt at decorous gravity on my part that I was obliged to secede; and, considering what the atmosphere was that we inhaled during the exhibition, it is only wonderful to me that we were not made ill by the double effort not to laugh, and, if possible, not to breathe.

[21 January 1839]
. . . We have, as a sort of under nursemaid and assistant of my dear Margery, whose white complexion, as I wrote you, occasioned such indignation to my Southern fellow-travellers, and such extreme perplexity to the poor slaves on our arrival here, a much more orthodox servant for these parts, a young woman named Psyche, but commonly called Sack, not a very graceful abbreviation of the divine heathen appellation.

She can not be much over twenty, has a very pretty figure, a graceful, gentle deportment, and a face which, but for its colour (she is a dingy mulatto), would be pretty, and is extremely pleasing, from the perfect sweetness of its expression. She is always serious, not to say sad and silent, and has always an air of melancholy and timidity, that has frequently struck me very much, and would have made me think some special anxiety or sorrow must occasion it, but that God knows the whole condition of these wretched people naturally produces such a deportment, and there is no necessity to seek for special or peculiar causes to account for it. . . .

I have never questioned Psyche as to her sadness, because, in the first place, as I tell you, it appears to me most natural, and is observable in all the slaves whose superior natural or acquired intelligence allows of their filling situations of trust or service about the house and family; and, though I can not and will not refuse to hear any and every tale of suffering which these unfortunates bring to me, I am anxious to spare both myself and them the pain of vain appeals to me for redress and help, which, alas! it is too often utterly out of my power to give them. . . .

Therefore, as I tell you, I asked Psyche no questions; but, to my great astonishment, the other day Margery asked me if I knew to whom Psyche belonged, as the poor woman had inquired of her with much hesitation and anguish if she could tell her who owned her and her children. She has two nice little children under six years old, whom she keeps as clean and tidy, and who are sad and as silent as herself.

My astonishment at this question was, as you will readily believe, not small, and I forthwith sought out Psyche for an explanation. She was thrown into extreme perturbation at finding that her question had been referred to me, and it was some time before I could sufficiently reassure her to be able to comprehend, in the midst of her reiterated entreaties for pardon, and hopes that she had not offended me, that she did not know herself who owned her.

She was, at one time, the property of Mr King, the former overseer. . . . He, like several of his predecessors in the management, has contrived to make a fortune upon it (though it yearly decreases in value to the owners, but this is the inevitable course of things in the Southern states), and has purchased a plantation of his own in Alabama, I believe, or one of the Southwestern states. Whether she still belonged to Mr King or not she did not know, and entreated me, if she did, to endeavour to persuade Mr Butler to buy her.

Now you must know that this poor woman is the wife of one of Mr Butler's slaves, a fine, intelligent, active, excellent young man, whose whole family are among some of the very best specimens of character and capacity of the estate.

I was so astonished at the (to me) extraordinary state of things revealed by poor Sack's petition, that I could only tell her that I had supposed all the negroes on the plantation were Mr Butler's property, but that I would certainly inquire, and find out for her, if I could, to whom she belonged, and if I could, endeavour to get Mr Butler to purchase her, if she really was not his. . . .

I did not see Mr Butler till the evening; but, in the mean time, meeting the overseer, with whom, as I believe I have already told you, we are living here, I asked him about Psyche, and who was her proprietor, when, to my infinite surprise, he told me that he had bought her and her children from Mr King, who had offered them to him, saying that they would be rather troublesome to him than otherwise down where he was going. 'And so,' said the overseer, 'as I had no objection to investing a little money that way, I bought them.'

With a heart much lightened, I flew to tell poor Psyche the news, so that, at any rate, she might be relieved from the dread of any immediate separation from her husband. You can imagine better than I can tell you what her sensations were; but she still renewed her prayer that I would, if possible, induce Mr Butler to purchase her, and I promised to do so.

Early the next morning, while I was still dressing, I was suddenly startled by hearing voices in loud tones in Mr Butler's dressing-room, which adjoins my bedroom, and the noise increasing until there was an absolute cry of despair uttered by some man.

I could restrain myself no longer, but opened the door of communication and saw Joe, the young man, poor Psyche's husband, raving almost in a state of frenzy, and in a voice broken with sobs and almost inarticulate with passion, reiterating his determination never to leave this plantation, never to go to Alabama, never to leave his old father and mother, his poor wife and children, and dashing his hat, which he was wringing like a cloth in his hands, upon the ground, he declared he would kill himself if he was compelled to follow Mr King.

I glanced from the poor wretch to Mr Butler, who was standing, leaning against a table with his arms folded, occasionally uttering a

143

few words of counsel to his slave to be quiet and not fret, and not make a fuss about what there was no help for.

I retreated immediately from the horrid scene, breathless with surprise and dismay, and stood for some time in my own room, with my heart and temples throbbing to such a degree that I could hardly support myself. As soon as I recovered myself I again sought the overseer, and inquired of him if he knew the cause of poor Joe's distress.

He then told me that Mr Butler, who is highly pleased with Mr King's past administration of his property, wished, on his departure for his newly-acquired slave plantation, to give him some token of his satisfaction, and had made him a present of the man Joe, who had just received the intelligence that he was to go down to Alabama with his new owner the next day, leaving father, mother, wife, and children behind.

You will not wonder that the man required a little judicious soothing under such circumstances, and you will also, I hope, admire the humanity of the sale of his wife and children by the owner who was going to take him to Alabama, because they would be encumbrances rather than otherwise down there. . . .

When I saw Mr Butler after this most wretched story became known to me in all its details, I appealed to him, for his own soul's sake, not to commit so great a cruelty.

Poor Joe's agony while remonstrating with his master was hardly greater than mine while arguing with him upon this bitter piece of inhumanity – how I cried, and how I adjured, and how all my sense of justice, and of mercy, and of pity for the poor wretch, and of wretchedness at finding myself implicated in such a state of things, broke in torrents of words from my lips and tears from my eyes! God knows such a sorrow at seeing any one I belonged to commit such an act was indeed a new and terrible experience to me, and it seemed to me that I was imploring Mr Butler to save himself more than to spare these wretches.

He gave me no answer whatever, and I have since thought that the intemperate vehemence of my entreaties and expostulations perhaps deserved that he should leave me as he did without one single word of reply; and miserable enough I remained.

Toward evening, my children having gone to bed, the overseer came into the room. I had but one subject in my mind; I had not been able to eat for it. I could hardly sit still for the nervous distress which every thought of these poor people filled me with. As he sat down looking over some accounts, I said to him, 'Have you seen Joe this afternoon?' (I give you our conversation as it took place.)

'Yes, ma'am; he is a great deal happier than he was this morning.'

'Why, how is that?' asked I, eagerly.

'Oh, he is not going to Alabama. Mr King heard that he had kicked up a fuss about it (being in despair at being torn from one's wife and children is called kicking up a fuss; this is a sample of overseer appreciation of human feelings), and said that if the fellow wasn't willing to go with him, he did not wish to be bothered with any niggers down there who were to be troublesome, so he might stay behind.'

'And does Psyche know this?'

'Yes, ma'am, I suppose so.'

I drew a long breath; and whereas my needle had stumbled through the stuff I was sewing for an hour before, as if my fingers could not guide it, the regularity and rapidity of its evolutions were now quite edifying.

The man was for the present safe, and I remained silently pondering his deliverance and the whole proceeding, and the conduct of every one engaged in it, and, above all, Mr Butler's share in the transaction, and I think, for the first time, almost a sense of horrible personal responsibility and implication took hold of my mind, and I felt the weight of an unimagined guilt upon my conscience; and yet, God knows, this feeling of self-condemnation is very gratuitous on my part, since when I married Mr Butler I knew nothing of these dreadful possessions of his, and even if I had I should have been much puzzled to have formed any idea of the state of things in which I now find myself plunged, together with those whose well-doing is as vital to me almost as my own.

With these agreeable reflections I went to bed. Mr Butler said not a word to me upon the subject of these poor people all the next day, and in the mean time I became very impatient of this reserve on his part, because I was dying to prefer my request that he would purchase Psyche and her children, and so prevent any future separation between her and her husband, as I supposed he would not again attempt to make a present of Joe, at least to any one who did not wish to be bothered with his wife and children.

In the evening I was again with the overseer alone in the strange, bare, wooden-walled sort of shanty which is our sitting-room, and revolving in my mind the means of rescuing Psyche from her miserable suspense; a long chain of all my possessions, in the shape of bracelets, necklaces, brooches, earrings, etc., wound in glittering procession through my brain, with many hypothetical calculations of the value of each separate ornament, and the very doubtful probability of the amount of the whole being equal to the price of this poor creature and her children. . . .

You will not wonder that when, in the midst of such cogitations, I suddenly accosted the overseer, it was to this effect: '. . . I have a particular favour to beg of you. Promise me that you will never sell Psyche and her children without first letting me know of your intention to do so, and giving me the option of buying them.'

The overseer is a remarkably deliberate man, and squints, so that, when he has taken a little time in directing his eyes to you, you are still unpleasantly unaware of any result in which you are concerned; he laid down a book he was reading, and directed his head and one of his eyes toward me and answered, 'Dear me, ma'am, I am very sorry – I have sold them.'

My work fell down on the ground, and my mouth opened wide, but I could utter no sound, I was so dismayed and surprised; and he deliberately proceeded: 'I didn't know, ma'am, you see, at all, that you entertained any idea of making an investment of that nature; for I'm sure, if I had, I would willingly have sold the woman to you; but I sold her and her children this morning to Mr Butler.'

My dear E, though Pierce had resented my unmeasured upbraidings, you see they had not been without some good effect, and though he had, perhaps justly, punished my violent outbreak of indignation about the miserable scene I witnessed by not telling me of his humane purpose, he had bought these poor creatures, and so, I trust, secured them from any such misery in future.

I jumped up and left the overseer still speaking, and ran to find Mr Butler, to thank him for what he had done, and with that will now bid you good-by.

Think, E, how it fares with slaves on plantations where there is no crazy Englishwoman to weep, and entreat, and implore, and upbraid for them, and no master willing to listen to such appeals.

[January 1839]
Dear E, . . . Rowing yesterday evening through a beautiful sunset
into a more beautiful moonrise, my two sable boatmen entertained
themselves and me with alternate strophe and antistrophe of
poetical description of my personal attractions, in which my 'wire
waist' recurred repeatedly, to my intense amusement. This is a
charm for the possession of which Margery (my white nursemaid)
is also invariably celebrated; and I suppose that the fine round
natural proportions of the uncompressed waists of the sable
beauties of these regions appear less symmetrical to eyes
accustomed to them than our stay-cased figures, since 'nothing
pleaseth but rare accidents'.

Occasionally I am celebrated in these rowing chants as 'Massa's
darling,' and Sally comes in for endless glorification on account of
the brilliant beautyof her complexion; the other day, however, our
poets made a diversion from the personal to the moral qualities of
their small mistress, and after the usual tribute to her roses and
lilies came the following rather significant couplet:

> Little Missis Sally,
> That's a ruling lady.

At which all the white teeth simultaneously lightened from the
black visages, while the subject of this equivocal commendation sat
with infantine solemnity (the profoundest, I think, that the human
countenance is capable of), surveying her sable dependants with
imperturbable gravity. . . .

I had rather a fright the other day in that same small craft, into
which I had taken Sally, with the intention of paddling myself a
little way down the river and back. I used to row tolerably well, and
was very fond of it, and frequently here take an oar, when the men
are rowing me in the long-boat, as some sort of equivalent for my
riding, of which, of course, I am entirely deprived on this little
dykeland of ours; but paddling is a perfectly different process, and
one that I was very anxious to achieve.

My first strokes answered the purpose of sending the boat off
from shore, and for a few minutes I got on pretty well; but
presently I got tired of shifting the paddle from side to side, a
manoeuvre which I accomplished very clumsily and slowly, and
yet, with all my precautions, not without making the boat tip
perilously.

The immense breadth and volume of the river suddenly seized my eyes and imagination as it were, and I began to fancy that if I got into the middle of the stream I should not be able to paddle myself back against it – which, indeed, might very well have proved the case. Then I became nervous, and paddled all on one side, by which means, of course, I only turned the boat round.

Sally began to fidget about, getting up from where I had placed her, and terrifying me with her unsteady motions and the rocking of the canoe. I was now very much frightened, and saw that I must get back to shore before I became more helpless than I was beginning to feel; so, laying Sally down in the bottom of the boat as a preliminary precaution, I said to her with infinite emphasis, 'Now lie still there, and don't stir, or you'll be drowned,' to which, with her clear grey eyes fixed on me, and no sign whatever of emotion, she replied deliberately, 'I shall lie still here, and won't stir, for I should not like to be drowned,' which, for an atom not four years old, was rather philosophical.

Then I looked about me, and of course having drifted, set steadily to work and paddled home, with my heart in my mouth almost till we grazed the steps, and I got my precious freight safe on shore again, since which I have taken no more paddling lessons without my slave and master, Jack. . . .

Yesterday evening the burial of the poor man Shadrach took place. I had been applied to for a sufficient quantity of cotton cloth to make a winding-sheet for him, and just as the twilight was thickening into darkness I went with Mr Butler to the cottage of one of the slaves whom I may have mentioned to you before – a cooper of the name of London, the head of the religious party of the inhabitants of the island, a Methodist preacher of no small intelligence and influence among the people – who was to perform the burial service.

The coffin was laid on trestles in front of the cooper's cottage, and a large assemblage of the people had gathered round, many of the men carrying pine-wood torches, the fitful glare of which glanced over the strange assembly, where every pair of large white-rimmed eyes turned upon Mr Butler and myself; we two poor creatures, on this more solemn occasion, as well as on every other when these people encounter us, being the objects of admiration and wonderment, on which their gaze is immovably riveted. Presently the whole congregation uplifted their voices in a hymn, the first high wailing notes of which – sung all in unison, in the midst of these unwonted surroundings – sent a thrill through all my nerves.

When the chant ceased, cooper London began a prayer, and all the people knelt down in the sand, as I did also. Mr Butler alone remained standing in the presence of the dead man and of the living God to whom his slaves were now appealing.

I can not tell you how profoundly the whole ceremony, if such it could be called, affected me; and there was nothing in the simple and pathetic supplication of the poor black artisan to check or interfere with the solemn influences of the whole scene. It was a sort of conventional Methodist prayer, and probably quite as conventional as all the rest was the closing invocation of God's blessing upon their master, their mistress, and our children; but this fairly overcame my composure, and I began to cry very bitterly; for these same individuals, whose implication in the state of things in the midst of which we are living, seemed to me as legitimate a cause for tears as for prayers.

When the prayer was concluded we all rose, and, the coffin being taken up, proceeded to the people's burial-ground, when London read aloud portions of the funeral service from the Prayer-book – I presume the American Episcopal version of our Church service, for what he read appeared to be merely a selection from what was perfectly familiar to me; but whether he himself extracted what he uttered I did not inquire. Indeed, I was too much absorbed in the whole scene, and the many mingled emotions it excited of awe and pity, and an indescribable sensation of wonder at finding myself on this slave soil, surrounded by MY slaves, among whom again I knelt while the words proclaiming to the living and the dead the everlasting covenant of freedom, 'I am the resurrection and the life,' sounded over the prostrate throng, and mingled with the heavy flowing of the vast river sweeping, not far from where we stood, through the darkness by which we were now encompassed (beyond the immediate circle of our torch-bearers).

There was something painful to me in Mr Butler's standing while we all knelt on the earth; for, though in any church in Philadelphia he would have stood during the praying of any minister, here I wished he would have knelt, to have given his slaves some token of his belief that – at least in the sight of that Master to whom we were addressing our worship – all men are equal.

149

The service ended with a short address from London upon the subject of Lazarus, and the confirmation which the story of his resurrection afforded our hopes. . . .

When the coffin was lowered the grave was found to be partially filled with water – naturally enough, for the whole island is a mere swamp, off which the Altamaha is only kept from sweeping by the high dykes all round it. This seemed to shock and distress the people, and for the first time during the whole ceremony there were sounds of crying and exclamations of grief heard among them.

Their chief expression of sorrow, however, when Mr Butler and myself bade them good-night at the conclusion of the service, was on account of my crying, which appeared to affect them very much, many of them mingling with their 'Farewell, good-night, massa and missis,' affectionate exclamations of 'God bless you, missis; don't cry!' 'Lor, missis, don't you cry so!'

Mr Butler declined the assistance of any of the torch-bearers home, and bade them all go quietly to their quarters; and as soon as they had dispersed, and we had got beyond the fitful and unequal glaring of the torches, we found the shining of the stars in the deep blue lovely night sky quite sufficient to light our way along the dykes.

I could not speak to Mr Butler, but continued to cry as we walked silently home; and, whatever his cogitations were, they did not take the usual form with him of wordy demonstration, and so we returned from one of the most striking religious ceremonies at which I ever assisted. . . .

February 1839

[Beginning of February 1839]
Returning from the hospital, I was accosted by poor old Teresa, the wretched negress who had complained to me so grievously of her back being broken by hard work and childbearing. She was in a dreadful state of excitement, which she partly presently communicated to me, because she said the overseer had ordered her to be flogged for having complained to me as she did.

It seems to me that I have come down here to be tortured, for this punishing these wretched creatures for crying out to me for help is really converting me into a source of increased misery to them. It is almost more than I can endure to hear these horrid stories of lashings inflicted because I have been invoked; and though I dare say Mr Butler, thanks to my passionate appeals to him, gives me little credit for prudence or self-command, I have some, and I exercise it, too, when I listen to such tales as these with my teeth set fast and my lips closed. Whatever I may do to the master, I hold my tongue to the slaves, and I wonder how I do it. . . .

[February 1839]
Dear E, – To-day I have the pleasure of announcing to you a variety of improvements about to be made in the Infirmary of the island. There is to be a third storey – a mere loft, indeed – added to the building; but, by affording more room for the least distressing cases of sickness to be drafted off into, it will leave the ground floor and room above it comparatively free for the most miserable of these unfortunates.

To my unspeakable satisfaction, these destitute apartments are to be furnished with bedsteads, mattresses, pillows, and blankets; and I feel a little comforted for the many heartaches my life here inflicts upon me – at least some of my twinges will have wrought this poor alleviation of their wretchedness for the slaves when prostrated by disease or pain.

I had hardly time to return from the hospital home this morning

151

before one of the most tremendous storms I ever saw burst over the island. . . .

The afternoon cleared off most beautifully, and Jack and I went out on the river to catch what might be caught. Jack's joyful excitement was extreme at my announcing to him the fact that Mr Butler had consented to try ploughing on some of the driest portions of the island instead of the slow and laborious process of hoeing the fields. This is a disinterested exultation on his part, for, at any rate, as long as I am here, he will certainly be nothing but 'my boy Jack', and I should think, after my departure, will never be degraded to the rank of a field-hand or common labourer. Indeed, the delicacy of his health, to which his slight, slender figure and languid face bear witness, and which was one reason of his appointment to the eminence of being 'my slave', would, I should think, prevent the poor fellow's ever being a very robust or useful working animal.

On my return from the river I had a long and painful conversation with Mr Butler upon the subject of the flogging which had been inflicted on the wretched Teresa. These discussions are terrible: they throw me into perfect agonies of distress for the slaves, whose position is utterly hopeless; for myself, whose intervention in their behalf sometimes seems to me worse than useless; for Mr Butler, whose share in this horrible system fills me by turns with indignation and pity.

But, after all, what can he do? How can he help it all? Moreover, born and bred in America, how should he care or wish to help it? And, of course, he does not; and I am in despair that he does not: *et voilà*, it is a happy and hopeful plight for us both.

He maintained that there had been neither hardship nor injustice in the case of Teresa's flogging; and that, moreover, she had not been flogged at all for complaining to me, but simply because her allotted task was not done at the appointed time. Of course this was the result of her having come to appeal to me instead of going to her labour; and as she knew perfectly well the penalty she was incurring, he maintained that there was neither hardship nor injustice in the case; the whole thing was a regularly established law, with which all the slaves were perfectly well acquainted; and this case was no exception whatever. The circumstance of my being on the island could not, of course, be allowed to overthrow the whole system of discipline established to secure the labour and obedience of the slaves; and if they chose to try experiments as to that fact, they and I must take the consequences. . . .

When I was thus silenced on the particular case under discussion, I resorted, in my distress and indignation, to the abstract question, as I never can refrain from doing; and to Mr Butler's assertion of the justice of poor Teresa's punishment, I retorted the manifest injustice of unpaid and enforced labour; the brutal inhumanity of allowing a man to strip and lash a woman, the mother of ten children; to exact from her toil which was to maintain in luxury two idle young men, the owners of the plantation. I said I thought female labour of the sort exacted from these slaves, and corporal chastisement such as they endure, must be abhorrent to any manly or humane man. Mr Butler said he thought it was disagreeable, and left me to my reflections with that concession.

My letter has been interrupted for the last three days – by nothing special, however. My occupations and interests here, of course, know no change; but Mr Butler has been anxious for a little while past that we should go down to St Simon's, the cotton plantation.

We shall suffer less from the heat, which I am beginning to find oppressive on this swamp island; and he himself wished to visit that part of his property, whither he had not yet been since our arrival in Georgia; so the day before yesterday he departed to make the necessary arrangements for our removal thither; and my time in the mean while has been taken up in fitting him out for his departure. . . .

In the afternoon I saw Mr Butler off for St Simon's; it is fifteen miles lower down the river, and a large island at the very mouth of the Altamaha. . . .

Mr Butler sat in the middle of a perfect chaos of freight; and as the boat pushed off, and the steersman took her into the stream, the men at the oars set up a chorus, which they continued to chant in unison with each other, and in time with their stroke, till the voices and oars were heard no more from the distance. . . .

That which I have heard these people sing is often plaintive and pretty, but almost always has some resemblance to tunes with which they must have become acquainted through the instrumentality of white men; their overseers or masters whistling Scotch or Irish airs, of which they have produced by ear these *rifacciamenti*.

153

The note for note reproduction of '*Ah! vous dirai-je, maman?*' in one of the most popular of the so-called negro melodies with which all America and England are familiar, is an example of this very transparent plagiarism; and the tune with which Mr Butler's rowers started him down the Altamaha, as I stood at the steps to see him off, was a very distinct descendant of 'Coming through the Rye'. The words, however, were astonishingly primitive, especially the first line, which, when it burst from their eight throats in high unison, sent me into fits of laughter.

> Jenny shake her toe at me,
> Jenny gone away;
> Jenny shake her toe at me,
> Jenny gone away.
> Hurrah! Miss Susy, oh!
> Jenny gone away;
> Hurrah! Miss Susy, oh!
> Jenny gone away.

What the obnoxious Jenny meant by shaking her toe, whether defiance or merely departure, I never could ascertain, but her going away was an unmistakable subject of satisfaction; and the pause made on the last 'oh!' before the final announcement of her departure, had really a good deal of dramatic and musical effect.

Except the extemporaneous chants in our honour, of which I have written to you before, I have never heard the negroes on Mr Butler's plantation sing any words that could be said to have any sense. To one, an extremely pretty, plaintive, and original air, there was but one line, which was repeated with a sort of wailing chorus:

> 'Oh! my massa told me, there's no grass in Georgia.'

Upon inquiring the meaning of which, I was told it was supposed to be the lamentation of a slave from one of the more northerly states, Virginia, or Carolina, where the labour of hoeing the weeds, or grass as they call it, is not nearly so severe as here, in the rice and cotton lands of Georgia.

Another very pretty and pathetic tune began with words that seemed to promise something sentimental:

> Fare you well, and good-by, oh, oh!
> I'm goin' away to leave you, oh, oh!

but immediately went off into nonsense verses about gentlemen in the parlour drinking wine and cordial, and ladies in the drawing-room drinking tea and coffee, etc.

I have heard that many of the masters and overseers on these plantations prohibit melancholy tunes or words, and encourage nothing but cheerful music and senseless words, deprecating the effect of sadder strains upon the slaves, whose peculiar musical sensibility might be expected to make them especially excitable by any songs of a plaintive character, and having any reference to their particular hardships. If it is true, I think it a judicious precaution enough – these poor slaves are just the sort of people over whom a popular musical appeal to their feelings and passions would have an immense power. . . .

This morning, instead of my usual visit to the Infirmary, I went to look at the work and workers in the threshing mill: all was going on actively and orderly under the superintendence of head man Frank, with whom, and a very sagacious clever fellow who manages the steam power of the mill, and is honourably distinguished as Engineer Ned, I had a small chat. . . .

After leaving the mill I prolonged my walk, and came, for the first time, upon one of the 'gangs', as they are called, in full field work. Upon my appearance and approach there was a momentary suspension of labour, and the usual chorus of screams and ejaculations of welcome, affection, and infinite desires for infinite small indulgences. I was afraid to stop their work, not feeling at all sure that urging a conversation with me would be accepted as any excuse for an uncompleted task, or avert the fatal infliction of the usual award of stripes; so I hurried off and left them to their hoeing.

On my way home I was encountered by London, our Methodist preacher, who accosted me with a request for a Prayer-book and Bible, and expressed his regret at hearing that we were so soon going to St Simon's.

I promised him his holy books, and asked him how he had learned to read, but found it impossible to get him to tell me. I wonder if he thought he should be putting his teacher, whoever he was, in danger of the penalty of the law against instructing the slaves, if he told me who he was; it was impossible to make him do so, so that, besides his other good qualities, he appears to have that most unusual one of all in an uneducated person – discretion. He certainly is a most remarkable man. . . .

After I had been in the house a little while, I was summoned out again to receive the petition of certain poor women in the family way to have their work lightened. I was, of course, obliged to tell them that I could not interfere in the matter; that their master was away, and that, when he came back, they must present their request to him: they said they had already begged 'massa', and he had refused, and they thought, perhaps, if 'missis' begged 'massa' for them, he would lighten their task. Poor 'missis,' poor 'massa,' poor woman, that I am to have such prayers addressed to me!

I had to tell them that, if they had already spoken to their master, I was afraid my doing so would be of no use, but that when he came back I would try; so, choking with crying, I turned away from them, and re-entered the house, to the chorus of 'Oh, thank you, missis! God bless you, missis!'

Elizabeth, I think an improvement might be made upon that caricature published a short time ago, called the 'Chivalry of the South.' I think an elegant young Carolinian or Georgian gentleman, whip in hand, driving a gang of 'lusty women,' as they are called here, would be a pretty version of the 'Chivalry of the South' – a little coarse, I am afraid you will say. Oh! quite horribly coarse, but then so true – a great matter in works of art, which nowadays appear to be thought excellent only in proportion to their lack of ideal elevation. That would be a subject, and a treatment of it, which could not be accused of imaginative exaggeration, at any rate. . . .

[13 February 1839]
Dearest E, – I think it right to begin this letter with an account of a most prosperous fishing expedition Jack and I achieved the other morning. It is true we still occasionally drew up huge catfish, with their detestable beards, and spikes, but we also captivated some magnificent perch, and the Altamaha perch are worth one's while both to catch and to eat. On a visit I had to make on the main land the same day, I saw a tiny strip of garden ground, rescued from the sandy road called the street, perfectly filled with hyacinths, double

jonquils, and snowdrops, a charming nosegay for February 11. . . .

You can not imagine how great a triumph the virtue next to godliness is making under my auspices and a judicious system of small bribery. I can hardly stir now without being assailed with cries of 'Missis, missis, me mind chile, me bery clean,' or the additional gratifying fact, 'and chile too, him bery clean.' . . .

In my afternoon's row today I passed a huge dead alligator, lying half in and half out of the muddy slime of the river bank – a most hideous object it was, and I was glad to turn my eyes to the beautiful surface of the mid stream, all burnished with sunset glories, and broken with the vivacious gambols of a school of porpoises. It is curious, I think, that these creatures should come fifteen miles from the sea to enliven the waters round our little rice swamp. . . .

[14 February 1839]
Dearest E, . . . In the afternoon I took my accustomed row. . . . On my return home I was met by a child (as she seemed to me) carrying a baby, in whose behalf she begged me for some clothes. On making some inquiry, I was amazed to find that the child was her own: she said she was married, and fourteen years old; she looked much younger even than that, poor creature. Her mother, who came up while I was talking to her, said she did not herself know the girl's age; how horridly brutish it all did seem, to be sure.

The spring is already here with her hands full of flowers. I do not know who planted some straggling *pyrus japonica* near the house, but it is blessing my eyes with a hundred little flame-like buds, which will presently burst into a blaze; there are clumps of narcissus roots sending up sheaves of ivory blossoms, and I actually found a monthly rose in bloom on the sunny side of one of the dykes; what a delight they are in the slovenly desolation of this abode of mine! What a garden one might have on the banks of these dykes, with the least amount of trouble and care!

In the afternoon I rowed over to Darien, and there procuring the most miserable vehicle calling itself a carriage that I had ever seen (the dirtiest and shabbiest London hackney-coach were a chariot of splendour and ease to it), we drove some distance into the sandy wilderness that surrounds the little town, to pay a visit to some of the resident gentry who had called upon us. . . .

157

From time to time a thicket of exquisite evergreen shrubs broke the monotonous lines of the countless pine shafts rising round us, and still more welcome were the golden garlands of the exquisite wild jasmine, hanging, drooping, trailing, clinging, climbing through the dreary forest, joining to the warm aromatic smell of the fir-trees a delicious fragrance as of acres of heliotrope in bloom. . . .

The house at which our call was paid was set down in the midst of the Pine Barren, with half-obliterated roads and paths round it, suggesting that it might be visited and was inhabited. It was large and not unhandsome, though curiously dilapidated, considering that people were actually living in it; certain remnants of carving on the cornices and paint on the panels bore witness to some former stage of existence less neglected and deteriorated than the present.

The old lady mistress of this most forlorn abode amiably inquired if so much exercise did not fatigue me; at first I thought she imagined I must have walked through the pine forest all the way from Darien, but she explained that she considered the drive quite an effort; and it is by no means uncommon to hear people in America talk of being dragged over bad roads in uneasy carriages as exercise, showing how very little they know the meaning of the word, and how completely they identify it with the idea of mere painful fatigue instead of pleasurable exertion. . . .

This morning I have been to the hospital to see a poor woman who has just enriched Mr Butler by *borning* him another slave. The poor little pickaninny, as they called it, was not one bit uglier than white babies under similarly novel circumstances, except in one particular, that it had a head of hair like a trunk, in spite of which I had all the pains in the world in persuading its mother not to put a cap upon it. I bribed her finally by the promise of a pair of socks instead, with which I undertook to endow her child, and, moreover, actually prevailed upon her to forego the usual swaddling and swathing process, and let her poor baby be dressed at its first entrance into life as I assured her both mine had been.

On leaving the hospital I visited the huts all along the street, confiscating sundry refractory baby caps among shrieks and outcries, partly of laughter and partly of real ignorant alarm for the consequences. I think, if this infatuation for hot head-dresses continues, I shall make shaving the children's heads the only condition upon which they shall be allowed to wear caps. . . .

[14–17 February 1839]

Dearest E, – Passing the rice mill this morning in my walk, I went in to look at the machinery, the large steam mortars which shell the rice, and which work under the intelligent and reliable supervision of Engineer Ned. I was much surprised, in the course of conversation with him this morning, to find how much older a man he was than he appeared. Indeed, his youthful appearance had hitherto puzzled me much in accounting for his very superior intelligence and the important duties confided to him. He is, however, a man upward of forty years old, although he looks ten years younger. He attributed his own uncommonly youthful appearance to the fact of his never having done what he called field-work, or been exposed, as the common gang negroes are, to the hardships of their all but brutish existence.

He said his former master had brought him up very kindly, and he had learned to tend the engines, and had never been put to any other work, but he said this was not the case with his poor wife. He wished she was as well off as he was, but she had to work in the rice-fields, and was 'most broke in two' with labour, and exposure, and hard work while with child, and hard work just directly after childbearing; he said she could hardly crawl, and he urged me very much to speak a kind word for her to massa. She was almost all the time in hospital, and he thought she could not live long. . . .

On my return to the house I found a terrible disturbance in consequence of the disappearance from under cook John's safe keeping of a ham Mr Butler had committed to his charge. There was no doubt whatever that the unfortunate culinary slave had made away in some inscrutable manner with the joint intended for our table: the very lies he told about it were so curiously shallow, childlike, and transparent, that while they confirmed the fact of his theft quite as much, if not more, than an absolute confession would have done, they provoked at once my pity and my irrepressible mirth to a most painful degree.

Mr Butler was in a state of towering anger and indignation, and, besides a flogging, sentenced the unhappy cook to degradation from his high and dignified position (and, alas! all its sweets of comparatively easy labour and good living from the remains of our table) to the hard toil, coarse scanty fare, and despised position of a common field-hand.

I suppose some punishment was inevitably necessary in such a plain case of deliberate theft as this, but, nevertheless, my whole soul revolts at the injustice of visiting upon these poor wretches a moral darkness which all possible means are taken to increase and perpetuate. . . .

I had a conversation the next morning with Abraham, cook John's brother, upon the subject of his brother's theft; and only think of the slave saying that 'this action had brought disgrace upon the family.' Does not that sound very like the very best sort of free pride, the pride of character, the honourable pride of honesty, integrity, and fidelity? But this was not all, for this same Abraham, a clever carpenter and much valued hand on the estate, went on, in answer to my questions, to tell me such a story that I declare to you I felt as if I could have howled with helpless indignation and grief when he departed and went to resume his work.

His grandfather had been an old slave in Darien, extremely clever as a carpenter, and so highly valued for his skill and good character that his master allowed him to purchase his liberty by money which he earned by working for himself at odd times, when his task-work was over.

I asked Abraham what sum his grandfather paid for his freedom: he said he did not know, but he supposed a large one, because of his being a 'skilled carpenter', and so a peculiarly valuable chattel. I presume, from what I remember Dr Holmes saying on the subject of the market value of negroes in Charleston and Savannah, that such a man in the prime of life would have been worth from 1,500 to 2,000 dollars. However, whatever the man paid for his ransom, by his grandson's account, fourteen years after he became free, when he died, he had again amassed money to the amount of 700 dollars, which he left among his wife and children, the former being a slave on Major Butler's estate, where the latter remained by virtue of that fact slaves also.

So this man not only bought his own freedom at a cost of at least 1,000 dollars, but left a little fortune of 700 more at his death; and then we are told of the universal idleness, incorrigible sloth, and brutish incapacity of this inferior race of creatures, whose only fitting and Heaven-appointed condition is that of beasts of burden to the whites. I do not believe the whole low white population of the State of Georgia could furnish such an instance of energy, industry, and thrift as the amassing of this laborious little fortune by this poor slave. . . .

. . . Called into the house to receive the return visit of old Mrs Spalding. As usual, the appearance, health, vigour, and good management of the children were the theme of wondering admiration; as usual, my possession of a white nurse the theme of envious congratulation; as usual, I had to hear the habitual senseless complaints of the inefficiency of coloured nurses.

If you are half as tired of the sameness and stupidity of the conversation of my Southern female neighbours as I am, I pity you; but not as much as I pity them for the stupid sameness of their most vapid existence, which would deaden any amount of intelligence, obliterate any amount of instruction, and render torpid and stagnant any amount of natural energy and vivacity. I would rather die – rather a thousand times – than live the lives of these Georgia planters' wives and daughters.

Mrs Spalding had brought me some of the delicious wild jasmine that festoons her dreary pine-wood drive, and most grateful I was for the presence of the sweet wild nosegay in my highly unorna-mental residence.

When my visitors had left me, I took the refreshment of a row over to Darien; and as we had the tide against us coming back, the process was not so refreshing for the rowers. The evening was so extremely beautiful, and the rising of the moon so exquisite, that instead of retreating to the house when I reached the island, I got into the *Dolphin*, my special canoe, and made Jack paddle me down the great river to meet the *Lily*, which was coming back from St Simon's with Mr Butler, who has been preparing all things for our advent thither.

[17 February 1839]
My letter has been interrupted, dear E, by the breaking up of our residence on the rice plantation, and our arrival at St Simon's, whence I now address you.

We came down yesterday afternoon, and I was thankful enough of the fifteen miles' row to rest in, from the labour of leave-taking, with which the whole morning was taken up, and which, combined with packing and preparing all our own personalities and those of the children, was no sinecure. At every moment one or other of the poor people rushed in upon me to bid me good-by; many of their farewells were grotesque enough, some were

161

pathetic, and all of them made me very sad. Poor people! How little I have done, how little I can do for them. . . .

Our voyage from the rice to the cotton plantation was performed in the *Lily*, which looked like a soldier's baggage-wagon and an emigrant transport combined. Our crew consisted of eight men. Forward in the bow were miscellaneous live-stock, pots, pans, household furniture, kitchen utensils, and an indescribable variety of heterogeneous necessaries. Enthroned upon beds, bedding, tables, and other chattels, sat that poor pretty chattel Psyche, with her small chattel children. Midships sat the two tiny free women and myself, and in the stern Mr Butler steering. And 'all in the blue unclouded weather' we rowed down the huge stream, the men keeping time and tune to their oars with extemporaneous chants of adieu to the rice-island and its denizens.

Among other poetical and musical comments on our departure recurred the assertion, as a sort of burden, that we were 'parted in body, but not in mind,' from those we left behind. Having relieved one set of sentiments by this reflection, they very wisely betook themselves to the consideration of the blessings that remained to them, and performed a spirited chant in honour of Psyche and our bouncing black housemaid, Mary.

At the end of a fifteen miles' row we entered one among a perfect labyrinth of arms or branches, into which the broad river ravels like a fringe as it reaches the sea, a dismal navigation along a dismal tract, called 'Five Pound', through a narrow cut or channel of water divided from the main stream. The conch was sounded, as at our arrival at the rice-island, and we made our descent on the famous long staple cotton island of St Simon's, where we presently took up our abode in what had all the appearance of an old, half-decayed, rattling farm-house.

This morning, Sunday, I peeped round its immediate neighbourhood, and saw, to my inexpressible delight, within hail, some noble-looking evergreen oaks, and close to the house itself a tiny would-be garden, a plot of ground with one or two peach-trees in full blossom, tufts of silver narcissus and jonquils, a quantity of violets and an exquisite myrtle bush; wherefore I said my prayers with especial gratitude.

[18 February 1839]
Dearest E, – The fame of my peculiar requisitions has, I find,

preceded me here, for the babies that have been presented to my admiring notice have all been without caps; also, however, without socks to their opposite little wretched extremities, but that does not signify quite so much. The people, too, that I saw yesterday were remarkably clean and tidy; to be sure, it was Sunday. The whole day, till quite late in the afternoon, the house was surrounded by a crowd of our poor dependants, waiting to catch a glimpse of Mr Butler, myself, or the children; and until, from sheer weariness, I was obliged to shut the doors, an incessant stream poured in and out, whose various modes of salutation, greeting, and welcome were more grotesque and pathetic at the same time than any thing you can imagine.

In the afternoon I walked with Mr Butler to see a new house in process of erection, which, when it is finished, is to be the overseer's abode and our residence during any future visits we may pay to the estate.

I was horrified at the dismal site selected, and the hideous house erected on it. It is true that the central position is the principal consideration in the overseer's location; but both position and building seemed to me to witness to an inveterate love of ugliness, or, at any rate, a deadness to every desire of beauty, nothing short of horrible; and, for my own part, I think it is intolerable to have to leave the point where the waters meet, and where a few fine picturesque old trees are scattered about, to come to this place even for the very short time I am ever likely to spend here. . . .

I observed, among the numerous groups that we passed or met, a much larger proportion of mulattoes than at the rice-island; upon asking Mr Butler why this was so, he said that there no white person could land without his or the overseer's permission, whereas on St Simon's, which is a large island containing several plantations belonging to different owners, of course the number of whites both residing on and visiting the place, was much greater, and the opportunity for intercourse between the blacks and whites much more frequent.

While we were still on this subject, a horrid-looking filthy woman met us with a little child in her arms, a very light mulatto, whose extraordinary resemblance to Driver Bran (one of the officials who had been duly presented to me on my arrival, and who was himself a mulatto) struck me directly. I pointed it out to Mr Butler, who merely answered, 'Very likely his child.'

'And,' said I, 'did you never remark that Driver Bran is the exact image of Mr King?'

'Very likely his brother,' was the reply: all which rather unpleasant state of relationships seemed accepted as such a complete matter of course, that I felt rather uncomfortable, and said no more about who was like who. . . .

I find here an immense proportion of old people; the work and the climate of the rice plantation require the strongest of the able-bodied men and women of the estate. The cotton crop is no longer by any means as paramount in value as it used to be, and the climate, soil, and labour of St Simon's are better adapted to old, young, and feeble cultivators than the swamp fields of the rice-island.

I wonder if I ever told you of the enormous decrease in value of this same famous sea-island long staple cotton. When Major Butler, Mr Butler's grandfather, first sent the produce of this plantation where we now are to England, it was of so fine a quality that it used to be quoted by itself in the Liverpool cotton market, and was then worth half a guinea a pound; it is now not worth a shilling a pound. This was told me by the gentleman in Liverpool who has been factor for this estate for thirty years.

Such a decrease as this in the value of one's crop, and the steady increase at the same time of a slave population, now numbering between 700 and 800 bodies to clothe and house, mouths to feed, while the land is being exhausted by the careless and wasteful nature of the agriculture itself, suggests a pretty serious prospect of declining prosperity; and, indeed, unless these Georgia cotton-planters can command more land, or lay abundant capital (which they have not, being almost all of them over head and ears in debt) upon that which has already spent its virgin vigour, it is a very obvious thing that they must all very soon be eaten up by their own property. . . .

[19–27 February 1839]
I find the people here much more inclined to talk than those on the rice-island; they have less to do and more leisure, and bestow it very liberally on me; moreover, the poor old women, of whom there are so many turned out to grass here, and of whom I have spoken to you before, though they are past work, are by no means past gossip, and the stories they have to tell of the former

government of the estate under old Massa King are certainly pretty tremendous illustrations of the merits of slavery as a moral institution.

This man, the father of the late overseer, Mr Roswell King, was Major Butler's agent in the management of this property, and a more cruel and unscrupulous one as regards the slaves themselves, whatever he may have been in his dealings with the master, I should think it would be difficult to find, even among the cruel and unscrupulous class to which he belonged. . . .

I was very sorry to hear to-day that the overseer at the rice-island, of whom I have made mention to you more than once in my letters, had had one of the men flogged very severely for getting his wife baptized. I was quite unable, from the account I received, to understand what his objection had been to the poor man's desire to make his wife at least a formal Christian; but it does seem dreadful that such an act should be so visited. I almost wish I was back again at the rice-island; for, though this is every way the pleasanter residence, I hear so much more that is intolerable of the treatment of the slaves from those I find here, that my life is really made wretched by it. . . .

Tuesday, the 26th [February 1839]
My dearest E, I write to you today in great depression and distress. I have had a most painful conversation with Mr Butler, who has declined receiving any of the people's petitions through me.

Whether he is wearied with the number of these prayers and supplications, which he would escape but for me, as they probably would not venture to come so incessantly to him, and I, of course, feel bound to bring every one confided to me to him, or whether he has been annoyed at the number of pitiful and horrible stories of misery and oppression under the former rule of Mr King, which have come to my knowledge since I have been here, and the grief and indignation caused, but which can not, by any means, always be done away with, though their expression may be silenced by his angry exclamations of 'Why do you listen to such stuff?' or 'Why do you believe such trash? Don't you know the niggers are all d—d liars?' etc., I do not know; but he desired me this morning to bring him no more complaints or requests of any sort, as the people had hitherto had no such advocate, and had done very well without,

165

and I was only kept in an incessant state of excitement with all the falsehoods they 'found they could make me believe.'

How well they have done without my advocacy, the conditions which I see with my own eyes, even more than their pitiful petitions, demonstrate. It is indeed true that the sufferings of those who come to me for redress, and, still more, the injustice done to the great majority who can not, have filled my heart with bitterness and indignation that have overflowed my lips, till, I suppose, Mr Butler is weary of hearing what he has never heard before, the voice of passionate expostulation and importunate pleading against wrongs that he will not even acknowledge, and for creatures whose common humanity with his own I half think he does not believe. But I must return to the North, for my condition would be almost worse than theirs – condemned to hear and see so much wretchedness, not only without the means of alleviating it, but without permission even to represent it for alleviation. This is no place for me, since I was not born among slaves, and can not bear to live among them. . . .

It was about now that Fanny ran away. 'She resolved to leave me,' Pierce later wrote, 'packed up her trunks, left the children in St Simon's Island without saying a word to them or the nurse, and came to the plantation near Darien to go away in the steamboat; as it happened no boat was to start for three or four days; for two days she shut herself up in a room, lay on a bed, and refused to eat or drink, because it was my food she would have to eat. . . .'[2]

[28 February 1839]
Dear E, – I can not give way to the bitter impatience I feel at my present position, and come back to the North without leaving my babies; and though I suppose their stay will not in any case be much prolonged in these regions of swamp and slavery, I must, for their sakes, remain where they are, and learn this dreary lesson of human suffering to the end. The record, it seems to me, must be utterly wearisome to you, as the instances themselves, I suppose, in a given time (thanks to that dreadful reconciler to all that is evil – habit), would become to me.

This morning I had a visit from two of the women, Charlotte and Judy, who came to me for help and advice for a complaint, which it really seems to me every other woman on the estate is cursed with, and which is a direct result of the conditions of their existence. The practice of sending women to labour in the fields in the third week after their confinement is a specific for causing this infirmity, and I know no specific for curing it under these circumstances.

As soon as these poor things had departed with such comfort as I could give them, and the bandages they especially begged for, three other sable graces introduced themselves, Edie, Louisa, and Diana. The former told me she had had a family of seven children, but had lost them all through 'ill luck,' as she denominated the ignorance and ill treatment which were answerable for the loss of these, as of so many other poor little creatures their fellows.

Having dismissed her and Diana with the sugar and rice they came to beg, I detained Louisa, whom I had never seen but in the presence of her old grandmother, whose version of the poor child's escape to, and hiding in the woods, I had a desire to compare with the heroine's own story. She told it very simply, and it was most pathetic.

She had not finished her task one day, when she said she felt ill, and unable to do so, and had been severely flogged by Driver Bran, in whose 'gang' she then was. The next day, in spite of this encouragement to labour, she had again been unable to complete her appointed work; and Bran having told her that he'd tie her up and flog her if she did not get it done, she had left the field and run into the swamp.

'Tie you up, Louisa!' said I. 'What is that?'

She then described to me that they were fastened up by their wrists to a beam or a branch of a tree, their feet barely touching the ground, so as to allow them no purchase for resistance or evasion of the lash, their clothes turned over their heads, and their backs scored with a leather thong, either by the driver himself, or, if he pleases to inflict their punishment by deputy, any of the men he may choose to summon to the office; it might be father, brother, husband, or lover, if the overseer so ordered it.

I turned sick, and my blood curdled listening to these details from the slender young slip of a lassie, with her poor piteous face and murmuring, pleading voice.

'Oh,' said I, 'Louisa; but the rattlesnakes – the dreadful rattlesnakes in the swamps; were you not afraid of those horrible creatures?'

'Oh, missis,' said the poor child, 'me no tink of dem; me forget all 'bout dem for de fretting.'

'Why did you come home at last?'

'Oh, missis, me starve with hunger, me most dead with hunger before me come back.'

'And were you flogged, Louisa?' said I, with a shudder at what the answer might be.

'No, missis, me go to hospital; me almost dead and sick so long, 'spec Driver Bran him forgot 'bout de flogging.'

I am getting perfectly savage over all these doings, E, and really think I should consider my own throat and those of my children well cut if some night the people were to take it into their heads to clear off scores in that fashion. . . .

1 March – 17 April 1839

Friday [1 March 1839]

Last night, after writing so much to you, I felt weary, and went out into the air to refresh my spirit. . . .

I have not felt well, and have been much depressed for some days past. I think I should die if I had to live here.

This morning, in order not to die yet, I thought I had better take a ride, and accordingly mounted the horse which I told you was one of the equestrian alternatives offered me here; but no sooner did he feel my weight, which, after all, is mere levity and frivolity to him, than he thought proper to rebel, and find the grasshopper a burden, and rear and otherwise demonstrate his disgust.

I have not ridden for a long time now; but Montreal's opposition very presently aroused the Amazon which is both natural and acquired in me, and made him comprehend that, though I object to slaves, I expect obedient servants; which views of mine being imparted by a due administration of both spur and whip, attended with a judicious combination of coaxing pats on his great crested neck, and endearing commendations of his beauty, produced the desired effect. Montreal accepted me as inevitable, and carried me very wisely and well up the island to another of the slave settlements on the plantation, called Jones's Creek. . . .

On my return from my ride I had a visit from Captain Fraser,* the manager of a neighbouring plantation. . . .

Captain Fraser told me that at St Clair General Oglethorpe,† the good and brave English governor of the State of Georgia in its colonial days, had his residence, and that among the magnificent live oaks which surround the site of the former settlement, there was one especially venerable and picturesque, which in his recollection always went by the name of General Oglethorpe's Oak.

---

* Former Captain in the British Army.

† General James Edward Oglethorpe (1696–1785), soldier and philanthropist and founder of the state of Georgia.

If you remember the history of the colony under his benevolent rule, you must recollect how absolutely he and his friend and counsellor Wesley opposed the introduction of slavery in the colony. How wrathfully the old soldier's spirit ought to haunt these cotton-fields and rice-swamps of his old domain, with their population of wretched slaves!

I will ride to St Clair and see his oak; if I should see him, he can not have much to say to me on the subject that I should not cry amen to. . . .

[Saturday, 2 March 1839]

Yesterday evening I had a visit that made me very sorrowful, if any thing connected with these poor people can be called more especially sorrowful than their whole condition; but Mr Butler's declaration that he will receive no more statements of grievances or petitions for redress through me makes me as desirous now of shunning the vain appeals of these unfortunates as I used to be of receiving and listening to them. The imploring cry, 'Oh missis!' that greets me whichever way I turn, makes me long to stop my ears now; for what can I say or do any more for them?

The poor little favours – the rice, the sugar, the flannel – that they beg for with such eagerness, and receive with such exuberant gratitude, I can, it is true, supply, and words and looks of pity, and counsel of patience, and such instruction in womanly habits of decency and cleanliness as may enable them to better, in some degree, their own hard lot; but to the entreaty, 'Oh, missis, you speak to massa for us! Oh, missis, you beg massa for us! Oh, missis, you tell massa for we, he sure do as you say!' I can not now answer as formerly, and I turn away choking and with eyes full of tears from the poor creatures, not even daring to promise any more the faithful transmission of their prayers. . . .

This settlement at St Annie's is the remotest on the whole plantation, and I found there the wretchedest huts, and most miserably squalid, filthy, and forlorn creatures I had yet seen here – certainly the condition of the slaves on this estate is infinitely more neglected and deplorable than that on the rice plantation.

Perhaps it may be that the extremely unhealthy nature of the rice cultivation makes it absolutely necessary that the physical condition of the labourers should be maintained at its best to enable them to abide it; and yet it seems to me that even the process of soaking the rice can hardly create a more dangerous miasma than the poor creatures must inhale who live in the midst of these sweltering swamps, half sea, half river slime.

Perhaps it has something to do with the fact that the climate on St Simon's is generally considered peculiarly mild and favourable, and so less protection of clothes and shelter is thought necessary here for the poor residents; perhaps, too, it may be because the cotton crop is now, I believe, hardly as valuable as the rice crop, and the plantation here, which was once the chief source of its owner's wealth, is becoming a secondary one, and so not worth so much care or expense in repairing and constructing negro huts and feeding and clothing the slaves. More pitiable objects than some of those I saw at the St Annie's settlement today I hope never to see. . . .

After reaching home I went to the house of the overseer to see his wife, a tidy, decent, kind-hearted little woman, who seems to me to do her duty by the poor people she lives among as well as her limited intelligence and still more limited freedom allow.

The house her husband lives in is the former residence of Major Butler, which was the great mansion of the estate. It is now in a most ruinous and tottering condition, and they inhabit but a few rooms in it. The others are gradually mouldering to pieces, and the whole edifice will, I should think, hardly stand long enough to be carried away by the river, which in its yearly inroads on the bank on which it stands has already approached within a perilous proximity to the old dilapidated planter's palace.

Old Molly, of whom I have often before spoken to you, who lived here in the days of the prosperity and grandeur of 'Hampton', still clings to the relics of her old master's former magnificence, and with a pride worthy of old Caleb of Ravenswood* showed me through the dismantled decaying rooms and over the remains of the dairy, displaying a capacious fish-box or well, where, in the good old days, the master's supply was kept in fresh salt water till required for table.

Her prideful lamentations over the departure of all this quondam glory were ludicrous and pathetic; but, while listening with some amusement to the jumble of grotesque descriptions, through which her impressions of the immeasurable grandeur and

---

* A character in Sir Walter Scott's *Bride of Lammermoor*.

nobility of the house she served was the predominant feature, I could not help contrasting the present state of the estate with that which she described, and wondering why it should have become, as it undoubtedly must have done, so infinitely less productive a property than in the old major's time.

Before closing this letter, I have a mind to transcribe to you the entries for to-day recorded in a sort of day-book, where I put down very succinctly the number of people who visit me, their petitions and ailments, and also such special particulars concerning them as seem to me worth recording. . . .

Fanny has had six children; all dead but one. She came to beg to have her work in the field lightened.

Nanny has had three children; two of them are dead. She came to implore that the rule of sending them into the field three weeks after their confinement might be altered.

Leah, Caesar's wife, has had six children; three are dead.

Sophy, Lewis's wife, came to beg for some old linen. She is suffering fearfully; has had ten children; five of them are dead. The principal favour she asked was a piece of meat, which I gave her.

Sally, Scipio's wife, has had two miscarriages and three children born, one of whom is dead. She came complaining of incessant pain and weakness in her back. This woman was a mulatto daughter of a slave called Sophy, by a white man of the name of Walker, who visited the plantation.

Charlotte, Renty's wife, had had two miscarriages, and was with child again. She was almost crippled with rheumatism, and showed me a pair of poor swollen knees that made my heart ache. I have promised her a pair of flannel trowsers, which I must forthwith set about making.

Sarah, Stephen's wife – this woman's case and history were alike deplorable. She had had four miscarriages, had brought seven children into the world, five of whom were dead, and was again with child. She complained of dreadful pains in the back, and an internal tumour which swells with the exertion of working in the fields; probably, I think, she is ruptured. She told me she had once been mad and had ran into the woods, where she contrived to elude discovery for some time, but was at last tracked and brought back, when she was tied up by the arms, and heavy logs fastened to her feet, and was severely flogged. . . .

This is only the entry for to-day, in my diary, of the people's complaints and visits. Can you conceive a more wretched picture than that which it exhibits of the conditions under which these women live?

[3 March 1839]

Dearest E, – When I told you in my last letter of the encroachments which the waters of the Altamaha are daily making on the bank at Hampton Point and immediately in front of the imposing-looking old dwelling of the former master, I had no idea how rapid this crumbling process has been of late years. . . . Within the memory of the slaves now living on the plantation, a grove of orange-trees had spread its fragrance and beauty between the house and the river . . . and just covered by the turbid waters of the in-rushing tide, were the heads of the poor drowned orange-trees, swaying like black twigs in the briny flood, which had not yet dislodged all of them from their hold upon the soil which had gone down beneath the water wearing its garland of bridal blossom.

As I looked at those trees a wild wish rose in my heart that the river and the sea would swallow up and melt in their salt waves the whole of this accursed property of ours. I am afraid the horror of slavery with which I came down to the South, the general theoretic abhorrence of an Englishwoman for it, has gained, through the intensity it has acquired, a morbid character of mere desire to be delivered from my own share in it.

I think so much of these wretches that I see, that I can hardly remember any others; and my zeal for the general emancipation of the slave has almost narrowed itself to this most painful desire that I and mine were freed from the responsibility of our share in this huge misery; and so I thought, 'Beat, beat, the crumbling banks and sliding shores, wild waves of the Atlantic and the Altamaha! Sweep down and carry hence this evil earth and these homes of tyranny, and roll above the soil of slavery, and wash my soul and the souls of those I love clean from the blood of our kind!' . . .

How I do defy you to guess the novel accomplishment I have developed within the last two days; what do you say to my turning butcher's boy, and cutting up the carcase of a sheep for the instruction of our butcher and cook, and benefit of our table?

You know, I have often written you word that we have mutton here – thanks to the short salt grass on which it feeds –that compares with the best South Down or *Prè salé*; but such is the barbarous ignorance of the cook, or rather the butcher who furnishes our kitchen supplies, that I defy the most expert anatomist to pronounce on any piece (joints they can not be called) of mutton brought to our table to what part of the animal sheep it originally belonged. . . .

. . . So the day before yesterday, while I was painfully dragging Sally through the early intellectual science of the alphabet and first reading lesson, Abraham appeared at the door of the room brandishing a very long thin knife, and with many bows, grins, and apologies for disturbing me, begged that I would go and cut up a sheep for him. My first impulse, of course, was to decline the very unusual task offered me with mingled horror and amusement. Abraham, however, insisted and besought, extolled the fineness of his sheep, declared his misery at being unable to cut it as I wished, and his readiness to conform for the future to whatever patterns of mutton 'de missis would only please to give him'. . . .

So I followed Abraham to the kitchen, when, with a towel closely pinned over my silk dress, and knife in hand, I stood for a minute or two meditating profoundly before the rather unsightly object which Abraham had pronounced 'de beautifullest sheep de missis eber saw'.

The sight and smell of raw meat are especially odious to me, and I have often thought that if I had had to be my own cook, I should inevitably become a vegetarian, probably, indeed, return entirely to my green and salad days. Nathless, I screwed my courage to the sticking-point, and slowly and delicately traced out with the point of my long carving-knife two shoulders, two legs, a saddle, and a neck of mutton; not probably in the most thoroughly artistic and butcherly style, but as nearly as my memory and the unassisted light of nature would enable me. And having instructed Abraham in the various boundaries, sizes, shapes, and names of the several joints, I returned to Sally and her *belles-lettres*, rather elated, upon the whole, at the creditable mode in which I flattered myself I had accomplished my unusual task, and the hope of once more seeing roast mutton of my acquaintance. . . .

[4 March 1839]

My Dearest E, – I have had an uninterrupted stream of women and children flowing in the whole morning to say 'Ha de, missis?' Among others, a poor woman called Mile, who could hardly stand for pain and swelling in her limbs; she had had fifteen children and two miscarriages; nine of her children had died; for the last three years she had become almost a cripple with chronic rheumatism, yet she is driven every day to work in the field.

She held my hands, and stroked them in the most appealing way while she exclaimed, 'Oh my missis! My missis! Me neber sleep till day for de pain,' and with the day her labour must again be resumed.

I gave her flannel and sal volatile to rub her poor swelled limbs with; rest I could not give her – rest from her labour and her pain – this mother of fifteen children.

Another of my visitors had a still more dismal story to tell. Her name was Die. She had had sixteen children, fourteen of whom were dead. She had had four miscarriages. One had been caused with falling down with a very heavy burden on her head, and one from having her arms strained up to be lashed.

I asked her what she meant by having her arms tied up. She said their hands were first tied together, sometimes by the wrists, and sometimes, which was worse, by the thumbs, and they were then drawn up to a tree or post, so as almost to swing them off the ground, and then their clothes rolled round their waist, and a man with a cowhide stands and stripes them.

I give you the woman's words. She did not speak of this as of any thing strange, unusual, or especially horrid and abominable; and when I said, 'Did they do that to you when you were with child?' she simply replied, 'Yes, missis.'

And to all this I listen – I, an English woman, the wife of the man who owns these wretches, and I can not say, 'That thing shall not be done again; that cruel shame and villainy shall never be known here again.'

I gave the woman meat and flannel, which were what she came to ask for, and remained choking with indignation and grief long after they had all left me to my most bitter thoughts. . . .

[c. 5 March 1839]

Dearest E, – I have found growing along the edge of the dreary inclosure where the slaves are buried such a lovely wild flower. It is a little like the euphrasia or eyebright of the English meadows, but grows quite close to the turf, almost into it, and consists of clusters of tiny white flowers that look as if they were made of the finest porcelain. I took up a root of it yesterday, with a sort of vague idea that I could transplant it to the North; though I can not say that I should care to transplant any thing thither that could renew to me the associations of this place – not even the delicious wild flowers, if I could. . . .

I have let my letter lie since the day before yesterday, dear E, having had no leisure to finish it. Yesterday morning I rode out to St Clair's, where there used formerly to be another negro settlement, and another house of Major Butler's.

I had been persuaded to try one of the mares I had formerly told you of, and to be sure a more 'curst' quadruped, and one more worthy of a Petruchio* for a rider I did never back. Her temper was furious, her gait intolerable, her mouth the most obdurate that ever tugged against bit and bridle. It is not wise any where, here it is less wise than any where else in the world – to say, '*Jamais de cette eau je ne boirai;*' but I think I will never ride that delightful creature Miss Kate again. . . .

Not far from the house, as I was cantering home, I met Sally, and took her up on the saddle before me, an operation which seemed to please her better than the vicious horse I was riding, whose various demonstrations of dislike to the arrangement afforded my small equestrian extreme delight and triumph.

My whole afternoon was spent in shifting my bed and bedroom furniture from a room on the ground floor to one above; in the course of which operation a brisk discussion took place between Margery and my boy Jack, who was nailing on the vallence of the bed, and whom I suddenly heard exclaim, in answer to something she had said, 'Well, den, I do think so; and dat's the speech of a man, whether um bond or free.'

A very trifling incident, and insignificant speech; and yet it came back to my ears very often afterward – 'the speech of a man, whether bond or free'.

They might be made conscious – some of them are evidently conscious – of an inherent element of manhood superior to the

* The hero of William Shakespeare's *The Taming of the Shrew.*

bitter accident of slavery, and to which, even in their degraded condition, they might be made to refer that vital self-respect which can survive all external pressure of mere circumstance, and give their souls to that service of God, which is perfect freedom, in spite of the ignoble and cruel bondage of their bodies.

My new apartment is what I should call decidedly airy; the window, unless when styled by courtesy shut, which means admitting of draught enough to blow a candle out, must be wide open, being incapable of any intermediate condition. The latch of the door, to speak the literal truth, does shut; but it is the only part of it that does – that is, the latch and the hinges; every where else its configuration is traced by a distinct line of light and air.

If what old Dr Physic used to say be true, that a draught which will not blow out a candle will blow out a man's life (a Spanish proverb originally I believe), my life is threatened with extinction in almost every part of this new room of mine, wherein, moreover, I now discover to my dismay, having transported every other article of bedroom furniture to it, it is impossible to introduce the wardrobe for my clothes. Well, our stay here is drawing to a close, and therefore these small items of discomfort can not afflict me much longer. . . .

[8 March 1839]
In the afternoon I made my first visit to the hospital of the estate, and found it, as indeed I find every thing else here, in a far worse state even than the wretched establishments on the rice-island, dignified by that name. So miserable a place for the purpose to which it was dedicated I could not have imagined on a property belonging to Christian owners.

The floor (which was not boarded, but merely the damp hard earth itself) was strewn with wretched women, who, but for their moans of pain, and uneasy, restless motions, might very well each have been taken for a mere heap of filthy rags. The chimney refusing passage to the smoke from the pine-wood fire, it puffed out in clouds through the room, where it circled and hung, only gradually oozing away through the windows, which were so far well adapted to the purpose that there was not a single whole pane of glass in them. My eyes, unaccustomed to the turbid atmosphere, smarted and watered, and refused to distinguish at first the different dismal forms, from which cries and wails assailed me in every corner of the place.

By degrees I was able to endure for a few minutes what they were condemned to live their hours and days of suffering and sickness through; and, having given what comfort kind words and promises of help in more substantial forms could convey, I went on to what seemed a yet more wretched abode of wretchedness.

This was a room where there was no fire because there was no chimney, and where the holes made for windows had no panes or glasses in them. The shutters being closed, the place was so dark that, on first entering it, I was afraid to stir lest I should fall over some of the deplorable creatures extended upon the floor.

As soon as they perceived me, one cry of 'Oh missis!' rang through the darkness; and it really seemed to me as if I was never to exhaust the pity, and amazement, and disgust which this receptacle of suffering humanity was to excite in me. The poor dingy supplicating sleepers upraised themselves as I cautiously advanced among them; those who could not rear their bodies from the earth held up piteous beseeching hands, and as I passed from one to the other I felt more than one imploring clasp laid upon my dress, to solicit my attention to some new form of misery.

One poor woman, called Tressa, who was unable to speak above a whisper from utter weakness and exhaustion, told me she had had nine children, was suffering from incessant flooding, and felt 'as if her back would split open.' There she lay, a mass of filthy tatters, without so much as a blanket under her or over her, on the bare earth in this chilly darkness.

I promised them help and comfort, beds and blankets, and light and fire – that is, I promised to ask Mr Butler for all this for them; and, in the very act of doing so, I remembered with a sudden pang of anguish that I was to urge no more petitions for his slaves to their master.

I groped my way out, and emerging on the piazza, all the choking tears and sobs I had controlled broke forth, and I leaned there crying over the lot of these unfortunates till I heard a feeble voice of 'Missis, you no cry; missis, what for you cry?' and, looking up saw that I had not yet done with this intolerable infliction.

A poor crippled old man, lying in the corner of the piazza, unable even to crawl toward me, had uttered this word of consolation, and by his side (apparently too idiotic, as he was too impotent, to move) sat a young woman, the expression of whose face was the most suffering, and, at the same time, the most horribly repulsive I ever saw.

I found she was, as I supposed, half-witted; and, on coming nearer to inquire into her ailments and what I could do for her, found her suffering from that horrible disease – I believe some form of scrofula – to which the negroes are subject, which attacks and eats away the joints of their hands and fingers – a more hideous and loathsome object I never beheld; her name was Patty, and she was granddaughter to the old crippled creature by whose side she was squatting. . . .

[16 March 1839]

Dear E, – This letter has remained unfinished, and my journal interrupted for more than a week. Mr Butler has been quite unwell, and I have been travelling to and fro daily between Hampton and the rice-island in the long-boat to visit him; for the last three days I have remained at the latter place, and only returned here this morning early.

My daily voyages up and down the river have introduced me to a great variety of new musical performances of our boatmen, who invariably, when the rowing is not too hard, moving up or down with the tide, accompany the stroke of their oars with the sound of their voices. . . . With a very little skilful adaptation and instrumentation, I think one or two barbaric chants and choruses might be evoked from them that would make the fortune of an opera. . . .

You can not think . . . how strange some of their words are: in one, they repeatedly chanted the 'sentiment' that 'God made man, and man makes' – what do you think? – 'money!' Is not that a peculiar poetical proposition? Another ditty to which they frequently treat me they call Caesar's song; it is an extremely spirited war-song, beginning 'The trumpets blow, the bugles sound – Oh, stand your ground!'

It has puzzled me not a little to determine in my own mind whether this title of Caesar's song has any reference to the great Julius, and if so, what may be the negro notion of him, and whence and how derived.

One of their songs displeased me not a little, for it embodied the opinion that 'twenty-six black girls not make mulatto yellow girl'; and as I told them I did not like it, they have omitted it since.

This desperate tendency to despise and undervalue their own race and colour, which is one of the very worst results of their abject condition, is intolerable to me. . . .

I have now to tell you of my hallowing last Sunday by gathering a congregation of the people into my big sitting-room, and reading prayers to them. I had been wishing very much to do this for some time past, and obtained Mr Butler's leave while I was with him at the rice-island, and it was a great pleasure to me. . . .

I was very anxious that it should not be thought that I ordered any of the people to come to prayers, as I particularly desired to see if they themselves felt the want of any Sabbath service, and would of their own accord join in any such ceremony; I therefore merely told the house servants that if they would come to the sitting-room at eleven o'clock, I would read prayers to them, and that they might tell any of their friends or any of the people that I should be very glad to see them if they liked to come. Accordingly, most of those who live at the Point, i.e., in the immediate neighbourhood of the house, came, and it was encouraging to see the very decided efforts at cleanliness and decorum of attire which they had all made.

I was very much affected and impressed myself by what I was doing, and I suppose must have communicated some of my own feeling to those who heard me. It is an extremely solemn thing to me to read the Scriptures aloud to any one, and there was something in my relation to the poor people by whom I was surrounded that touched me so deeply while thus attempting to share with them the best of my possessions, that I found it difficult to command my voice, and had to stop several times in order to do so.

When I had done, they all with one accord uttered the simple words, 'We thank you, missis,' and instead of overwhelming me as usual with petitions and complaints, they rose silently and quietly, in a manner that would have become the most orderly of Christian congregations accustomed to all the impressive decorum of civilized church privileges. . . .

I have resumed my explorations in the woods with renewed enthusiasm, for during my week's absence they have become more lovely and enticing than ever: unluckily, however, Jack seems to think that fresh rattlesnakes have budded together with the tender spring foliage, and I see that I shall either have to give up my wood walks and rides, or go without a guide.

Lovely blossoms are springing up every where – weeds, of course, wild things, impertinently so called. Nothing is cultivated here but cotton; but in some of the cotton-fields beautiful creatures are peeping into blossom, which I suppose will all be duly hoed off the surface of the soil in proper season. Meantime I rejoice in them, and in the splendid, magnificent thistles, which would be in flower-gardens in other parts of the world, and in the wonderful, strange, beautiful butterflies that seem to me almost as big as birds, that go zigzagging in the sun. I saw yesterday a lovely monster, who thought proper, for my greater delectation, to alight on a thistle I was admiring, and as the flower was purple, and he was all black velvet fringed with gold, I was exceedingly pleased with his good inspiration. . . .

[17–22 March 1839]
My letter has been lying unfinished for the last three days. I have been extraordinarily busy, having emancipated myself from the trammels of Jack and all his terror, and as I fear no serpents on horseback, have been daily riding through new patches of woodland without any guide, taking my chance of what I might come to in the shape of impediments.

Last Tuesday I rode through a whole wood of burned and charred trees, cypresses and oaks, that looked as if they had been each of them blasted by a special thunderbolt, and whole thickets of young trees and shrubs perfectly black and brittle from the effect of fire, I suppose the result of some carelessness of the slaves.

As this charcoal woodland extended for some distance, I turned out of it, and round the main road through the plantation, as I could not ride through the blackened boughs and branches without getting begrimed. It had a strange, wild, desolate effect, not without a certain gloomy picturesqueness. . . .

After my return home I had my usual evening reception, and, among other pleasant incidents of plantation life, heard the following agreeable anecdote from a woman named Sophy, who came to beg for some rice.

In asking her about her husband and children, she said she had never had any husband; that she had had two children by a white man of the name of Walker, who was employed at the mill on the rice-island. She was in the hospital after the birth of the second child she bore this man, and at the same time, two women, Judy and Sylla, of whose children Mr King was the father, were recovering from their confinements.

It was not a month since any of them had been delivered, when Mrs King came to the hospital, had them all three severely flogged, a process which she personally superintended, and then sent them to Five Pound – the swamp Botany Bay of the plantation, of which I have told you – with farther orders to the drivers to flog them every day for a week.

Now, E, if I make you sick with these disgusting stories, I can not help it; they are the life itself here. Hitherto I have thought these details intolerable enough, but this apparition of a female fiend in the middle of this hell I confess adds an element of cruelty which seems to me to surpass all the rest. Jealousy is not an uncommon quality in the feminine temperament; and just conceive the fate of these unfortunate women between the passions of their masters and mistresses, each alike armed with power to oppress and torture them.

Sophy went on to say that Isaac was her son by Driver Morris, who had forced her while she was in her miserable exile at Five Pound.

Almost beyond my patience with this string of detestable details, I exclaimed – foolishly enough, heaven knows – 'Ah! but don't you know – did nobody ever tell or teach any of you that it is a sin to live with men who are not your husbands?'

Alas! E, what could the poor creature answer but what she did, seizing me at the same time vehemently by the wrist: 'Oh yes, missis, we know – we know all about dat well enough; but we do any thing to get our poor flesh some rest from de whip; when he made me follow him into de bush, what use me tell him no? He have strength to make me.'

I have written down the woman's words; I wish I could write down the voice and look of abject misery with which they were spoken. . . .

It is Wednesday, the 20th of March; we can not stay here much longer; I wonder if I shall come back again! and whether, when I do, I shall find the trace of one idea of a better life left in these poor people's minds by my sojourn among them. . . .

I must tell you that I have been delighted, surprised, and the very least perplexed, by the sudden petition on the part of our young waiter, Aleck, that I will teach him to read. He is a very intelligent lad of about sixteen, and preferred his request with an urgent humility that was very touching. I told him I would think about it.

I mean to do it. I will do it; and yet, it is simply breaking the laws of the government under which I am living. Unrighteous laws are made to be broken – pehaps – but then, you see, I am a woman, and Mr Butler stands between me and the penalty. If I were a man, I would do that and many a thing besides, and doubtless should be shot some fine day from behind a tree by some good neighbour, who would do the community a service by quietly getting rid of a mischievous incendiary; . . .

I certainly intend to teach Aleck to read. I certainly won't tell Mr Butler any thing about it. I'll leave him to find it out. . . .

[24–28 March 1839]
In the afternoon I took a long walk with the chicks in the woods – long at least for the little legs of Sally and Margery, who carried baby.

We came home by the shore, and I stopped to look at a jutting point, just below which a sort of bay would have afforded the most capital position for a bathing-house. If we staid here late in the season, such a refreshment would become almost a necessary of life, and any where along the bank just where I stopped to examine it to-day an establishment for that purpose might be prosperously founded.

I am amused, but by no means pleased, at an entirely new mode of pronouncing which Sally has adopted. Apparently the negro jargon has commended itself as euphonious to her infantile ears, and she is now treating me to the most ludicrous and accurate imitations of it every time she opens her mouth.

Of course I shall not allow this, comical as it is, to become a habit. This is the way the Southern ladies acquire the thick and inelegant pronunciation which distinguishes their utterances from the Northern snuffle, and I have no desire that Sally should adorn her mother tongue with either peculiarity. . . .

The day before yesterday I took a disagreeable ride, all through swampy fields, and charred, blackened thickets, to discover nothing either picturesque or beautiful; the woods in one part of the plantation have been on fire for three days, and a whole tract of exquisite evergreens has been burnt down to the ground. . . .

183

I have been having a long talk with Mr Butler about Ben and Daphne, those two young mulatto children of Mr King's, whom I mentioned to you lately. Poor pretty children! they have refined and sensitive faces as well as straight, regular features; and the expression of the girl's countenance, as well as the sound of her voice, and the sad humility of her deportment, are indescribably touching.

Mr Butler expressed the strongest interest in and pity for them, *because of their colour*: it seems unjust almost to the rest of their fellow-unfortunates that this should be so, and yet it is almost impossible to resist the impression of the unfitness of these two forlorn young creatures for the life of coarse labour and dreadful degradation to which they are destined. In any of the Southern cities the girl would be pretty sure to be reserved for a worse fate; but even here, death seems to me a thousand times preferable to the life that is before her. . . .

[27 March 1839]

Last Wednesday we drove to Hamilton, by far the finest estate on St Simon's Island. The gentleman to whom it belongs lives, I believe, habitually in Paris; but Captain Frazer resides on it, and, I suppose, is the real overseer of the plantation.

All the way along the road (we traversed nearly the whole length of the island) we found great tracts of wood all burnt or burning. The destruction had spread in every direction, and against the sky we saw the slow rising of the smoky clouds that showed the pine forest to be on fire still. . . .

We found that there had been a most terrible fire in the Hamilton woods – more extensive than that on our own plantation. It seems as if the whole island had been burning at different points for more than a week.

What a cruel pity and shame it does seem to have these beautiful masses of wood so destroyed! I suppose it is impossible to prevent it. The 'field-hands' make fires to cook their midday food wherever they happen to be working, and sometimes through their careless neglect, but sometimes, too, undoubtedly on purpose, the woods are set fire to by these means.

One benefit they consider that they derive from the process is the destruction of the dreaded rattlesnakes that infest the woodland all over the island; but really the funeral pyre of these hateful reptiles is too costly at this price. . . .

We drove home by moonlight; and as we came toward the woods in the middle of the island, the fireflies glittered out from the dusky thickets as if some magical golden veil was every now and then shaken out into the darkness. The air was enchantingly mild and soft, and the whole way through the silvery night delightful. . . .

To-day . . . my visit to the Infirmary was marked by an event which has not occurred before – the death of one of the poor slaves while I was there.

I found, on entering the first ward – to use a most inapplicable term for the dark, filthy, forlorn room I have so christened – an old negro called Friday lying on the ground. I asked what ailed him, and was told he was dying. I approached him, and perceived, from the glazed eyes and the feeble rattling breath, that he was at the point of expiring.

His tattered shirt and trousers barely covered his poor body; his appearance was that of utter exhaustion from age and feebleness; he had nothing under him but a mere handful of straw that did not cover the earth he was stretched on; and under his head, by way of pillow for his dying agony, two or three rough sticks just raising his skull a few inches from the ground. The flies were all gathering around his mouth, and not a creature was near him.

There he lay – the worn-out slave, whose life had been spent in unrequited labour for me and mine, without one physical allevia-tion, one Christian solace, one human sympathy, to cheer him in his extremity – panting out the last breath of his wretched existence like some forsaken, overworked, wearied-out beast of burden, rotting where it falls!

I bent over the poor awful human creature in the supreme hour of his mortality; and while my eyes, blinded with tears of unavailing pity and horror, were fixed upon him, there was a sudden quivering of the eye-lids and falling of the jaw – and he was free. . . .

[1 April 1839]
I rode all through the burnt district and the bush to Mrs Wylly's field. . . .

A horrible quarrel has occurred quite lately upon the subject of the ownership of this very ground I was skirting, between Dr Hazzard and young Mr Wylly; they have challenged each other, and what I am going to tell you is a good sample of the sort of spirit which grows up among slave-holders. So read it, for it is curious to people who have not lived habitually among savages.

The terms of the challenge that has passed between them have appeared like a sort of advertisement in the local paper, and are to the effect that they are to fight at a certain distance with certain weapons – fire-arms, of course; that there is to be on the person of each a white paper, or mark, immediately over the region of the heart, as a point for direct aim; and whoever kills the other is to have the privilege of cutting off his head, and sticking it up on a pole on the piece of land which was the origin of the debate. So that, some fine day, I might have come hither as I did today, and found myself riding under the shadow of the gory locks of Dr Hazzard or Mr Wylly, my peaceful and pleasant neighbours. . . .

Yesterday, Sunday, I had my last service at home with these poor people; nearly thirty of them came, all clean, neat, and decent, in their dress and appearance.

Sally had begged very hard to join the congregation, and upon the most solemn promise of remaining still she was admitted; but, in spite of the perfect honour with which she kept her promise, her presence disturbed my thoughts not a little, and added much to the poignancy of the feeling with which I saw her father's poor slaves gathered round me. . . .

Dear E, bless God that you have never reared a child with such an awful expectation . . . at the end of the prayers, the tears were streaming over their faces, and one chorus of blessings rose round me and the child – farewell blessings, and prayers that we would return; and thanks so fervent in their incoherency, it was more than I could bear, and I begged them to go away and leave me to recover myself.

And there I remained with Sally, and for quite a long while even her restless spirit was still in wondering amazement at my bitter crying. I am to go next Sunday to the church on the island, where there is to be a service; and so this is my last Sunday with the people. . . .

[2–4 April 1839]
I must give you an account of Aleck's first reading lesson, which

took place at the same time that I gave Sally hers this morning. It was the first time he had had leisure to come, and it went off most successfully. He seems to me by no means stupid.

I am very sorry he did not ask me to do this before; however, if he can master his alphabet before I go, he may, if chance favour him with the occasional sight of a book, help himself on by degrees.

Perhaps he will have the good inspiration to apply to Cooper London for assistance; I am much mistaken if that worthy does not contrive that Heaven shall help Aleck, as it formerly did him, in the matter of reading. . . .

I must tell you of something which has delighted me greatly. I told Jack yesterday that, if any of the boys liked, when they had done their tasks, to come and clear the paths that I want widened and trimmed, I would pay them a certain small sum per hour for their labour. And behold, three boys have come, having done their tasks early in the afternoon, to apply for work and wages: so much for a suggestion not barely twenty-four hours old, and so much for a prospect of compensation! . . .

I have given Aleck a second reading lesson with Sally, who takes an extreme interest in his newly-acquired alphabetical lore. He is a very quick and attentive scholar, and I should think a very short time would suffice to teach him to read; but, alas! I have not even that short time.

When I had done with my class I rode off with Jack, who has become quite an expert horseman, and rejoices in being lifted out of the immediate region of snakes by the length of his horse's legs. I cantered through the new wood paths, and took a good sloping gallop through the pine land to St Annie's. The fire is actually still burning in the woods. I came home quite tired with the heat, though my ride was not a long one. . . .

I drove home, late in the afternoon, through the sweet-smelling woods, that are beginning to hum with the voice of thousands of insects.

My troop of volunteer workmen is increased to five – five lads working for my wages after they have done their task-work; and this evening, to my no small amazement, Driver Bran came down to join them for an hour, after working all day at Five Pound, which certainly shows zeal and energy.

Dear E, I have been riding through the woods all the morning with Jack, giving him directions about the clearings, which I have some faint hope may be allowed to continue after my departure.

I went on an exploring expedition round some distant fields, and then home through the St Annie's woods. They have almost stripped the trees and thickets along the swamp road since I first came here. I wonder what it is for; not fuel surely, nor to make grass-land of, or otherwise cultivate the swamp.

I do deplore these pitiless clearings; and as to this once pretty road, it looks 'forlorn,' as a worthy Pennsylvania farmer's wife once said to me of a pretty hill-side from which her husband had ruthlessly felled a beautiful grove of trees. . . .

I have spent the whole afternoon at home; my 'gang' is busily at work again. Sawney, one of them, came to join it nearly at sundown, not having got through his day's task before.

In watching and listening to these lads, I was constantly struck with the insolent tyranny of their demeanour toward each other. This is almost a universal characteristic of the manner of the negroes among themselves. They are diabolically cruel to animals too, and they seem to me, as a rule, hardly to know the difference between truth and falsehood.

These detestable qualities, which I constantly hear attributed to them as innate and inherent in their race, appear to me the direct result of their condition. The individual exceptions among them are, I think, quite as many as would be found, under similar circumstances, among the same number of white people. . . .

[5–7 April 1839]
Dear E, – This is the fourth day that I have had a 'gang' of lads working in the woods for me after their task hours for pay; you can not think how zealous and energetic they are; I dare say the novelty of the process pleases them almost as much as the money they earn. I must say they quite deserve their small wages. . . .

The day was exquisitely beautiful, and I explored a new wood path, and found it all strewed with a lovely wild flower not much unlike a primrose. I spent the afternoon at home. . . .

To-day, – Saturday – I took another ride of discovery round the fields by Jones's. I think I shall soon be able to survey this estate, I have ridden so carefully over it in every direction; but my rides are drawing to a close, and even were I to remain here this must be the case, unless I got up and rode under the stars in the cool of the night. . . .

To-day is Sunday, and I have been to the little church on the island. It is the second time since I came down to the South that I have been to a place of worship. A curious little incident prefaced my going thither this morning. I had desired Israel to get my horse ready and himself to accompany me, as I meant to ride to church; and you can not imagine any thing droller than his horror and dismay when he at length comprehended that my purpose was to attend divine service in my riding-habit.

I asked him what was the trouble; for, though I saw something was creating a dreadful convulsion in his mind, I had no idea what it was till he told me, adding that he had never seen such a thing on St Simon's in his life – as who should say, such a thing was never seen in Hyde Park or the Tuileries before. You may imagine my amusement; but presently I was destined to shock something much more serious than poor Israel's sense of *les convenances et bienséances*, and it was not without something of an effort that I made up my mind to do so.

I was standing at the open window speaking to him about the horses, and telling him to get ready to ride with me, when George, another of the men, went by with a shade or visor to his cap exactly the shape of the one I left behind at the North, and for want of which I have been suffering severely from the intense heat and glare of the sun for the last week. I asked him to hand me his cap, saying, 'I want to take the pattern of that shade.'

Israel exclaimed, 'Oh, missis, not to-day; let him leave the cap with you to-morrow, but don't cut pattern on de Sabbath day!'

It seemed to me a much more serious matter to offend this scruple than the prejudice with regard to praying in a riding-habit; still, it had to be done.

'Do you think it wrong, Israel,' said I, 'to work on Sunday?'

'Yes, missis, parson tell we so.'

'Then, Israel, be sure you never do it. Did your parson never tell you that your conscience was for yourself and not for your neighbours, Israel?'

'Oh yes, missis, he tell we that too.'

'Then mind that too, Israel.'

The shade was cut out and stitched upon my cap, and protected my eyes from the fierce glare of the sun and sand as I rode to church. . . .

[8–12 April 1839]
Dear E, – I still go on exploring, or rather surveying the estate, the aspect of which is changing every day with the unfolding of the leaves and the wonderful profusion of wild flowers. The cleared ground all round the new building is one sheet of blooming blue of various tints; it is perfectly exquisite. But in the midst of my delight at these new blossoms, I am most sorrowfully bidding adieu to that paragon of parasites, the yellow jasmine; I think I must have gathered the very last blossoms of it to-day. . . .

The men and women had done their work here by half past three. The chief labour in the cotton-fields, however, is both earlier and later in the season. At present they have little to do but let the crop grow.

In the evening I had a visit from the son of a very remarkable man, who had been one of the chief drivers on the estate in Major Butler's time, and his son brought me a silver cup which Major Butler had given his father as a testimonial of approbation, with an inscription on it recording his fidelity and trustworthiness at the time of the invasion of the coast of Georgia by the English troops. Was not that a curious reward for a slave who was supposed not to be able to read his own praises? And yet, from the honourable pride with which his son regarded this relic, I am sure the master did well so to reward his servant, though it seemed hard that the son of such a man should be a slave.

Maurice himself came with his father's precious silver cup in his hand, to beg for a small pittance of sugar, and for a Prayer-book, and also to know if the privilege of a milch cow for the support of his family, which was among the favours Major Butler allowed his father, might not be continued to him. He told me he had ten children 'working for massa', and I promised to mention his petition to Mr Butler.

Saturday, the 13th [April 1839]
Dear E, – I rode to-day through all my wood paths for the last time with Jack, and I think I should have felt quite melancholy at taking leave of them and him but for the apparition of a large black snake, which filled me with disgust and nipped my other sentiments in

the bud. Not a day passes now that I do not encounter one or more of these hateful reptiles; it is curious how much more odious they are to me than the alligators that haunt the mud banks of the river round the rice plantation. It is true that there is something very dreadful in the thickeless mass, uniform in colour almost to the black slime on which it lies basking, and which you hardly detect till it begins to move. But even those ungainly crocodiles never sickened me as those rapid, lithe, and sinuous serpents do.

Did I ever tell you that the people at the rice plantation caught a young alligator and brought it to the house, and it was kept for some time in a tub of water? It was an ill-tempered little monster; it used to set up its back like a cat when it was angry, and open its long jaws in a most vicious manner. . . .

Sunday, 14th [April 1839]

My dear E, – That horrid tragedy with which we have been threatened, and of which I was writing to you almost jestingly a few days ago, has been accomplished, and apparently without any thing but the most passing and superficial sensation in this community.

The duel between Dr Hazzard and Mr Wylly did not take place, but an accidental encounter in the hotel at Brunswick did, and the former shot the latter dead on the spot. He has been brought home and buried here by the little church close to his mother's plantation; and the murderer, if he is even prosecuted, runs no risk of finding a jury in the whole length and breadth of Georgia who could convict him of any thing. It is horrible. . . .

I stopped before going into church to look at the new grave that has taken its place among the defaced stones, all overgrown with briers, that lie round it. Poor young Wylly! Poor widowed mother, of whom he was the only son! What a savage horror! And no one seems to think any thing of it, more than of a matter of course. My devotions were any thing but satisfactory or refreshing to me. My mind was dwelling incessantly upon the new grave under the great oaks outside, and the miserable mother in her home.

The air of the church was perfectly thick with sand-flies; and the disgraceful carelessness of the congregation in responding and singing the hymns, and the entire neglect of the Prayer-book regulations for kneeling, disturbed and displeased me even more than the last time I was at church; but I think that was because of

191

the total absence of excitement or feeling among the whole population of St Simon's upon the subject of the bloody outrage with which my mind was full, which has given me a sensation of horror toward the whole community. . . .

I had service at home in the afternoon, and my congregation was much more crowded than usual; for I believe there is no doubt at last that we shall leave Georgia this week.

Having given way so much before when I thought I was praying with these poor people for the last time, I suppose I had, so to speak, expended my emotion, and I was much more composed and quiet than when I took leave of them before. But, to tell you the truth, this dreadful act of slaughter done in our neighbourhood by one man of our acquaintance upon another, impresses me to such a degree that I can hardly turn my mind from it, and Mrs Wylly and her poor young murdered son have taken almost complete possession of my thoughts.

After prayers I gave my poor people a parting admonition, and many charges to remember me and all I had tried to teach them during my stay. They promised with one voice to mind and do all that 'missis tell we;' and with many a parting benediction, and entreaties to me to return, they went their way.

I think I have done what I could for them – I think I have done as well as I could by them; but when the time comes for ending any human relation, who can be without their misgivings? Who can be bold to say, I could have done no more, I could have done no better? . . .

[17 April 1839]
Dear E, – We shall leave this place next Thursday or Friday [18 or 19 April] and there will be an end to this record; meantime I am fulfilling all sorts of last duties, and especially those of taking leave of my neighbours, by whom the neglect of a farewell visit would be taken much amiss. . . .

. . . On Sunday we rode out to a place called Frederica . . . How can I describe to you the exquisite spring beauty that is now adorning these woods, the variety of the fresh, new-born foliage, the fragrance of the sweet, wild perfumes that fill the air? Honeysuckles twine round every tree; the ground is covered with a low, white-blossomed shrub more fragrant than lilies of the valley. The accacnas are swinging their silver censers under the green roof of these wood temples; every stump is like a classical altar to the sylvan gods, garlanded with flowers; every post, or stick, or slight stem, like a Bacchante's thyrsus, twined with wreaths of ivy and wild vine waving in the tepid wind. Beautiful butterflies flicker like flying flowers among the bushes, and gorgeous birds, like winged jewels, dart from the boughs, and – and – a huge ground snake slid like a dark ribbon across the path while I was stopping to enjoy all this deliciousness, and so I became less enthusiastic, and cantered on past the little deserted church-yard, with the new-made grave beneath its grove of noble oaks. . . .

I rode today, after breakfast, to Mrs Anne Demere's, another of my neighbours, who lives full twelve miles off. During the last two miles of my expedition I had the white sand hillocks and blue line of the Atlantic in view.

The house at which I called was a tumble-down barrack of a dwelling in the woods, with a sort of poverty-stricken pretentious air about it, like sundry 'proud planters' dwellings that I have seen. I was received by the sons as well as the lady of the house, and could not but admire the lordly rather than manly indifference with which these young gentlemen, in gay guard-chains and fine attire, played the gallants to me, while filthy, barefooted, half-naked negro women brought in refreshments, and stood all the while fanning the cake, and sweetmeats, and their young masters, as if they had been all the same sort of stuff. I felt ashamed for the lads.

The conversation turned upon Dr Hazzard's trial; for there had been a trial as a matter of form, and an acquittal as a matter of course; and the gentlemen said, upon my expressing some surprise at the latter event, that there could not be found in all Georgia a jury who would convict him, which says but little for the moral sense of 'all Georgia.' . . . I took my leave and rode home.

I met my babies in the wood-wagon, and took Sally up before me, and gave her a good gallop home. Having reached the house with the appetite of a twenty-four miles' ride, I found no preparation for dinner, and not so much as a boiled potato to eat, and the sole reply to my famished and disconsolate exclamations was, 'Being that you order none, missis, I not know.' I had

* Fanny did not fill in this name.

forgotten to order my dinner, and my slaves, unauthorized, had not ventured to prepare any.

Wouldn't a Yankee have said, 'Wal, now, you went off so uncommon quick, I kinder guessed you forgot all about dinner,' and have had it all ready for me? But my slaves durst not, and so I fasted till some tea could be got for me.

This was the last letter I wrote from the plantation, and I never returned there, nor ever saw again any of the poor people among whom I lived during this winter but Jack, once, under sad circumstances. The poor lad's health failed so completely that his owners humanely brought him to the North, to try what benefit he might derive from the change; but this was before the passing of the Fugitive Slave Bill, when, touching the soil of the Northern states, a slave became free; and such was the apprehension felt lest Jack should be enlightened as to this fact by some philanthropic Abolitionist, that he was kept shut up in a high upper room of a large empty house, where even I was not allowed to visit him. I heard at length of his being in Philadelphia; and upon my distinct statement that I considered freeing their slaves the business of the Messrs Butler themselves, and not mine, I was at length permitted to see him. Poor fellow! Coming to the North did not prove to him the delight his eager desire had so often anticipated from it; nor, under such circumstances, is it perhaps much to be wondered at that he benefited but little by the change – he died not long after. . . .

5

The Road to Another Life

1839–49

They arrived home to face the slow but inexorable break-up of their marriage. For marriage, as then lived, had become highly toxic to Fanny.

Some time before, she had submitted there was no justice in the theory that one rational creature should be subservient to another. 'Dear Pierce,' she had asked, 'upon what ground should you exercise this control over me?'[1] Thereafter she made it a point of honour to resist his dominion and fight for what she termed 'an equal relationship'. Long before, she had even doubted that she should marry at all. For this she blamed her early life for allowing her sexual development, or what she more delicately termed 'the healthy affections', to starve and diminish in the interests of 'cultivation'. Certainly on her engagement to Pierce an old family friend had bluntly commented that although a 'perfect lady,' she was troublesome and self-willed, and he for one was sorry for her future husband. The adverse qualities he had attributed to her now came into play.

Her tragedy was that she was emotionally riven. While despising Pierce and his indolent life style, she was at the same time passionately attracted to him. In a letter to a friend she described this passion as 'violent', and had confided that marriage had in no way rendered it 'calmer'. Her sadly modern-seeming dilemma made it as impossible for her to leave as to stay with him, and she accordingly suffered a torment which Pierce was totally unable to comprehend. She nevertheless sought to enlighten him: 'We have intellects – and we have passions . . . as for retorting "What need of intellectual converse, have you not an affectionate husband and

195

two sweet babies?" you might as well say to a man, who told you he had no arms "Oh! no, but you have legs!" '[2]

Only a few weeks after their return from Georgia, Fanny was threatening to sail home to England on the *Great Western* and resume her stage career.

'You can never repair the injury you have done in marrying me,' she wrote, 'I will not remain here to be your housekeeper, your child's nurse, or what you make me [referring to their sex life] that is still more degrading and revolting.'[3] The letter was left on Pierce's pillow.

He had by now confided to their friends, the Sedgwicks, that he feared she was going mad. '. . . Deep, true free and well tried love . . . caused us to marry,' he wrote, 'yet her life is passed in constant tears.'[4] It wasn't long before Fanny's tantrums coupled with a severe attack of rheumatism drove him to recuperate at a West Virginian spa, after which he trundled down to Georgia, leaving Fanny at Butler Place. Here Fanny solaced herself teaching little Sally her letters and reading Gibbon's *Decline and Fall*, 'sliding through my days in a state of external quietude', as she expressed it.

Sidney George Fisher, a Philadelphian, was to glimpse her at this time '. . . on horseback and alone. She is very independent and rides about constantly unattended. . . . Never saw her look so well.' He then went on to describe her costume, surely a clear expression of the fascinatingly androgynous side of her nature. 'Her costume was becoming and peculiar. A green cloth riding habit with rolling collar and open in front, under it a *man's* waistcoat with yellow and gilt buttons, a calico shirt collar and breast, blue striped and turned over, and a black silk cravat tied sailor fashion, with a man's hat and veil . . . mounted on a beautiful horse highly groomed. . . .'[5]

It was about now that her friend, Elizabeth Sedgwick, probably hoping to effect a reconciliation, showed Fanny some of the unhappy letters she had been receiving from Pierce. Appalled, Fanny for a moment surfaced from her well of self-absorption: '. . . forgive me my dearest, dearest Pierce if I have so bitterly cursed your existence,'[6] she managed to get down before she went blind with crying. Thoughts of travelling to Georgia to be with him raced through her head, but these were hastily scotched by John Butler who saw her only as a source of distress to herself, an annoyance to others, and a danger, moreover, to the property.

By the winter of 1840 the relationship seems to have marginally improved, for when news came through of the illness of Fanny's father they managed to agree sufficiently to pack up and sail for England, the first crossing, as it happened, taken under steam.

They were to remain in England for nearly three years. Fanny's former success had not been forgotten, and there opened before them a brilliant social prospect, which was to impress even the torpid Pierce. Before long the house they had rented off Piccadilly was opening its doors to the Egertons, Normanbys, Ellesmeres, Wiltons – 'nothing under the rank of a viscount . . .' They attended the magnificent ball given by the Duke of Wellington for the King of Prussia, and both were presented at Court, Fanny in a new gown and £700 worth of hired diamonds.

'I kissed a soft white hand, which I believe was hers. I saw a pair of very handsome legs in white silk stockings . . . which I am convinced were not hers . . .'[7]

That autumn Pierce and Fanny made plans to join her sister Adelaide who was in Germany on a concert tour with Liszt. The party met at Frankfurt and continued up the Rhine together, but the heavy German cuisine upset Pierce's stomach, and he and Fanny bickered for most of the trip.

The following spring they clashed again on familiar ground. *Bentley's Miscellany* had written to Fanny asking if they might publish excerpts from her *Georgian Journal*. This Pierce had expressly forbidden. But although declining to let them have descriptions of life on the plantation, Fanny did permit them to publish her account of the hazardous journey from Philadelphia to Georgia. For this she received thirty guineas. Pierce was furious at what he considered both a defiant breach of their privacy, and treacherous involvement in the Abolitionist issue. To anticipate further disclosures he began reading her private correspondence, and finally suppressed it. Fanny found him out, was outraged, and instantly got on a train to Liverpool with the intention of absconding – this time to America. Pierce followed hotfoot and just managed to dissuade her – but only for the time being. That summer she ran away, and returned – twice. When not bolting, letters of a somewhat histrionic nature passed regularly between them.

Her unhappy situation had by now become very public. 'She has discovered that she has married a weak, dawdling, ignorant, violent-tempered man, who is utterly unsuited to her,' wrote Charles Greville (the diarist), 'she is aware that she has outlived his liking, as he has outlived her esteem and respect. . . . The consequence is she is supremely and hopelessly wretched!'[8]

Yet the flame of their unhappy attraction was still not wholly snuffed. Following yet another impetuous bolt on Fanny's part, this time from the Clarendon Hotel at midnight, they were reported living together once more. Perhaps by way of celebration, they threw an enormous farewell party in mid-April, on the eve of their departure for the States, and during which police had to be summoned to restrain the enthusiastic crowds. More significant for Fanny's future, however, was one of the last parties they attended before leaving England, at which, for the first time, she read aloud from Shakespeare's *Much Ado About Nothing*, to entertain her fellow guests. It was an unqualified success, and a pointer for the years ahead. By early summer of 1843 they were once more back in the States.

The next two years were to be entirely taken up with painful, and curiously modern wrangles as to whether or not they should separate, and in the ensuing dramas it is impossible to decide which party was the more foolish, though Fanny had both the insight and the grace to comment 'my trials are what they are because of what I am.'[9] Pierce exhibited no such insight, and though he had been undeniably tried, that fatal friend of his, Henry Berkeley, who had been the cause of their meeting at all, had this to say of him: 'but he is mad. I do not use the word in any but its literal sense. I have known him ever since he was eighteen intimately, and I know he is mad!'[10]

There were now furious claims and counter claims of irreparable injury. Pierce was surprised, perhaps understandably, philandering. A duel was fought between Pierce and the wronged husband, 'each fired twice', it was reported, but fortunately 'all shots missed', after which Fanny decided they must part for ever.

When the time came this was found to be impossible. There followed a fatuous arrangement, in lieu of separation, whereby they would live under one roof for the sake of the children, but as separate individuals, and Fanny would abide by the terms of the contract that Pierce would draw up. And here one begins to understand the assertions of Henry Berkeley. The terms were little more than a recapitulation, with savage prohibitions, of former grievances. Fanny was to receive no letters from outside, was to publish nothing without Pierce's consent, have nothing to do with the cause of Abolition, never even mention going on the stage again. Desperate not to be parted from her children, Fanny unwisely signed, and went to live with Pierce and the girls at Miss McPherson's depressing lodging house.

For a time they soldiered on, communicating only by scribbled notes, eating their glum meals in total silence, Fanny under virtual house arrest. Then the prohibitions became progressively wilder. Fanny was to have 'nothing to say or do' with Sally, the eldest child, finally it was not long before both children were to be removed altogether from her tainting presence.

At this Fanny snapped. She had no money, but managed to borrow the requisite sum from a friend. On 16 October 1845 she did her final bolt, and sailed for England. At Liverpool she was met by the devoted Harriet St Leger.

There lay ahead what Fanny was to call 'her year of consolation.' This was spent with Adelaide, who was now living in Italy. In heightened mood Fanny would attend the Roman Carnival, returning home with her stays full of confetti, and in calmer frame evoke the white oxen of the *campagna*, near Frascati, slowly winding their way through the arched gate of the farmyard, and how, 'leaning their serious-looking heads upon the stone basin', they soberly drank, their eyes fixed on her.

By December she had sufficiently recovered her strength to return to England, and by the following February of 1847 she was acting once more. It was her first appearance for thirteen years, and the play was *The Hunchback* in Manchester.

Her new audience saw 'a quiet unassuming lady of middle age, with pale classic features dominated by a pair of dark lustrous eyes which wore an eerie expression – imperious one moment, pleading the next . . .'[11]

Imperious she still was. Not long after *The Hunchback*, surgical treatment for piles became necessary. The suggestion that she should have an anaesthetic for the exceedingly painful operation was regally brushed aside.

'Though torture is a serious thing,' she told her medical advisers, 'to lose all self government is a still more serious thing, and I would rather know what I suffer than not to know what I was saying or doing.'[12] It was perhaps a significant comment, hinting at concealed sexual fears or possible guilt.

But confidence had returned. Fanny was now receiving £54 a performance, sufficient not only to put money aside to build a home of her own, but to lend to her soldier brother. Offers of work were coming in from New York, and at home she was invited to play opposite Macready, by now the most popular actor in England.

This, with some foreboding, she accepted. Actors' eyes had been all but gouged out, others nearly throttled during his furious fighting in *Macbeth*, while actresses' arms had been in danger of being wrenched from their sockets as a consequence of his passionate love-making. Given she was to play Desdemona to his Othello, Fanny had grounds for her fears, and considered herself fortunate to escape with only a fractured little finger. To make matters worse, the two were incompatible: Fanny complained that 'he growls and prowls and roams and foams about the stage',[13] while Macready found her as an actress '. . . so bad, so unnatural, so affected and conceited . . .'[14] But Rachel, the great French actress, commented of Fanny's work at this time, 'Ah, bien, bien, tres bien. . .' and stage hands everywhere tended to burst into tears with emotion at her presentations.

Fanny herself continued to protest her loathing of the stage. 'The sound of the applause sets my teeth on edge,' she complained, and went on to grumble, 'Plasterboard and paint, for the thick breathing orange groves of the south; green silk and oiled parchment for the solemn splendour of her moon at night . . .'[15]

Meanwhile, back in the States, Pierce had been working out a strategy for divorce, and on 29 March 1848, filed his application on the grounds of Fanny's desertion of him and their family.

As Pierce intended, Fanny was caught on the wrong foot. She had as yet only managed to save £1,500; she received Pierce's legal summons a month late and so had little time to prepare a defence. 'I shall come however,' she promised 'at the appointed time and go thro' this ordeal with what courage and patience I may say.'[16]

The divorce, when it came, was all that could be expected – a portentous array of lawyers on both sides, the principals in the case violently contradicting one another. Delays. Procrastinations. Postponements. When the lid was lifted off Pierce's affairs they were discovered to be in a ruinous state, with debts amounting to more than half a million dollars and the southern property mortgaged – the consequence of inept stock exchange gambling and misfortunes at poker. It was a state of affairs that finally persuaded Fanny not to contest the divorce, at the price of saving what she could for the children from the wreckage. In exchange for withdrawing her defence, she was to retain an interest on the mortgage of the family home at Butler Place, together with an annual allowance from Pierce, and the right to see her daughters for two months every summer.

'In England . . . a statute of lunacy would have been taken out against him,' she remarked of Pierce. Nonetheless, she begged friends to excise from her correspondence with them all reference to the bitter differences between herself and her husband, all accounts of past misconduct and misery, 'so as not to grieve the hearts of those after us'.[17]

In the September of 1849 Pierce obtained his divorce. Well before this, however, Fanny had embarked on her new career. At the beginning of the year she had given her first public reading from Shakespeare in Boston Masonic Hall to an enthusiastic audience. From now on a second and successful life lay before her. She was forty.

6

Postscript

With her Shakespeare readings Fanny sprang Phoenix-like from the ashes of her unhappy marriage. Wearing white satin for *Romeo and Juliet*, soft green for *A Winter's Tale*, wine-red for *Hamlet*, she would ascend the dais, curtsey, then sitting down open her book saying 'I have the honour to read . . .' naming the play and the cast of characters. She would then begin to read.

The play she enjoyed reading most was *Henry V*. 'Her splendid tones and her face like that of a war goddess seemed to fill the performance with the hurry of armies and the sound of battle,'[1] Henry James remembered. She had indeed always loved matters martial. 'A fortress is always delightful to me,' she had written, 'my destructiveness rejoices in guns and drums, and all the circumstance of glorious war.'[2]

Readings were given in Boston, New York, Chicago, Indianapolis, Philadelphia, and soon enough money was saved to build herself a cottage. The humorously named 'Perch' was at Lenox in Massachusetts, and Nathaniel Hawthorne and Herman Melville were near neighbours.

Throughout the 1850s and 1860s Fanny was to go from strength to strength, though people, otherwise charmed and interested by her, were to find her increasingly eccentric. At Lenox she was frequently glimpsed fishing in a man's shirt and hat, and when Elizabeth Barrett Browning met her, staying with Adelaide, in Rome, she noticed that Fanny wore her dresses in strict rotation: 'nothing ever induced her to put on Monday's dress on Tuesday!'[3] she recorded. Apparently Fanny had become such a creature of habit that she would put on flannel and light fires on a given day of the year whether the day was wintry or not. 'Somewhat inelastic,' commented Mrs Browning, lightly. Nonetheless she was much taken with Fanny's radiant smile and lustrous black eyes. Others of the English colony were also impressed, especially the painter,

Lord Leighton, who asked her to pose for him – as Jezebel.
Probably more to her taste was hiring a carriage to drive into the
campagna, often with the Thackeray girls whose father, as Fanny
pithily expressed it, she continued 'to admire but not to endure'.

'Where shall I drive?' the man would ask.

'*Andate al Diavolo!*'* Fanny would gaily reply, and, singing arias,
she and the girls would vanish into the landscape.[4]

'Bohème exquise!' someone remarked of her at Adelaide's Paris
salon, where Liszt, Mendelssohn and Dessauer[†] were frequent
visitors.

Yet even now life was not all plain sailing. In 1854 her father
died, to be followed three years later by her elder brother John,
who left behind a destitute family. As she had helped her brother
Henry in the past, so now she helped John's children, keeping
herself solvent by her readings.

> '. . . Round as a butt',

wrote Adelaide affectionately as the decade drew to a close,

> 'full of fire from top to toe,
> Cock of the walk to the village I strutt
> And scare them all wherever I go.'[5]

Meanwhile the star of the unfortunate Pierce continued its
gloomy descent. He and the two girls were reduced to living in
shabby boarding houses, business becoming so desperate on the
plantation that in 1859 it was decided the slaves must be sold. At
this time the price of slaves was high, so high that to mitigate the
shortage, some enterprising Southerners were contemplating
reopening the slave trade with West Africa.

The sale took place in pouring rain on the Savannah racecourse:
429 men, women and children on view in the stables and carriage-
sheds, with the humanitarian proviso, however, that families and
husbands and wives should not be split up. The sale fetched over
300,000 dollars, and afterwards, to the popping of champagne
corks, Pierce personally handed out four shiny new quarter-dollar
pieces to each of his former slaves.

Fanny, back in the States to keep an eye on this event, kept her
hand grimly on the purse-strings, sensibly refusing, in the girls'

---

* Go to the devil!

† Ludwig Dessauer (1810–74), German actor.

interest, to render up the mortgage of Butler Place in exchange for Pierce's offer to pay the huge arrears of payments he owed her. The girls themselves were by now going separate ways, the younger, Frances, with her father, Sarah, the elder, with her mother.

Two years later the long-threatened war between North and South broke out. Not long before, Pierce, determined to fight for his Southern property, had been briefly imprisoned on a charge of smuggling arms into Georgia. Fanny, on the point of returning to England, contributed to the Northern offensive by giving readings to wounded Yankees, following this up by the publication of her journal *Residence on a Georgian Plantation*. This, with its frank exposure of their life together thirty years before, must have been a bitter pill for Pierce, and worse was to follow as Sherman marched through Georgia, occupied Savannah and crushed the Confederate forces at Nashville.

It was now that their younger daughter showed her metal. With an aplomb reminiscent of her mother's, young Fanny returned to Butler Island, hung a portrait of Robert E. Lee over the fireplace, and set to work.

During the war years the plantation had fallen into neglect, much of it returning to swamp, with a scattering of former slaves drifting back to lead a hand-to-mouth existence hunting and trying to cultivate their gardens. Together, Pierce and his daughter planted a rice crop, and new orange trees. In the spring of 1867 young Fanny went north to avoid the 'sickly season', leaving her father to follow. This he never did. Left alone but for a handful of his former slaves, he contracted malaria, grew worse and died.

Undaunted, young Fanny returned, and for four years ran the plantation single-handed. People were to remember how she went about followed everywhere by her horse, an abandoned Yankee deserter's mount, and how, like her mother, she rode everywhere alone through the length and breadth of St Simon's Island.

Her mother, for her part, had by now given up her public readings, and was addressing herself to serious authorship, something she had always wanted to do. She was by now well on her way to making a name for herself in the political sphere. Had not the president of America's National Woman's Suffrage Association listed her along with Mary Wollstonecraft, Fanny Wright, Victoria Woodhull and George Sand, as a woman 'crucified' by her fellow women, who still blindly observed man-made taboos and conventions? But Fanny, while liking George Sand ('very like myself!'), was not eager to espouse the Suffragette cause, preferring that the battle should be won by 'education' rather than 'the vote'.

By the spring of 1875 she was ensconced at York Farm, across the road from Butler Place, where Sally, her elder daughter, now lived with her husband. She had begun her memoirs. At seven she rose and took a four-mile walk, returning to write and edit for several hours. In winter she worked in the conservatory, allowing her canary to fly free as she typed. 'I sit upright to it,' she wrote of her machine, 'as I should at my piano, and it tires neither my eyes nor my back.'[6] In 1876 *Records of a Girlhood* came out and was a 'quite immense success'. A year later she sailed for England, following her younger daughter, who had married an English parson. She did not know it, but she had left the States for the last time.

From now on she was to live in London, taking long breaks from June to September in Switzerland. This was the country of her maternal grandmother, with whose shade, in later life, she discovered an affinity. Close on seventy, she much enjoyed climbing and walking, and was given to singing lustily as she went, so that the mountain guides knew her as 'la dame qui va chantant par les montagnes.'[7]

Time began to catch up with her, however. She experienced a puzzling and unfamiliar exhaustion; found, horrors, that she could not hear unless she used an ear-trumpet.

'A half mile *crawl* when the pavement is dry is my utmost on foot,' she found herself writing in 1889, going on to complain how she rested 'from the *exertion* of doing nothing all day and prepare myself by changing my dress for the *exertion* of doing nothing all night . . .'[8] There were still friends, however, and in particular, Henry James.

They had met in 1872 at Rome. At the time he had recorded seeing '. . . the terrific Kemble herself, whose splendid hand-someness of eyes, nostril and mouth were the best things in the room . . .'[9] The friendship, he was to explain years later, was as of an aunt and favourite nephew. They corresponded frequently. She signed herself 'Katharine of Russia'.

'It is . . . a kind of rest and refreshment,' James wrote to his mother, 'to see a woman who (extremely annoying as she sometimes is) gives one a positive sense of having a deep, rich, human nature, and having cast off all vulgarities!'[10]

Three volumes of *Records of a Girlhood* were already published. In 1882, when Fanny was seventy-one, two volumes of later memoirs followed, with a third in 1891. She now lived permanently with her younger daughter in Portman Square, and one wonders how harmonious this could have been, since the younger Fanny detested England and the English, and was perpetually homesick for the freedom of Georgia.

But it was in Portman Square that, early in January 1893, Fanny Kemble was taken suddenly ill. Characteristically, her desired death had been 'to break my neck off the back of my horse at a full gallop on a fine day!'[11] As it was, she died in the arms of her devoted maid, Ellen. She was eighty-two.

'I am conscious of a strange bareness and a kind of evening chill in the air as if some great object that had filled it for long had left an emptiness,' wrote Henry James of her death. 'It seemed quite like the end of some reign, or the fall of some empire!'[12]

Sources

Books

There are a number of now rather elderly biographies of Fanny Kemble, but by far the best accounts of her life are her own books of reminiscences: *Records of a Girlhood*, in three volumes (London, 1878); *Records of a Later Life*, in three volumes (London, 1882); and *Journal of a Residence on a Georgian Plantation 1838–39*, ed. J. A. Scott (London, 1961.)

Recent biographies of interest are: J. C. Furnas, *Fanny Kemble. Leading Lady of the Nineteenth Century Stage* (The Dial Press, New York, 1982);* and *Fanny the American Kemble. Her Journals and Unpublished Letters*, ed. Fanny Kemble Wister (Tallahassee, 1972).†

* Abbreviated in Notes to Furnas.
† Abbreviated in Notes to Wister.

Notes

Introduction

1. Wister, p. 125.
2. Ibid., p. 14.
3. *Records of a Girlhood*, Vol. II, p. 158.
4. Ibid., Vol. III, p. 16.
5. Furnas, p. 153.
6. Ibid., p. 162.
7. Ibid., p. 163.
8. Ibid., p. 164.
9. Ibid.,
10. Ibid.,
11. Ibid., p. 200.
12. Ibid., p. 401.
13. *Georgian Plantation*, p. 61.
14. Furnas, p. 117.
15. Wister, p. 169.
16. Furnas, p. 264.

Chapter 1

1. Wister, p. 16.
2. Furnas, p. 130.
3. *Records of a Girlhood*, Vol. I, p. 16.
4. Ibid., p. 43.
5. Ibid.
6. Ibid., p. 63.
7. Ibid., p. 74.
8. Ibid., Vol. II, p. 22.
9. Wister, p. 34.
10. Ibid., p. 35.
11. *Records of a Girlhood*, Vol. II, p. 22.
12. Ibid., p. 59.
13. Wister, p. 42.
14. Furnas, p. 50.
15. Wister, p. 42.
16. Ibid., p. 56.
17. Ibid., p. 53.
18. Ibid., p. 58.

19. Ibid., p. 61.
20. *Records of a Girlhood*, Vol. II, p. 237.
21. Ibid., p. 254.
22. Ibid., p. 257.
23. Ibid., Vol. III, p. 28.
24. Ibid., p. 39.
25. Ibid., p. 49.
26. Ibid., p. 59.
27. Ibid., p. 65.
28. Ibid., p. 207.
29. Ibid., p. 213.
30. Ibid., p. 223.
31. Ibid.
32. Ibid., p. 231.

Chapter 2

1. Wister, p. 26.
2. Furnas, p. 35.
3. Wister, p. 86.
4. Furnas, p. 104.
5. Wister, p. 84.
6. Ibid., p. 108.
7. Furnas, p. 117.
8. Wister, p. 98.
9. Furnas, p. 122.
10. Wister, p. 108.
11. *Records of a Girlhood*, Vol. III, p. 260.

12. Furnas, p. 129.
13. Wister, p. 116.
14. Furnas, p. 140.
15. Ibid., p. 141.
16. *American Journal*, Vol. ii, p. 226.
17. Wister, p. 137.
18. Furnas, p. 136.
19. Wister, p. 137.
20. *American Journal*, Vol. ii, p. 231.
21. *Records of a Girlhood*, Vol. iii, p. 311.

Chapter 3

1. Wister, p. 121.
2. *Records of a Girlhood*, Vol. iii, p. 320.
3. Ibid., p. 320.
4. Furnas, p. 144.
5. Ibid.
6. Ibid., p. 172.
7. Ibid., p. 164.
8. Ibid., p. 167.
9. Wister, p. 149.
10. Furnas, p. 171.
11. Wister, p. 152.
12. Ibid., p. 154.
13. Ibid., p. 157.
14. Furnas, p. 188.
15. Wister, p. 158.
16. Furnas, p. 177.
17. *Records of a Later Life*, Vol. i, p. 207.

Chapter 4

1. Furnas, p. 209.
2. Ibid., p. 227.

Chapter 5

1. Furnas, p. 185.
2. Ibid., p. 229.
3. Ibid., p. 230.
4. Ibid., p. 231.
5. Wister, p. 168.
6. Furnas, p. 241.
7. Furnas, p. 249.
8. Ibid., p. 258.
9. Ibid., p. 269.
10. Wister, p. 108.
11. Furnas, p. 303.
12. Ibid., p. 307.
13. Furnas, p. 314.
14. Ibid.
15. Ibid., p. 319.
16. Wister, p. 201.
17. Ibid., p. 206.

Chapter 6

1. Wister, p. 208.
2. *American Journal*, Vol. i, p. 301.
3. Furnas, p. 359.
4. Ibid., p. 367.
5. Ibid., p. 370.
6. Ibid., p. 421.
7. Ibid.
8. Ibid., p. 433.
9. Ibid., p. 435.
10. Wister, p. 215.
11. Furnas, p. 3.
12. Wister, p. 216.

Index